New Men

RECONSTRUCTING AMERICA
Andrew L. Slap, series editor

New Men

Reconstructing the Image of the Veteran in Late-Nineteenth-Century American Literature and Culture

John A. Casey Jr.

FORDHAM UNIVERSITY PRESS
NEW YORK   2015

Copyright © 2015 Fordham University Press

All rights reserved. No part of this publication may be reproduced, stored in a retrieval system, or transmitted in any form or by any means—electronic, mechanical, photocopy, recording, or any other—except for brief quotations in printed reviews, without the prior permission of the publisher.

Fordham University Press has no responsibility for the persistence or accuracy of URLs for external or third-party Internet websites referred to in this publication and does not guarantee that any content on such websites is, or will remain, accurate or appropriate.

Fordham University Press also publishes its books in a variety of electronic formats. Some content that appears in print may not be available in electronic books.

Visit us online at www.fordhampress.com.

Library of Congress Cataloging-in-Publication Data

Casey, John A., Jr.
  New men : reconstructing the image of the veteran in late nineteenth-century American literature and culture / John A. Casey, Jr. — First edition.
      pages cm — (Reconstructing America)
   Includes bibliographical references and index.
   ISBN 978-0-8232-6539-8 (hardback)
   1. American literature—19th century—History and criticism. 2. Veterans in literature. 3. Veteran reintegration—United States—History. 4. United States—History—Civil War, 1861–1865—Literature and the war. 5. Veterans—United States—History. I. Title. II. Title: Reconstructing the image of the veteran in late nineteenth-century American literature and culture.
   PS217.V48C37 2015
   810.9′352697—dc23
                                                                 2014045375

Printed in the United States of America

17 16 15   5 4 3 2 1

First edition

To my paternal grandfather, the late Martin E. Casey Jr.,
whose extensive collection of illustrated military history books
started my interest in the Civil War and its soldiers, as well as to
my Uncle Paul, who was the first living historian I ever met.
Hic Placet.

Contents

List of Illustrations ix
Acknowledgments xi

Introduction | 1

1 Demobilization, Disability, and the Competing Imagery of the Wounded Warrior and the Citizen-Soldier | 17

2 Veterans, Artisanal Manhood, and the Quest for Postwar Employment | 48

3 Narrating Traumatic Experience in Civil War Memoir | 74

4 The Glorious Burden of the Aging Civil War Veteran | 104

5 Racial Uplift and the Figure of the Black Soldier | 130

Epilogue | 163

Notes 167
Bibliography 195
Index 227

Illustrations

1 *Petersburg, VA. Dead Confederate Soldier, in Trench Beyond a Section of Chevaux-de-frise* 7
2 Mathew Brady. *Washington, D.C., Infantry Units with Fixed Bayonets Passing on Pennsylvania Avenue near the Treasury* 25
3 Winslow Homer. "Our Watering Places—The Empty Sleeve at Newport" 31
4 *Point Lookout, MD—View of Hammond General Hospital and U.S. General Depot for Prisoners of War* 45
5 Winslow Homer. *The Veteran in a New Field* 52
6 Charles L. Cummings. *The Great War Relic* 56
7 Charles L. Cummings. *The Great War Relic* 57
8 F. O. C. Darley. *Sherman's March to the Sea* 88
9 War Department. Office of the Chief of Engineers. *Sketch of the Battle Field of Shiloh Showing the Disposition of the Troops Under the Command of Major General D. C. Buell on the 6th and 7th of April 1862* 97
10 *Hazen Brigade Monument* 102
11 George E. Lemon. "Pension Advertisement" 108
12 G. Kauffman. "The Veteran's Memories" 112
13 "An American Goddess Between Veterans of Two Wars" 128
14 *24th Regiment U.S. Colored Troops. Let Soldiers in War, Be Citizens in Peace* 134
15 "Teaching the Negro Recruits the Use of the Minie Rifle" 137
16 *Distinguished Colored Men* 143

Acknowledgments

Writing a book of any kind is far from a solitary endeavor. Doing so requires the patience and assistance of all those whose lives are touched by the author. This project is no different.

New Men began as a seminar paper in a graduate-level Civil War literature class I attended in the fall of 2000 at the University of Illinois at Chicago. In that class I first encountered John William De Forest through his novel *Miss Ravenel's Conversion*. I owe both the professor of that seminar, Terence Whalen, and the author he introduced me to for the first time, John William De Forest, a great debt. Whalen's engaging course provided me with more than just a research topic; it also provided a methodology that continues to shape my scholarship.

I have incurred numerous other obligations to generous scholars who have helped me locate resources for this project as well as sharpen the ideas presented in these pages. My particular thanks go out to Michael Perman and Robin Grey. I was honored to earn the respect of such a well-known historian as Professor Perman through my extensive primary research. The careful reading by my mentor, Robin Grey, of the innumerable drafts of each chapter I sent her has helped make this a solid piece of scholarship. I'd also like to thank Brian Mornar and Jennifer Joan Smith. I gained much from their observant commentary on each chapter.

Turning my research into a book has required the assistance of innumerable libraries and librarians along the way. Special thanks are due to Teri Embrey and Devin Hunter at the Pritzker Military Library, Teresa Yoder in the Special Collections Department at the Chicago Public Library, and the reading room staff at the William L. Clements Library—Terese Austin, Valerie Proehl, and Diana Sykes—who brought me countless boxes of soldiers' letters during my summer visit to their archives. I'd also like to express my appreciation to the staffs at the Newberry Library, the Filson Historical Society, and the Special Collections Departments at Washington and Lee University and the Virginia Military Institute.

Grants provided by the University of Illinois at Chicago Alumni Association, the Filson Historical Society, and the Upton Foundation supplied much-needed funding for my research. I am grateful to the journals *American Literary Realism* and *Civil War History*, in which earlier versions of Chapters 1 and 4 of this book appeared, for their publication permissions.

The staff at Fordham University Press has been both patient with and helpful to this first-time author. Series editor Andy Slap deserves particular mention, as it was he who contacted me about publishing this project and has ushered it through the early stages of the publication process.

And finally, to all those friends and colleagues who listened to me complain about the difficulties I faced during the research and writing of this book, you have my undying love and admiration. The book's done. I promise I'll be quiet now, at least until the next project.

Introduction

> My enthusiasm was pretty well aroused Monday—it being "Memorial Day"—and it was a beautiful sight to see the Grand A.R. observe the ceremonies consequent on that day. I think on one occasion on that day, and I don't know but more than one, the thought came to me that perhaps we as soldiers would be as much thought of if we were under the turf as well—but of course live soldiers don't deserve as much credit as dead ones.
>
> —Letter from James C. Bolles to Charles Maxim

The question of what the living owe to the dead is central to the healing process for any culture following war. Cemeteries, monuments, and rituals such as parades are all pieces of the attempt by a society to remember the sacrifices of those who gave their lives in its defense. From these commemorations, a public memory develops of the war, its causes, and its larger significance. This public memory becomes the story of the war that a society tells its future generations. What civilians owe to veterans is a much thornier question. Unlike dead soldiers, veterans endure as everyday reminders of the conflict in which they participated and often require considerable medical and financial aid to help them adjust to postwar life. Veterans also tend to complicate the portrait of war created by public memory. Their diverse experiences remind a society of the messiness of war at a time when most members of that society are searching for closure.

Each war has its unique characteristics, but they all seem to share this conundrum of how to address living veterans. *New Men* explores this problem in the context of the post–Civil War–era United States. In this book we see the tangled reintegration process of former soldiers from the North and South as they attempted to reenter civilian life. We also see the growing tension that develops between the well-meaning civilians who attempted to understand those who fought in the war and Civil War veterans who sensed they were perceived as different following discharge from the army but struggled to explain how and why. From that tension emerged a new understanding of what it meant to be a "veteran." No longer the marker of a temporary status, "veteran" came to connote a new identity that was associated with a new state of consciousness. This shift in the understanding of what it meant to be a veteran was a different type of reconstruction that would influence how later generations of U.S. authors wrote about war. Not simply one event in a man's life, military service in time of war became a defining experience.

Through studying this shift in the conception of "the veteran," the research in *New Men* engages two entrenched narratives associated with scholarship on the post–Civil War era in the United States. The first is connected to literary history and the theme of the "unwritten war." Having its origin in the statement by the American poet Walt Whitman that "the real war will never get in the books," this theme has long been used as the starting point for examinations of why no "great" literature of the Civil War was written in the three decades following its close.[1] Feminist scholarship has done much to undermine this belief by showing how female authors published hundreds of popular novels, short stories, and poems that until relatively recently have not been classified by scholars as Civil War fiction.[2] Nonetheless, the theme of the unwritten war still has a strong hold on the critical imagination as scholars continue to study the gaps in the literary record for clues about how the war was represented in fiction and why authors chose to represent it the way they did.[3]

New Men addresses the theme of the unwritten war by uncovering the origins of veteran claims to representational authority of "their war."[4] Veterans of the war experienced a gap between what language could describe and what they had survived. Some former soldiers attempted to ignore this gap, writing conventional narratives that belied their experience. Others explored it in an attempt to reshape language and narrative structure to better conform to their lives. What all veterans shared, however, was a sense that only those who had participated in the war could truly understand the conflict. Civilians often laughed at the tendency of old soldiers to argue with one another endlessly over minute details associated with a Civil War battle, but the arguments of these veterans signaled a challenge for anyone attempting to write about the war in the late-nineteenth-century United States. The war was not left unwritten. Instead, the terms of representation shifted in such a way that nonveterans were discouraged from writing.

INTRODUCTION

The second narrative addressed by my research comes from historiography, a theme often referred to as the "road to reunion." The road to reunion assumes that the central issues of the war—slavery and black civil rights—were hidden in the late nineteenth century through a focus on white solidarity. That solidarity was represented for many Americans by the image of soldiers from the North and South reuniting on their former battlefields as friends in Blue–Gray gatherings.[5] Recent studies of Civil War veterans have begun to call into question the dominant interpretation of the role veterans played in the road to reunion. They highlight the tensions that persisted between Union and Confederate veterans well into the twentieth century as well as the importance of questions surrounding manhood and disability.[6] These studies encourage future scholars to move beyond an approach to analyzing the war that often tells us more about dead soldiers than it does about living veterans.

What we learn from the experience of veterans described in *New Men* is that historians have overestimated the degree of amity between former soldiers and civilians. At the same time, they have also underestimated the degree of understanding that existed between northern and southern veterans. Even though veterans were not willing to forget the issues that motivated them to fight and divided them from their foes on the battlefield, both Union and Confederate veterans shared the experience of camp and combat. What we see in photos of Blue–Gray reunions is filtered through the lens of late-nineteenth- and early-twentieth-century civilian political needs. For the nation to become an international power, it first needed to unite around a common mythology. Johnny Reb and Billy Yank's shaking hands with each other at Gettysburg provided that foundation. However, veterans took a different meaning from their reunions. As *New Men* shows, veterans of the North and South shared a survivor's sense of changed identity and an ongoing determination to understand the force that had reshaped the course of their lives.

A few words are in order at this point about the scope of this project. *New Men* is a qualitative rather than a quantitative study. Even in this era of digitized texts, it still isn't possible to view, much less analyze, every narrative written by a Civil War veteran. Moreover, the experiences of veterans are often so different in the details that thus far the only successful quantitative studies of Civil War veterans have been limited to regional histories of states and counties.[7] My interest throughout this book has been in larger trends that illustrate the way many veterans understood themselves and their war experiences. I have also sought to expose patterns in the way civilians responded to veteran claims of exceptionalism. These trends have then been used as a way to understand the literature and culture of the postwar era. Veteran reintegration thus provides a new heuristic for cultural historians, an alternative to examining the era's cultural production exclusively through the lens of race and reconciliation or sectionalist politics.

Because this new heuristic depends on an altered conception of what it meant to be a veteran, it is necessary to consider briefly how this term was used prior to the Civil War. The term "veteran" appears in relation to fiction and nonfiction writings associated with the three major wars that preceded the Civil War: the Revolutionary War, the War of 1812, and the Mexican War. In these wars, however, the term reflected the length of service or technical expertise of a soldier rather than represented a unique state of consciousness or altered sense of social identity in relation to civilians. This less exclusionary use of the term reflected the fact that divisions existed within the soldiery between officers and enlisted men as well as regulars, militia, and volunteers.[8] Politics also proved to be more of a dividing factor for soldiers than their military service.[9] Consequently, veterans of wars before the Civil War felt a greater affinity with groups outside the ranks of the army than they did with other former soldiers. All of this meant, of course, that "veterans" would not become objects of social interest in their own right. Instead, they would be discussed as a subsidiary factor related to larger social issues.

These issues varied in each of the three major wars that preceded the Civil War. Revolutionary War veterans would initially be ignored to emphasize the character of that conflict as a "people's war." Distrustful of standing armies, the leaders of the new republic wanted to enshrine in public memory the image of the Revolutionary War as a struggle won by all the people mobilized in defense of their homes.[10] Over time this vision of the war would change, in part because of the poor performance of the militia in the War of 1812, whose veterans were frequently lumped together in nineteenth-century public memory with those of the Revolutionary War, and also because of the rise of a new generation for whom the Revolutionary War was part of a distant past. This new generation looked with pity on the aging veterans of the Revolutionary War and sought inspiration in their record of service to the nation.[11] Mexican War veterans would initially be understood as torchbearers of the Revolutionary War veterans' legacy. Their military service showed that the patriotic spirit of the founding generation had not faded away. What that legacy might have become remains an object of speculation as public memory of the Mexican War was quickly elided into that of the Civil War that soon followed.

Literary history also reflects the changed usage of the term "veteran." Studies of war literature as a distinct genre in the United States tend to begin after the Civil War.[12] Far from accidental, this indicates the changed status of war as a concept in American culture and of the men who fight in the nation's wars. Before war was conceptualized as a transformative experience and the veteran as the possessor of a unique form of consciousness, it was not unusual for civilians to write about veterans. Among the better-known antebellum works of fiction addressing the topic of veterans in the early republic are Washington Irving's *Rip Van Winkle* (1819) and Herman Melville's *Israel Potter* (1855), the latter of which was based on a memoir titled *The Life and Remarkable Adventures of Israel R. Potter* (1824). This perspective changed to such a degree after the Civil War, thanks to the reintegration experience of Civil War veterans, that by the 1890s it was impossible for Americans to conceive of a young man like Stephen Crane, who had not served in the war, writing so "realistic" an account of combat. Not simply a watershed moment in national politics and race relations, the Civil War also proved itself the dividing point between two distinct ways of writing about war. Finding the "real" war would now become the obsession of American authors writing about combat, and possession of that reality was assumed to be under the control of those who had "gone to see the elephant."[13]

The change in conception of what it meant to be a "veteran" and the belief that this status came with a unique perspective on war were due to the exceptional nature of the Civil War in comparison with the wars that preceded it. There is considerable disagreement among historians over what made the Civil War different from earlier conflicts in the United States. Some have even claimed that the Civil War was not, in fact, very different from prior wars. Much of this disagreement hinges on the question of whether the Civil War was the first "modern" or "total" war in the United States.[14] How one defines a war as modern or total depends on a number of factors. Chief among them is the degree of involvement of civilians in the conflict. Major General William Tecumseh Sherman's "march to the sea" has often been used as evidence that civilians became legitimate targets in the last years of the Civil War. By destroying their property, Sherman hoped to hasten the war's end and make sure that the South would think hard before engaging in another conflict with the "legitimate" government.[15] Another key factor is the use of technology on the battlefield. Rifled muskets and artillery increased the range of fire for soldiers in the Civil War. Breech-loading versions of these weapons increased the rate of fire. Trenches became far more elaborate in part to help infantry deal with these new threats.[16]

For the purposes of this book, modernity and totality are not understood as absolutes. Recent scholarship on the Civil War has shown the limits of our assumptions about Sherman's march and the lethality of the rifled musket. What this proves, however, is not that the Civil War was not a modern or total war but rather that no war can live up to the abstract ideal represented by these terms. The U.S. Civil War contained within it elements of a modern or total war that coexisted (often uncomfortably) with tactics and strategies present in prior conflicts. This makes sense, as many of the commanding officers during the war had fought in the Mexican War using tactics based on the Napoleonic tradition as it was passed down by Antoine-Henri Jomini.[17]

Although few Civil War generals were conscious practitioners of Jomini's principles, they instinctively applied them in the preparation of their battles. Battles were planned on the assumption that the terrain would be open and relatively flat. This would allow the army to maneuver around the enemy, threatening their communications and supply, and forcing it into a decisive engagement. Troops would then move toward the enemy massed in straight lines with artillery close behind them to provide covering fire. Once the battle was concluded, the armies would disengage and begin the process of recovery before starting a new campaign. This tactical pattern remained fairly consistent throughout the war despite tortuous terrain that often made its application a nightmare for common soldiers. Rosters of the dead from battles such as Shiloh, Antietam, Gettysburg, and Chickamauga indicate the real cost in lives of the significant gap that frequently existed between a general's plan of battle and actual battlefield conditions.[18]

When Ulysses S. Grant became general of the army in 1864, the first alteration he made was strategic rather than tactical. Frustrated by the lack of coordination between armies in the various theaters of war, Grant sought to craft a plan that would attack Confederate forces on all fronts in a synchronized fashion. This would put maximum stress on the supplies for Confederate soldiers and prevent armies in different regions from sending reinforcements to one another.[19] The decision to fight a series of continual battles on every front was understandable as part of a larger plan for the war. From the beginning, the Confederacy saw its primary goal as survival. If they could maintain an army in the field and gain international recognition, Confederate leaders believed, the North would have no choice but to let the southern states form a new nation distinct from the United States.

This strategy was not dramatically different from that followed by the Continental Congress in the Revolutionary War, which was ultimately successful in creating the fledging United States as a republic. Union war strategy thus far had played into the hands of the Confederacy. By fighting southern armies and then disengaging, the North had allowed them a chance to marshal their resources in terms of men and supplies for the longest war possible. Grant intended to break that cycle and end the war quickly while keeping the nation intact.

One of the few significant tactical changes made by Grant appears minor upon surface examination. Beginning with the Overland Campaign in May 1864, the Army of the Potomac maintained continual contact with the Army of Northern Virginia. No longer would the armies fight a battle and disengage to recuperate. Grant would drive his army to follow General Robert E. Lee's troops wherever they went. For seven weeks the Army of the Potomac maneuvered in an attempt to cut Lee off from his base of supplies or force him into a major battle. What they eventually accomplished was to drive Confederate forces into entrenchments around Petersburg.[20] There the Army of the Potomac settled in for a siege while Grant in his role as general of the army encouraged his subordinates to follow his example and give all the southern armies no rest.

Figure 1. *Petersburg, VA. Dead Confederate Soldier, in Trench Beyond a Section of Chevaux-de-frise*. Photograph. April 3, 1865. Library of Congress. Washington, D.C.

In the end, Grant's plan for the war succeeded. Southern will to fight declined as both territory and supplies were lost to the North. That success, however, came at a price. Casualties remained fairly consistent in relation to those of earlier battles. At Gettysburg, for instance, 3,155 were killed, 14,531 wounded, and 5,369 captured or missing. During the Battle of Cold Harbor, which supposedly cemented Grant's reputation as a butcher, casualties were 1,844 killed, 9,077 wounded, and 1,816 captured or missing.[21] Nonetheless, the psychic toll on the living was greatly magnified by the increased tempo of combat. After the Battle of Gettysburg, the Army of the Potomac would not fight a major engagement with the Army of Northern Virginia for more than three months. Following Cold Harbor, the northern army made one last attempt to flank Lee's command. Then it settled down for a long siege of Confederate forces near Petersburg. Although no longer engaging their opponents in the open, neither side found respite in the trenches. Under near-constant shelling, Private Daniel Bond of the First Minnesota confided to his diary, "Oh! I am sick of war. God save me that I may oppose this slaughter of human beings."[22] Just one day later, he was a prisoner of war on his way to Andersonville. It would take nearly another year before his prayers were answered.

"Modern" war is not simply about technological change or depredations against civilians. Nor is it solely about casualty statistics. In the context of the U.S. Civil War, it is the changed rhythm of war more than anything that marks it as different from earlier national conflicts. As soldiers are driven from battle to battle, something elemental in them changes. Instinct takes over as fatigue wears down consciousness. Even today, we only partially understand these changes. Neuroscience still struggles to determine the physiological alterations that occur in battle. Civil War–era soldiers had none of this knowledge at their disposal. All they had were the comrades they had fought beside and the stories they began to tell before the last of the war's battles had even ended. What these soldiers possessed, however, they used to great effect. Leaving the ranks of the army, Civil War veterans left a trail of writings that document their uneven process of reintegration into civilian life. From examining that process we do not necessarily arrive at an answer about how the changed tempo of war had altered them, but it soon becomes clear how they came to understand the ways in which they had become new men.

To analyze the trail of writings that illustrate veteran reintegration in the Civil War era, *New Men* relies on a selective pairing of literary works. Most of these were chosen because they had been written by veterans of the war who wanted to better understand the conflict they had survived. The issues in these texts matched nicely with the nonfiction writings of Civil War veterans attempting a similar task in a different genre. This allowed me the opportunity to explore some of the differences between representing war in fiction versus nonfiction forms. Additional texts were chosen based on their engagement with veterans' issues in the postwar era. These were written largely by civilians attempting to understand the statements of Civil War veterans about their experience. They appear in the text primarily at moments when veterans were a matter of public concern, such as during the period of army demobilization, during the debates over pension expansion, and in the Jim Crow era as African Americans debated the best role models for racial uplift. The narratives written by these civilian authors are meant to provide a greater context for issues that veterans faced at each stage of their reintegration.

Blending an analysis of such a wide variety of fiction and nonfiction narratives alters our conception of many classics of Civil War literature such as *The Red Badge of Courage*, *Tales of Soldiers and Civilians*, and *Miss Ravenel's Conversion from Secession to Loyalty*. Suddenly it becomes clear how these works were involved in the task of documenting and defining what it meant to be a veteran in the late-nineteenth-century United States. In addition, the juxtaposition of these fiction and nonfiction texts offers an explanation for why war literature as a distinct genre in American fiction seems to begin only after the Civil War. Without a conception of veteran uniqueness, war is simply one event out of many in a man's life. Civil War veterans came to see their war service as a defining "experience" rather than as simply an "event." This perspective and the narratives used to describe it made possible a new way of writing about war in literary forms. Military service came to be viewed as analogous to religious conversion. Writers of the "Lost Generation" such as Ernest Hemingway and John Dos Passos would find this new way of writing influential to their own conception of war as a subject for literature.

Understanding how Civil War veterans came to see their war service as an "experience" rather than as an "event" requires a systematic and coherent analysis. In order to achieve this goal, *New Men* is organized both chronologically and thematically, with each chapter marking a particular stage in the process of veteran reintegration. The first of these stages, explored in Chapters 1 and 2, comprises the initial period of army demobilization (1865–67) and the search for employment among white veterans of the North and South that soon followed (1867–77). Subsequent to this initial stage is a period (1877–90) of growing awareness among veterans that their memories of the war set them apart from the civilian population. This growing sense of apartness among veterans led to the final stage (1890–1900) examined in *New Men*, wherein civilians of the rising generation responded with mingled appreciation and resentment to former soldiers' claims of a unique and privileged identity. It is worth noting that these periods are meant to be descriptive rather than proscriptive. Some overlap exists between themes explored in each period or stage. However, specific themes appear with greater frequency during the periods in which they are examined.

Additionally worth noting is the fact that *New Men* examines black veterans in their own chapter rather than spread an analysis of their reintegration process throughout the book. This decision was not made lightly, given the segregation that black veterans and the African American community as a whole faced during the nineteenth century. Research indicated, however, that the postwar reintegration experience of former soldiers in the U.S. Colored Troops differed enough to warrant distinct examination. Consequently, even though we will see that many of the same themes discussed at each stage of the reintegration process of white veterans appear in the discussion of the reintegration of black veterans, the details of each stage will vary significantly. This variance is due, in no small part, to the fact that while white veterans were fighting as one of the duties of their citizenship in the nation, black veterans were fighting in large part to attain citizenship status in the first place. Moreover, those who had only recently been freed from chattel slavery saw the war as an opportunity to prove that they were men and not property.

An examination of the stages of white veteran reintegration begins in Chapter 1. Here the initial period of army demobilization and civilian uneasiness about soldiers returning home is described.

Union veteran John William De Forest's novel *Miss Ravenel's Conversion from Secession to Loyalty* and Confederate veteran Sidney Lanier's *Tiger-Lilies* serve as examples of a veteran reaction against early postwar civilian claims that the majority of recently demobilized soldiers were disabled by their wartime service. Powerfully evoked in images such as Winslow Homer's engraving for *Harper's Weekly*, "The Empty Sleeve at Newport," the pervasive sentimental image of the wounded warrior in need of civilian care was created to allay anxieties concerning the dangerous and "demoralizing" effects of army life, which civilians believed exposed soldiers both to violence and to vice. Civil War veterans resisted the widespread belief circulating in newspapers and popular periodicals such as *Harper's* that former soldiers were victims of war in need of civilian caretakers to nurse them back to health and normalcy. They sought ways to prove that the war had simply been an interlude in their prewar lives.

De Forest addresses these issues in his novel through an unflattering comparison of the heroic amateur soldier, the citizen-soldier Edward Colburne, with the stigmatized professional soldier John Carter. Colburne is sober, dutiful, and self-controlled, traits the author believes necessary for success in civilian life. Carter, in contrast, is improvident and a slave to his passions. The heroine of the novel, Lillie Ravenel, finds this out, much to her chagrin, when she marries Carter; she discovers that he is incapable of supporting a family economically and is an adulterer, engaging in an affair with Lillie's aunt. At the conclusion of the narrative, Carter is killed in battle, an ending the author suggests is appropriate for this hapless old soldier. Following her first husband's death, Lillie, finally seeing the error of her ways, goes on to marry the heroic citizen-soldier Edward, who the narrative assumes will succeed at establishing himself in a postwar civilian career.

Despite De Forest's optimism, however, the narrative struggles to convince the reader near its conclusion why one veteran will succeed in postwar civilian life whereas the other could not. This dilemma is made all the more acute by the author's subconscious doubt concerning the actual differences between citizen-soldier volunteers and the professional soldiers of the Regular Army. Both types of soldiers had survived the same campaigns and engaged in the same wartime actions. The author, consequently, can only reiterate his earlier claim that Colburne's status as an amateur rather than a professional warrior is a good omen for his ability to live a normal life in peacetime society.

Lanier's response to civilian anxiety focused less on a citizen's military duty and the distinctions among soldiers that followed from that sense of obligation. Instead, he envisioned a shared narrative of suffering that would join southern soldiers and civilians. That narrative would move beyond civilian pity for veterans and instead cultivate empathy. As the survivor of a Union prisoner-of-war camp and suffering from tuberculosis, Lanier shows less resistance than De Forest to the sentimental image of the wounded warrior that the postwar civilian populace embraced. Nonetheless, his novel *Tiger-Lilies* demonstrates the emergence of the belief that even though civilians could sympathize with former soldiers, they would never fully understand what soldiers had lived through. The love of his friends and family allow the Confederate veteran Phil Sterling, the protagonist in the narrative, to reclaim his name and, along with it, the identity he had lost in the prisoner-of-war camp. There he had simply become number four and then later answered to another man's name during roll call in order to attain better sleeping quarters. But being recognized by his friends and family and thereby reclaiming his name is a far cry from feeling "at home." Already in the days following the war's end, Phil Sterling senses a wall of experience that has dropped between him and the ones he loves.

Chapter 2 examines the assumption held by white Civil War veterans of both the North and the South that civilian employment would function as the cornerstone of a normal life. This belief emerged in part as a reaction to the civilian anxieties surrounding the soldier's homecoming that are examined in the first chapter. It emerged also in response to their own doubts about the war's lasting influence on their character. Union veteran Albion Tourgée's novel *Figs and Thistles* and Confederate veteran John Esten Cooke's novel *The Heir of Gaymount* reveal that finding a civilian career was a highly conflicted process. Union as well as Confederate veterans sought to hold onto their prewar assumptions about autonomous, self-employed work, which they believed shaped their sense of manhood. Born into a largely agrarian world comprising self-sufficient regions that were largely detached from a national market, veterans confronted with deep uncertainty the rapidly industrializing and nationalizing economy of the 1870s United States.

Tourgée's main character, Union veteran Markham Churr, becomes a politician, ostensibly in order to manage these troubling changes in ways that would be favorable to northern veterans. The narrative tries to imagine a way to preserve the small town as veterans knew it before the war. This would ensure that the values they fought for would not become obsolete. Cooke's hero, the southern veteran Edmund Cateret, cautiously enters the new postwar economy by turning his family's ruined Virginia plantation into a produce farm. In contrast to Tourgée's corporate jeremiad, which calls the northern reader back to the values of the prewar nation while attempting to hold on to its postwar economic growth, Cooke's narrative embodies a tentative exploration for a New South among southern survivors of the war. Cateret attempts to find a way to blend core southern cultural values such as gentility with the antebellum vision of political economy championed by the northern victors.

Despite their differences, these narratives share an initial optimism about the future that gradually fades into disillusionment. Confronted with the perceived egoism and self-indulgence of what would come to be known as the Gilded Age, these fictional veterans discover that reentry into society depended on the acceptance of a set of new values they were either unwilling to accept or unable to implement. When faced with the prospect that they might have to abandon the values of autonomous manhood that had led many of them to war, these authors turned to the past for comfort—Tourgée, in the hope that others might follow the example of his corporate jeremiad in order to change the wayward, materialist course of the postwar nation; Cooke, in the belief that a southern alternative to the Gilded Age narrative of success might be found.

Both works bear within them the signs of growing veteran disillusionment with the post–Civil War nation and serve as early harbingers of what would become the second stage in the veteran reintegration process, the turn to memory (1877–90). Chapter 3 examines the troubled nature of veterans' memories. Veterans initially turned in self-defense to their memories of both the war and their prewar youth. They desperately wanted to escape the sordid economic realities that confronted them in the postwar nation and led them to believe they no longer had a place in American society. However, it was impossible for them to remember the idealized world of their antebellum youth without being confronted by the traumas of their wartime experiences. While searching for succor in the past, veterans dredged up long-buried psychic wounds that threatened their health and, in some cases, their public legacies.

The traumatic nature of veterans' memories are central to the analysis of William Tecumseh Sherman's *Memoirs*, Confederate veteran Sam Watkins's personal narrative *Company Aytch*, and a selection of stories from the Union veteran Ambrose Bierce. Combat narratives promised a way to organize the traumatic events of the past into something coherent that could then be reconciled with the former soldiers' present-day lives. The cathartic results of these narratives, however, proved to be mixed, as authors like Sherman were compelled to choose reputation over exposure, revealing trauma in slips of the tongue. Moreover, among those veterans who were willing or able to reveal traumatic memories, like Watkins and Bierce, the exposure of traumatic events in their narratives had the unintended consequence of separating them from those who had not suffered in the same way, confirming rather than dispelling their sense of isolation and difference.

Watkins, in particular, struggled to explain to civilian readers in his community the violation of key social norms during the war, such as those prohibiting theft and murder. He was haunted more by the memory of stealing a pig from a widowed woman and her children in Tennessee, knowing that they would probably starve to death as a result, than he was by the sudden death of a close friend due to artillery fire. This callousness of emotion toward the phenomenon of death becomes a key subject of examination for Bierce and Watkins. Watkins, like Sherman, tries to apply socially acceptable explanations to the death and despoliation that surround him. This allows him to argue, at least on the surface, that he is not materially different from his readers in sentiment. Bierce shocks his civilian readers with the reality of sudden, brutal, and unheroic death. In his works, death is taken for granted and survival becomes an end in itself. The dead, he suggests, are lucky, as their troubles are over.

Whether they attempted to connect with their civilian readers, as in the case of Sherman and Watkins, or embraced the gulf that divided them, as in Bierce, these authors nonetheless seem to arrive at the same conclusion—only those who had experienced the Civil War battlefield could understand them and their troubled memories. This led former soldiers increasingly to talk about the war primarily with other veterans, not just in writing but also in veterans' reunions and through associations such as the Grand Army of the Republic and United Confederate Veterans. In doing so, Civil War veterans came to adopt a distinct and exclusive sense of self. This altered understanding of their identity bore religious undertones, as is evidenced in Union veteran Oliver Wendell Holmes's oft-cited phrase "touched by fire," which drew a comparison between Civil War veterans and the Apostles who had been touched by the Holy Spirit with "tongues of fire." War had made them into new men, and many of them chose to view that metamorphosis as a sign of cultural superiority.

The third stage of veteran reintegration (1890–1900) involved society's growing awareness of this new veteran sense of self as a "chosen people" and the pressing need on the part of society to come to terms with it. Chapter 4 examines the societal consequences of this new veteran identity, uncovering both the growing resentment among members of the succeeding generations of middle-class white males toward the exclusionary language espoused by Civil War veterans, and the burdens their unique self-conception placed on American society. These burdens were both literal, in the form of pension costs, as well as figurative, through the constraints placed on young men's maturation by the rhetoric of singularity and sacredness attached to military service in the Civil War.

Stephen Crane's novel *The Red Badge of Courage* and the sequel short story "The Veteran" demonstrate that the argument regarding the unique social status of veterans, employed by veterans and grudgingly accepted by society as a whole, excluded succeeding generations of young middle-class white men from participating in one of the crucial rituals of manhood. Lacking a chance to wage a war of their own, young men were thereby denied an active leadership role in the nation, which had been governed by Civil War veterans for nearly thirty years. Moreover, they were asked—in the form of pensions, monuments, and parades—to help further the heritage that continued to exclude them from the pantheon of American manhood.

As a member of the younger generation, Crane confronted the burdensome legacy of the Civil War veteran in his writings. Borrowing from a public discourse saturated with panegyrics to the heroes of the Civil War, Crane developed an indirect mode of narration that allowed him to undercut subtly the pretensions of these old soldiers. On the surface, his writings seemed to praise veterans of the Civil War. Yet underneath the façade of filial piety was a rejection of their monopoly on the ideals of American manhood. By highlighting the ludicrous ordinariness of the Civil War veteran Henry Fleming in *The Red Badge of Courage* and "The Veteran," Crane contended that his generation contained just as much manly potential as the one that had come before—all that was required was a chance to prove it. They could not do so, however, as long as the prior generation stood in the way.

When Crane portrays the death of the now-aged Civil War veteran Henry Fleming in "The Veteran," it seems that a path has now been cleared for the younger generation to prove its mettle. This is reflected in Crane's choice to cease trying to understand the heroism and manhood of the Civil War generation. Instead, he decided to experience war firsthand, serving as a war correspondent first in the Greco-Turkish War and later in the Spanish–American War. On the field of battle, Crane, along with many other young men of his era, found a way to transcend the obstacle represented by the Civil War veteran. Accepting the logic held by veterans of the Civil War that "war made men," the rising generation had succeeded in its struggle with their forebears. They had found a war of their own and thereby facilitated entry into the pantheon of real American men.

Chapter 5 examines the reintegration experience of African Americans who served in the ranks of the Union army. The decision to study in a separate chapter the struggles of black soldiers in the U.S. Colored Troops to enter civilian life acknowledges the unique nature of their wartime service, which of necessity influenced their understanding of the return "home." Black men did indeed, as Barbara Gannon suggests, share with white northern veterans a commitment to the "won cause": the Union effort to end slavery and preserve the Union and the ongoing quest to remember that accomplishment.[23] Freedom's soldiers, however, hoped through their military service to convince white Americans of more than just their capability to practice discipline and stand up under fire. Many learned to read and write in camp and prepared themselves for citizenship and postwar social integration even more so than combat. These non-combat-related experiences filled black veterans with the confidence to speak out after the war in defense of their rights as citizens, including the right to vote.

Ironically, the voices of black veterans began to fade just as those of white veterans began to dominate American publishing in the 1880s and '90s. This growing silence has been alternately explained by the successful passage of the Fourteenth and Fifteenth amendments or the growing virulence of white racism. The passage of the constitutional amendments affirming black citizenship and the black male right to vote, as the historian Christian Samito notes, seemed to resolve the issues that black soldiers had initially set out to address through their military service.[24] Therefore, unlike their white comrades who were struggling with the discordant values of the Gilded Age, there seemed to be little need for black veterans to publish memoirs of their military experiences during the "renaissance" in white veteran–written narratives about the war. Furthermore, white racism, at a time when most publishers and readers were not African Americans, would have discouraged black male authors in the publication of such war narratives as they sought to avoid becoming targets of mob violence.

What these explanations of the shortage of black veteran memoirs do not adequately address, however, is the curious avoidance of black military service during the Civil War as a topic of discussion within the writings published by civilians in the African American community. By reviewing black veteran Joseph Wilson's history of black troops during the war, *The Black Phalanx*, alongside Paul Laurence Dunbar's novel *The Fanatics* and Frances Harper's *Iola Leroy*, Chapter 5 demonstrates that near the end of the nineteenth century and the beginning of the twentieth, the perceived value of black military service in the Civil War had declined within the African American community. This was especially true among those black civilians engaged in the project of racial uplift. Dunbar saw the black veteran "Nigger Ed" in *The Fanatics* as an unpleasant reminder of what northern free blacks had lost in social status through their association with emancipated slaves during the war. Harper, in contrast, felt that evoking the image of the black soldier would only encourage more violence in an era plagued by lynch mobs and race riots.

These negative connotations led each author to search for a way to champion the values once associated with the black soldier, such as equality before the law and the ability to succeed or fail based on merit rather than on identity, without actually representing him. African American veterans fought a rearguard action in the struggle for relevance both within their communities and in the nation as a whole. Yet even with the help of their comrades in the Grand Army, black veterans were never able to regain the social power and prestige they possessed in the early postwar years.

An epilogue serves in place of a conclusion to *New Men*. There I discuss the lessons that can be drawn from the Civil War veterans' reintegration experience and the relevance of those lessons to our own time.

1

Demobilization, Disability, and the Competing Imagery of the Wounded Warrior and the Citizen-Soldier

> The Indians die of civilization. So does many a returned soldier. You will have to be careful of yourself for a long time to come.
>
> —JOHN WILLIAM DE FOREST, *Miss Ravenel's Conversion*

The end of the U.S. Civil War brought with it a whole new set of problems for the nation. Among these was the question of how the armies would be disbanded and if the soldiers of the northern and southern armies could successfully assimilate back into the civilian population. Civilians were afraid that soldiers returning home, having been exposed to the violence of combat and the "demoralizing" influences of army life, might fail to adjust to the ways of peacetime life. Publications from the early postwar period illustrate that these fears varied in specific details and intensity. Some periodicals such as *The Nation* and the *New York Herald* speculated that returning soldiers might dominate postwar politics to such an extent that civil and military distinctions would be erased. Other civilian writers such as the editors at the *Washington Daily Intelligencer* imagined a class of men that while not injurious to our nation's political future would nonetheless be disruptive to its social well-being.[1] Time would eventually prove these civilian fears to have been unfounded, but in the immediate postwar years relations between soldiers and civilians were tinged with misunderstanding and uneasiness mixed in with the joy at having loved ones home from battlefield and camp. These ambivalent emotions were expressed most clearly in the imagery of the wounded warrior, which rendered all veterans as potentially disabled and in need of civilian care rather than as a potentially disruptive social force.

This turn toward sympathy fit naturally with the sentimental ethos that dominated antebellum culture, particularly in its discussion of social ills such as slavery and drunkenness.[2] It also echoed the approach of a previous generation toward veterans of the nation's much earlier "people's war"—the American Revolution. In his study *Suffering Soldiers*, the historian John Resch notes that the image of the "suffering soldier" was used by a new generation to adjust the relationship between civilians and the military. After the suspicions of the wartime generation toward the Continental Army, the iconography of the suffering soldier "evoked the sentiment of gratitude" in a new generation following the Revolutionary War and helped that generation to "affirm its place as worthy heirs to the Revolution."[3] What made the use of wounded warrior imagery in the aftermath of the Civil War so different from its use in prior wars, however, was its adoption just months after the war's end, in contrast to the nearly twenty-year interval that preceded the emergence of the Revolutionary War's suffering soldier. Clearly, civilians were desperately reaching for the familiar while charting the uncertain waters of the postwar era.

Even though a significant number of soldiers returning home were wounded, veterans resented the assumption perpetuated by the imagery of the wounded warrior that all of them were disabled and needed civilian care to nurse them back into postwar life.[4] The most expansive reaction to the imagery of the wounded warrior came from Union veteran John William De Forest. His novel *Miss Ravenel's Conversion from Secession to Loyalty* illustrates one veteran's attempt to answer civilian concerns about returning soldiers. De Forest combats the image of the wounded warrior/suffering soldier with the equally hoary one of the citizen-soldier.[5] Through a contrast in the narrative between the fictional Regular Army officer Colonel John Carter and the Volunteer officer Captain Edward Colburne, De Forest resurrects in his novel the rhetoric against professional soldiers that dominated the Jacksonian era but had much earlier origins in the founding generation's inherited fear of standing armies.[6] De Forest interpreted that cautionary tale the same way his ancestors did. He attempted to show his readers that not all soldiers were alike: temporary or citizen-soldiers were defenders of their invaded homes and communities, whereas Regular Army soldiers were professional killers and disruptive to normal life.

Another response to the imagery of the wounded warrior came from the Confederate veteran Sidney Lanier. Known primarily for his poetry written before and after the war, Lanier crafted in his only novel, *Tiger-Lilies*, a less coherent but nonetheless moving expression that represented how southern veterans felt in relation to the civilian population after the war. He uses the life of a fictional member of the South's social elite, Philip Sterling, to represent the experience of southern veterans. Captured by the northern army and sent to Point Lookout prison camp, Sterling undergoes a not-so-subtle transformation in identity as a result of his privations. Upon his release at the end of the war, Sterling returns to the ruins of the onetime Confederate capital. Here he is eventually recognized by his friends, but he struggles to imagine a place for himself in the postwar United States. Not only have his sufferings displaced his once-strong sense of self, but the destruction of the social order that buttressed his public image also makes Philip Sterling's recovery problematic. Lanier, like De Forest, wants to see the veteran Sterling through the lens of the citizen-soldier, but finds empathy rather than duty a better salve for the sting of defeat. Thus, instead of rejecting the wounded warrior imagery outright, Lanier attempts to map out a distinction between the empathy he felt was needed by returning soldiers such as Philip Sterling and the pity into which that emotion too often degenerated.

The discourse surrounding the imagery of the wounded warrior/suffering soldier and the responses to that imagery by veterans like De Forest and Lanier expose the complex relationship between white soldiers and civilians in the years immediately following the Civil War. Peaceful relations between the nation and its former soldiers were not foreordained at the close of the war. Each group needed to become reacquainted with the other. The process of social reintegration would begin with army demobilization and would gradually move into the realm of representation. Civilians would craft figures they felt explained the veterans' experience, while former soldiers started to explore how they understood the events they had survived. Soon there would develop a gap between these interpretations that would set the tone for veteran reentry in the decades to come.

Reversing the Engine of War: Civil War Demobilization

Before we consider civilian attitudes in the early postwar period toward the returning armies of the North and the South, we must first review how Civil War armies were disbanded.[7] Confederate army demobilization was so ad hoc in nature that it is almost impossible to re-create a "typical" experience of the phenomenon. One of the few things that all southern veterans had in common, however, was that they were compelled to find their own way home. George Henry Mills, a former captain of the Sixteenth North Carolina, recalled telling his men that "they had better get away from that crowd [i.e., the regiment as a whole] as soon as possible, as I had fears that they would suffer for food if they kept with it [and] that I expected to take the first road I saw leading to the right." After giving this exhortation to his men, Captain Mills walked what he estimated to be a total of 310 miles from the site of his regiment's surrender at Appomattox to his home town of Rutherfordton, North Carolina.[8]

Units fighting either in their home states or close to their communities did not have to deal with the difficulties of travel in a war-torn land, but in many of those units anecdotal evidence suggests a large portion of the men had already left the army's ranks. C. I. Walker, a former lieutenant colonel of the Tenth South Carolina, observed that well before the official surrender of General Joseph E. Johnston's army, of which his regiment was a part, enlisted men were fast disappearing from the ranks: "The Army arrived at Augusta [Georgia] a mere skeleton. Its operations were paralyzed, and it was necessary to retain a large number of officers there, under Gen. [Benjamin F.] Cheatham, to gather up the men . . ." Because they were fighting so close to home, it was too much to ask these soldiers to forget that they were also husbands, sons, and brothers, especially when Sherman was taking the war to their front doors.[9]

Besides concerns for family safety, there was also a growing sense at all levels of the Confederate army that the war was a lost cause. Sergeant Jonas Curry of the Fortieth Alabama spoke to the mind-set of the average Confederate soldier near the end of the war when he said, "Lee, of Virginia, had already surrendered, and great demoralization was manifest, especially among those so near to their homes as the Carolinians. We remained doing picket duty until the day of our surrender, May 5, 1865. We were to march home in regular order, but after the first day or two, every man was his own commander and went his own way."[10] The tone of this passage blends a mixture of exhaustion, futility, sadness, and relief. Before May 5 these men knew the war was over, but for the sake of honor they decided to wait for official disbandment rather than to desert. Yet as soon as the ink was dry on their paroles, all pretenses to unit cohesion were gone. The southern army simply disappeared.

Union army units preparing to demobilize went through a series of formal steps established by the army adjutant general's office in Washington, D.C., on May 15, 1865. The process of disbandment, which commonly took anywhere from three to four weeks, began with a unit's traveling to a designated field rendezvous site. These locations were created to facilitate the initial stage of demobilization, which included the completion of paperwork mustering the unit out of federal service, accounting of government property, and listing of the full unit roster for purposes of back pay and bounties. There were a total of nineteen field rendezvous sites, chosen for their proximity to an army unit's area of operations.[11] Upon the successful completion of this paperwork in multiple copies, a unit could leave its field rendezvous site and move on to the next stage in the process of Union demobilization: the state rendezvous site. These locations were chosen based on where a regiment had originally been mustered into federal service, typically a state capital, major city, or county seat. Depending on how long it took the members of a regiment to travel from its field rendezvous point to the state rendezvous site, back pay and bounty money might already be waiting for them when they arrived. If not, the unit would wait in camps set up at the state rendezvous site for final payment and official discharge papers.

The amount of time needed for a unit to travel from its field rendezvous site to the state rendezvous was determined largely by where they needed to travel. One regiment, the Forty-Ninth Ohio, which had taken part in Sherman's march to the sea, stayed at a field rendezvous site outside Washington, D.C., for two weeks before boarding a westbound train for Columbus, Ohio. They arrived at the state rendezvous site in Columbus in about ten days. The experience of another regiment in Sherman's army, the Fifth Connecticut, was quite different. The members of this unit remained at the same field rendezvous site outside of Washington for almost two months because of congestion in the northeast travel corridor and the lack of an adequate number of ships and trains to carry them home. Captain Edwin Marvin noted that, "as the summer dragged slowly along under a Washington sun in June and July of 1865, [the men of the unit] took French leave of their lousy encampment and returned to their homes."[12] Even though the impatience of the men of the Fifth Connecticut was understandable, their abrupt departure from the field rendezvous site jeopardized any future claims to back pay and bounties. They would need official discharge papers to obtain these monetary rewards for their service. Knowing this, many soldiers in other units were encouraged to wait no matter how bad conditions were in camp and how impatient they were to return home.

Impatience was not limited to the wait for transportation from the field rendezvous site to the state rendezvous site. Many soldiers chafed while waiting in state camps to receive their pay. B. F. Blakeslee remembered the comments of one of the men of the Sixteenth Connecticut regiment, who were standing in line waiting to receive their pay and be mustered out. The man said that "while it did not take long to enlist, it took a long time to get mustered out." Blakeslee then commented on this soldier's remarks, saying, "It proved quite true; for while we enlisted for three years, it was not supposed that we should be out more than three or six months at the most; and many of the men enlisted expecting to return in a short time."[13] Joseph Field, a lieutenant in the Second Massachusetts Heavy Artillery, complained in a letter to his wife, Kittie, that "we are yet held up on this island waiting for our final discharge papers and I get quite angry."

He was particularly annoyed by the cause of his long wait to be mustered out—paperwork errors made by the regimental officers at the field rendezvous site. Field told his wife, "It provokes me to think that officers who have been in the service nearly four years cannot make correct papers at this late hour . . . I am afraid it might be Tuesday before they begin to pay off the men."

Stuck on an island in Boston Harbor, Field might have been tempted to leave and find some other way to obtain his pay. Instead, he chose to wait and asked his wife to come to Boston in order to make that wait more pleasant. He said, "I wish you could come down here and go right to the United States Hotel where Frank Pray sleeps and I would get away late Monday afternoon. So if you get this in time to take the noon train Saturday or the night express which arrives in Boston at Midnight. I will meet you at the Depot."[14] Although no record exists to indicate that Kittie went to Boston to be with her husband, government paperwork shows that Joseph Field was finally paid late in September 1865 and went home.

John William De Forest, a former captain in the Twelfth Connecticut, captured something of the frantic mood that must have gripped regimental officers during the demobilization process in a passage from his novel *Miss Ravenel's Conversion*. He also shows that misfiling paperwork to the War Department was not simply an annoyance for the enlisted men in a unit but a subject of concern for company-level commanders who typically were the main administrators of the demobilization process for most of the Union army's personnel. In this passage we see the novel's hero, Union volunteer Captain Colburne, "dressed, and looking over a mass of company records, preparatory to commencing his muster-out roll." Although dressed, he was lying in a sickbed in the fictional New England town of New Boston. Colburne had been temporarily separated from his company at this point in the narrative as a result of a recurrence of the malaria he contracted during the Red River Campaign but, because he had not resigned his commission, was still held accountable for his company's demobilization paperwork. Moreover, Colburne knew he would be held personally liable for any government property that was not properly recorded as damaged, lost, or returned. He told his friend and future father-in-law Doctor Ravenel that "I have six months' unfinished business to write up, or I am a disgraced man. The Commissary of Musters will report me to the Adjutant-General and the Adjutant-General will dismiss me from the service."[15]

Doctor Ravenel scolded his future son-in-law, telling him, "You ought not to do that. You are very feverish and weak. All the strength that you have is from opiates, and you tax your brain fearfully by driving it on such fuel." He also made the observation that as a company commander on leave for illness Colburne needed an officer to whom he could delegate this task. Colburne replied to the doctor, "There is not a man of my original company who has not either re-enlisted as a veteran [in another regiment], or deserted, or died, or been killed, or been discharged because of wounds, or breaking down under hardships... That Shenandoah campaign cut up our regiment wonderfully. We went there with four hundred men, and we had less than one hundred and fifty when I left." He went on to say that "I must have the name of every officer and man that ever belonged to the company—where, when, and by whom enlisted—where, when and by whom mustered in—when and by whom last paid—what bounty paid and what bounty due—balance of clothing account—stoppages of all sorts—facts and dates of very promotion and reduction, discharge, death and desertion—number and date of very important order. Five copies!" Following Colburne's explanation, the doctor volunteered his services and those of his daughter, Colburne's soon-to-be wife. He told him, "Make your original, which is, I suppose, the great difficulty; and my daughter and I will make the four others."[16]

Although this passage comes from a work of fiction, Colburne's frantic response to the mustering-out process illustrates not simply one Union officer's devotion to duty but also the future value of those papers to the unit's officers and enlisted men. Without filing the proper paperwork with the War Department in Washington, an entire unit ran the risk of forfeiting the back pay and bounties due to it, which were often substantial. An original discharge certificate would also serve as proof in later years that a soldier had in fact served with a specific unit during a set period. These certificates would be crucial when soldiers began applying for pensions. In the case of Colburne's fictional unit, which he asserted now consisted of him alone as a result of attrition, this would appear to be less of a concern. However, even in units that essentially ceased to exist because of casualties or expiration of service, having all the names of that unit's members from its inception listed on a mustering-out roll was necessary. Not always the most efficient bureaucracy, the U.S. Army nonetheless, as De Forest's novel illustrates, was zealous to keep track not only of its materiel but also of its men.

Once the mustering-out process was finished, former soldiers displayed a wide variety of emotions. Corporal Aaron S. Turner of the Ninety-Fourth Ohio offers us one example. He wrote in his diary, "Got my eagle. Struck out for home immediately. Arrived home about dark. So ends the chapter. I am a citizen now. I think I feel a change."[17] The last line of this final entry from Turner's war diary captures the anticlimactic nature of his demobilization experience. An official change had occurred in his life, but Turner still did not know what it really meant. Consequently, although he believed he should feel something more as he returned to civilian life, he did not.

In contrast to Turner's brevity is a passage from the regimental history of the Fifty-Fifth Illinois. Here the writer captured something of the conflicting emotions that must have been present at many other state rendezvous sites as fellow soldiers prepared to go their separate ways: "Notwithstanding the members of the regiment had all anxiously looked with longing for the day of final discharge, when the time for their separation came there were struggles with the emotions which showed themselves, although not in words, for no language can express the feelings of sorrow at parting between comrades whose regard for each other has grown from long companionship amid the scenes of a bloody war. We were civilians again."[18] An emotional conflict is illustrated in this excerpt as soldiers felt the draw of two homes—the temporary one they had constructed in their unit during the war and the one they had left behind following enlistment but to which they were soon to return. Having anticipated their homecoming during the war, these men were now reluctant to separate from one another and return to their wives and families. The reluctance these men felt was due in part to questions of whether the homes they were returning to would live up to the dreams they had fashioned during the darkest days of the war. They also couldn't help but wonder how their civilian families would compare to the families in the field they were leaving behind. Soldiers had been brought together by sufferings both in camp and in battle. Could those at home understand and accept these unheroic aspects of army life that members of the regimental family had shared?

Henry Grimes Marshall addressed these concerns in a letter to his sister Hattie. He confided to her that "I don't feel like the same man as when I entered the service. I feel old and cold-blooded."[19] Writing to his aunt, William Harrison Barber, a private in the Forty-Ninth Pennsylvania, expressed a similar feeling of dissonance. Describing to her the spectacle of victory that was the Grand Review, which took place in Washington, D.C., on May 23–24, 1865, Barber confessed to a lack of interest. From the context of his letter, it seems clear that his aunt had read about the event in the papers and wanted firsthand information about it from her nephew. Barber, however, told her that he didn't focus his attention on the ranks of soldiers, to which he was accustomed, but instead looked out on the civilians who were watching him. He noticed "all descriptions of forms, faces, classes and there were many fair, pretty faces alive with excitement, wonder, and admiration on the avenue that day." Underlying this moment of celebration for Union

Figure 2. Mathew Brady. *Washington, D.C., Infantry Units with Fixed Bayonets Passing on Pennsylvania Avenue near the Treasury*. Photograph. May 1865. Library of Congress. Washington, D.C.

veterans like Barber were hints of a subtle wall that would come to divide them from civilians in the postwar era. Turning his face back from the civilian crowd to the soldiers for a moment, Barber asserted that "society applauds [the returning soldiers] yet how little conception has society of the hardships, [and] misery, endured by these men and the dangers faced to maintain society."[20]

The hardships and misery to which Barber referred included not only the incidents associated with combat but also the filth associated with life in an army camp. De Forest illustrates this in a scene from *Miss Ravenel's Conversion* wherein Doctor Ravenel seeks to congratulate his future son-in-law, Colburne, for his heroism and the victory of his cause. Doctor Ravenel says to Colburne, "We are all ready here to worship your very rags." To this, Colburne replies brusquely, "Well. After I get rid of them. I must have a citizen's suit as soon as possible."[21] Colburne's negative reaction to his future father-in-law's praise sounds like a rejection of his past rather than simply a desire for clean clothes. It is almost as if he wishes to throw away with his filthy uniform the events that have transpired in the last four years.

The visceral reaction to the worn uniform expressed by De Forest's fictional hero echoes the real-life response of Union veterans such as Edwin Finch, who wrote in a letter to his sister that "I will have to buy a suit of clothes for my blues are rather lousy and where I am now it is impossible to keep rid of them for the ground is covered alive with them. You see we have been on the march all the spring and we got lousy and no chance to wash any clothes and when we came here it was some time before we could draw any clothes and our blankets and tents got full of them."[22] Like many other soldiers, Edwin Finch was anxious to be clean again. However, as the abrupt tone of De Forest's fictional protagonist suggests, cleanliness was a category fraught with meaning for soldiers. The historian Reid Mitchell notes that dirt and "infestation," which had typically been associated with "sloth and poverty," became one of the "hallmarks" of being a Civil War soldier.[23] It was a sign for some that army life threatened rather than sustained or boosted their social standing as "citizens" and men. In a letter written by an Alabama officer on the prospects of leaving behind the filth of army life for the cleaner settings of the domestic sphere, he told his sister that he couldn't wait to return home so that he could "put on a white shirt and have my shoes blacked and ride on horseback or perhaps be exalted to a seat in a buggy and then I could sit down in a chair like white man, and eat at a table like a white man and feel for a little while like a white man once again!!"[24] Here racial prejudice joins with class bias in a soldier's imaginings about future cleanliness and renewed social stature.

Although Mitchell ultimately downplays the long-term impact of this assault on a soldier's identity, it seems unlikely that as a veteran he would forget this stigma. If anything, it would tend to make him more sensitive following discharge about his social status. Many veterans, in fact, overcompensated to address anxieties about social status, arguing that they were better citizens than those who had stayed home. Lieutenant Colonel Hicks, former commander of the Ninety-Fifth Illinois, displayed this overcompensation in a speech delivered to his men at a banquet not long after the surrender. He told them that:

> no longer soldiers, you are now, as citizens, to mingle with your fellow citizens, and join with them in pursuing the arts of peace, and maintaining the blessings of our land. Those blessings are theirs and yours in common; theirs by inheritance, but yours by purchase, and, knowing the dear price of that

purchase, you will not fail to maintain them inviolate. I need not urge you to the fulfillment of every duty which pertains to the citizen. I know you will cherish your reputations as soldiers so highly that you will be especially careful to do nothing which will in the least tarnish or efface it [sic].[25]

On the surface Hicks's exhortation seems like a simple admonishment to his men to return peacefully to civilian life. His speech, however, also presented a unique understanding of what it meant to be a citizen, one that reflected poorly on the civilian populace. Whereas these former soldiers had "purchased" their status as citizens, others, presumably civilians and other noncombatants, had "inherited" it.[26] This sentiment was shared by many other veterans who tried to ignore the changes to themselves, which many felt but did not fully understand. It aided them emotionally as they left the sites of their mustering out, but it also fed into a heightened state of civilian anxiety. Noncombatants were suspicious of the role that former soldiers would play in the postwar nation. They attempted to allay those fears by interpreting veterans through the image of the wounded warrior—a soldier disabled by the war and in need of civilian care.

The Image of the Wounded Warrior

Even though the alternative families created within army regiments did not replace blood ties to families back home, the perceived insularity and attitude of social superiority held by many returning soldiers helped fuel civilian misgivings about the negative effects of army life. These doubts had roots that were far older than the Civil War, dating back to the founding of the nation and debates regarding the dangers of standing armies.[27] Added to these long-standing uncertainties about the negative influence of a standing army to both its members and the republic as a whole were vestiges of the crisis mentality necessary to prosecute the war. Political leaders encouraged civilians to see potential enemies hiding in every corner, to prepare them for sacrifices—to both their comfort and their personal liberties—that would be needed to win the war. During the early postwar period civilian emotions swung wildly in many directions, not a few of which were highly contradictory. Soldiers and their officers were easy targets on which to project these anxieties and helped explain for many civilians the emotional state they were experiencing.

The moderate Republican magazine *The Nation*, which began publication in the last year of the war, reflected in many of its editorials the contradictory emotions that drove civilian discourse about the military at the end of the Civil

War. An editorial published on October 11, 1866, argued for a connection between military leaders, the expanded powers of the presidency, and the perils of an uninformed electorate. The editor said that "the danger of the interference of military men in political affairs must be apparent to every thinking mind," and pointed out that civilian impatience with the legislative process, which was encouraged during the war, might pave the way for a demagogue. A "thinking mind," the editorial argued, was needed to counter the "danger" of a potential military dictator's taking the reins of power in the United States.[28] Ironically, however, the explicit reference to the potential for this danger made such dispassionate thought difficult if not impossible on the part of the civilian reader. Instead, it opened the door to further paranoia and invective, including an editorial attack several weeks later on President Lincoln's former postmaster general Montgomery Blair.

The article "Have We Come to Caesarism?" examined statements made by Blair that indicated his support of "Caesarism" in American politics. This term appears to signify for *The Nation*'s editors an abuse of executive power up to and including an absolute dictatorship.[29] The author of this editorial accused Blair of placing too much faith in the executive as the "true voice of the people" rather than in the legislative branch. Blair, the author claimed, had fallen into the trap represented by the French experience of 1848, wherein "the Nation, by universal suffrage, gives over all power and sovereignty to one man, saying, Be Thou our sultan." Paradoxically, Montgomery Blair had been forced from his position as postmaster general prior to the 1864 election because he was not, according to the Radical Republicans, radical enough. Now, in contrast, he was being accused of being too radical and consequently un-American. As the editorial concluded, "Mr. Blair and all who side with him are not only unrepublican in their views, they are anti-representative, they are unconstitutional, and ought to emigrate to France." There, the author suggested, Mr. Blair and his ilk could have all the demagoguery their hearts desired.[30]

Through their attack on Blair and the inflammatory references to military dictators, *The Nation*'s editors showed that they were not immune to the lingering crisis mentality of the war years even as they decried its effect on postwar American politics. In fact, they risked making it worse by moving away from innuendo and directly reminding their readers about the wartime crises that had surrounded the presidential election of 1864, when it was feared that Union soldiers would vote for their former commander, George McClellan, rather than for Lincoln. McClellan was on record as favoring peace with the Confederacy. His election would have led to a permanent partition of the United States. Many wondered as well if Lincoln would step down from power should his rival win as a result of the soldier vote.[31]

Long after the 1864 election the public remained suspicious of the "soldier vote." *The Nation*'s editors decided to make use of this distrust in an editorial from the October 25, 1866, issue titled "Ought Soldiers to Vote?" The writer was clear in his assertion that soldiers ought to be denied the franchise in the postwar nation, even though most of them possessed it during the war, because of the demoralization of army life. He argued that "whenever an army exists for any length of time, it becomes a caste, in which are prevalent peculiar motives of action and peculiar habits of thought, but all dangerous to liberty." The "peculiar motive of action" the author referred to in this article was the soldier's impatience with the slow process of civil law and procedure. With soldiers, "debate is decried and action exalted." A desire to take quick action would not be a bad thing in itself, the writer suggested, but the "peculiar habit of thought" he saw the soldier as possessing made such swift action a danger to liberty. Army life, the article claimed, had nurtured in the former soldier a "blind unreasoning obedience to authority," which made him more susceptible to a charismatic and forceful leader.[32]

What makes the line of argument presented in this editorial particularly intriguing is that the editors had only recently suggested that civilians were susceptible to these same "peculiar habits" both of thought and of action. Former soldiers, however, seemed to provide a more appealing target. The idea that soldiers occupied a marginal space in society was not new and thus was more palatable than the elitism implied by making the same comment about high-strung and irrational civilian voters. Despite the large number of native-born Americans in its ranks, the Union army was still perceived by many in the North to be a collection of disreputable foreigners. This belief was enhanced by the antebellum reputation of the army as an outcast profession suitable only for those who had failed in pursuing or were unwilling to pursue the "American Dream" of entrepreneurial success.[33]

The debates surrounding "the soldier vote" were thus simply one aspect of a larger discussion in the United States surrounding the social status of soldiers, particularly that of enlisted men. Another component of civilians' negative image of the army was their perception of military life's demoralizing effect on an individual's character. In newspaper articles that addressed the vices of gambling, drinking, and profanity we can see a pattern of concern that developed surrounding army life.[34] That pattern involved habits of idleness and dependency, which sap the strength of a man's initiative and destroy him at both the economic and moral level. These civilian perceptions taken together all suggested that with so many soldiers reentering civil society, a great potential threat to the health of the republic was nigh.

Before the Civil War, the concept of the citizen-soldier had helped civilians to address these concerns. A small standing army was seen as necessary even as the general populace stigmatized it. The professional soldiers of this army were assumed the most prone to demoralizing influence because enlisting in the army was for them a career choice rather than a temporary action taken in defense of one's home. Sending these men off to the frontier was a reflection not just of the need for soldiers on the edge of civilization but also of American society's unease with the defenders it had created. Scapegoating or marginalizing Regular Army soldiers and officers, however, was considerably more difficult in the post–Civil War nation. The inevitable mixing of volunteers with draftees and Regular Army personnel exposed them to corrupting influences and threatened to confuse any meaningful distinctions between volunteer soldiers and professionals. Consequently, this method of addressing civilian anxiety was merely another avenue that fed into their paranoia. How could one tell a "good" soldier from a "bad" one anymore when all men belonged to one army?

Civilians needed a new way to understand returning soldiers that did not perpetuate the crisis-laden discourse of the wartime years. The image of the wounded warrior provided this new interpretive lens. With its roots in the early Republican figure of the "suffering soldier" and the ethos of antebellum sentimentalism, wounded warrior imagery provided a symbolic resolution to a populace that felt its world spinning out of control.[35] By viewing all soldiers as potentially disabled and in need of civilian care, noncombatants could imagine themselves as in charge of the fate of the postwar nation. *They* would steer the future course of the United States, not the hordes of armed men returning from the battlefield to a nervous home front.

Perhaps the best example of the image of the wounded warrior and how it functioned to dispel civilian anxieties in the postwar nation is Winslow Homer's engraving "Our Watering Places—The Empty Sleeve at Newport."[36] Appearing in the August 26, 1865, issue of *Harper's Weekly*, Homer's work was commissioned to accompany a short story, "The Empty Sleeve at Newport; or, Why Edna Ackland Learned to Drive." Homer's image shows a man, presumably the short story's hero, Union veteran Captain Harry Ash, and his prewar sweetheart, Edna Ackland, riding in a horse carriage along the seashore at Newport, Rhode Island, a popular nineteenth-century resort for the nation's elite. The viewer can observe sails in the distance, gliding calmly on the waters of the Atlantic Ocean, and what appears to

The Wounded Warrior and the Citizen-Soldier 31

Figure 3. Winslow Homer. "Our Watering Places—The Empty Sleeve at Newport." Engraving. August 26, 1865. *Harper's Weekly.*

be a sandy beach. As we shift our view away from the background and look to the foreground of the engraving, we see Edna driving the coach with a determined look on her face, focused on her task. She is also holding the reins with both hands, which are stretched out to their full length, along with a rather menacing whip. Harry, whose kepi, in addition to his missing arm, identifies him as a former soldier, seems distant and somewhat grim. His expression could be the result of illness, suggested by his slouching posture and prominent cheekbones. Or it might be a reflection of his annoyance at the situation in which he has been placed: the woman is doing all the work; he is merely going along for the ride.

Homer has drawn the woman's arms in this engraving in such a way that it is impossible not to focus on what she possesses and what the man lacks. Her arms are at the center of the image, but the man's empty sleeve is closest to the viewer. These two components of the engraving compete with each other for the viewer's attention and help to create its meaning. Homer forces the viewer's gaze on the empty sleeve while at the same time refusing to allow us the chance to ignore the woman's intact arms holding the reins just behind him.

This contrast leaves the viewer to draw two conclusions prior to reading the story, which appears one page after Homer's engraving. The first is the most obvious, which is that the war is an omnipresent phenomenon in postwar life: it has even found its way to popular vacation destinations. The second is that gender relations have changed with the end of the war, and so, too, has the relationship between soldiers and civilians. The woman in this image is quite literally "holding the reins," and the wounded hero of the republic is subject to either her power or her care. Using the prewar concept of the "separate spheres" as an interpretive guide, Homer's image tells the viewer that home life is dominant now that the war is over.[37]

The short story fully supports the first of these interpretations of Homer's image and partially confirms the second. Having traveled to Newport for his health, former Union captain Harry Ash instead finds himself a minor celebrity worn out by playing the public role of "disabled veteran" for a largely civilian and female crowd. The narrator of the story tells us that "at best he hated the endless questioning and commiseration—the answering of inquiries as to his health, and how and where and when that sleeve became empty. He did not enjoy the role of hero, nor the admiring pity of simpering misses and stout mamas." Harry had hoped to blend in with the vacationing crowd but instead finds himself intensely visible because of both his military service and his disability.

The former soldier is also disturbed to see his onetime sweetheart from before the war driving a carriage. We are told that "he had, young as he was, old-fashioned prejudices. He liked womanly women." To Harry Ash, Edna's driving of her own carriage seems both a "new freak," representing the upended gender rules of the postwar nation, and also a sign that she is spending her time with a "fast" crowd of "fops and roués." Instead of the homecoming Harry imagined with Edna Ackland rushing into his arms upon his return home, he finds her at the beach enjoying herself with a loose group of acquaintances and pursuing what he interprets as "unwomanly" activities.

Disgusted, Harry retreats to his hotel room to contemplate his future. He tells himself, "I have borne much; I can bear more." Harry plans to leave Newport the next day without speaking to Edna. Her heart, he believes, has been given to others more fashionable than he. Before he goes, however, he decides to take one last walk along the beach. Harry becomes easily exhausted during his walk and sits down under a tree. Disgusted with himself, he says, "I am getting no stronger. I shall never live to see the flowers die." Just as this thought crosses his lips, he hears a gentle sobbing coming from a tree nearby. As fate would have it, the sobs are coming from Edna Ackland. She says to Harry in between her sobs, "I feared you were very ill. You have been here a whole week and have never been near us." He responds to her concern with an observation on Edna's new activities, saying, "Were Miss Ackland a gentleman I should complement her." She is offended by these remarks and turns to leave, but she stops for a moment to ask "Are you really angry that I've learned to drive?"

Before Harry can answer, Edna pours her heart out, stating, "I must tell you first why I learned. I knew you loved me; I felt sure that you would tell me so when you returned . . . So when they told me you had lost an arm, the first thought that came to my mind was this. He will be so helpless! There will be so many things he cannot do for himself. I must be left hand and right hand also." Edna then tells her beloved that she spent the days awaiting his return from the war learning activities that would be helpful to him. Among them was asking her servant "old Mark" to teach her how to drive. Unable to remain angry at his love, Harry Ash rushes into her arms and "his one arm stole about her waist and drew her close to him" as they shower each other in kisses. The narrator concludes the tale by saying, "They are married now, and you may see them any day driving upon the Newport Beach in the pleasant August afternoons. Her hands guide the reins, and he sits with his empty sleeve beside her. Yet, for all that, his eye is on the road and his voice guides her; so that, in reality, she is only his left hand, and he, the husband, drives."[38]

The unsettled gender relations that Homer represents in his engraving are clearly oversimplified by the short story that is paired with it. The anonymous author of the tale is quick to assert that the husband remains in control of the carriage even though the woman is driving. Yet the image suggests otherwise. Harry's mouth is closed and his expression downcast. He seems more intent on not falling out of the carriage than he does at directing Edna's driving. The story also suggests marital happiness for Edna and Harry, but, again, the image seems to represent a couple that at best is numb. They have both survived the war and remain uncertain about what will happen next. A future of any kind seems distant and uncertain in this image. Yet when compared with the hysterical tomorrows of the paranoid discourse fostered by publishers and politicians during the war, this relatively sedate postwar scene of disability seems to represent paradise. Edna will take care of her wounded warrior, and through his lover's sympathy Harry Ash will become whole again in spirit if not in body.

The idea of creating social harmony between soldiers and civilians through female sympathy and the power of the private sphere helped calm civilian anxiety about the disbandment of armies and the massive influx of veterans who soon would be returning home. However, the gender inversion implied by the image of the wounded warrior would have been distasteful to veterans. Whether they were disabled or not, veterans would not be spectators to postwar life: they would steer the carriage regardless of its passengers.

Two veterans who responded to the imagery of the wounded warrior in their fiction were John William De Forest and Sidney Lanier. A historian and minor novelist before the war, De Forest wrote *Miss Ravenel's Conversion from Secession to Loyalty*, which contains many biographical details.[39] Like his hero Edward Colburne, De Forest was proud of his status as a citizen-soldier. He also suffered from recurring bouts of fever, which he had contracted in Louisiana, and a wide range of intestinal ailments. This blending of fact and fiction adds passion to De Forest's narrative as he asserts the distinction between citizen-soldiers and Regular Army soldiers. Reaffirming the ability of the citizen-soldier to succeed in peace as well as in war is crucial to the author. He rejects any metaphor for former soldiers that involves illness, seeing in it a diminishment of his manhood and with it his social status in the postwar nation.

Best known for his poems, Sidney Lanier served as a private in the Confederate army. For most of his time in the army he operated as a scout and blockade runner along the James River in Virginia. It was during one of his blockade-running missions that Union forces captured Lanier and sent him to the prisoner-of-war camp at Point Lookout, Maryland. At some point during his captivity, Lanier contracted the tuberculosis that would eventually end his life.[40] These events appear in fictionalized form in his only novel, *Tiger-Lilies*. Unlike De Forest, Lanier does not reject being viewed as a wounded warrior. Instead, he seeks to find true empathy between southern veterans and civilians, both of whom have been wounded by war.

The writings of both authors represent an ongoing quest for self-definition as those who fought in the war tried to understand how their combat experiences shaped their postwar sense of self. De Forest and Lanier wanted to see themselves as unchanged by the war. This meant coming to terms not only with the real illnesses they faced but also with the larger social implications attached to veterans being ill. Representations of wounded former soldiers implied their marginal social status during times of peace. De Forest approached this task through substitution, replacing one metaphor with another. The duty-infused image of the citizen-soldier is meant to supplant the sickly figure of the wounded warrior. Lanier, in contrast, looked for ways to reshape the image of the wounded soldier that moved beyond both the duty envisioned by De Forest and the pity aroused by the image of the wounded warrior.

Defending the Concept of the Citizen-Soldier in *Miss Ravenel's Conversion*

Miss Ravenel's Conversion from Secession to Loyalty has not traditionally been viewed as a novel concerned with issues of veteran representation. Part of the reason for this lies in the title, which prepares the reader for a genre that would come to be known as "reconciliation romance." In the reconciliation romance, the courtship and marriage of a northern man to a southern woman symbolizes the potential for national reunion and regional harmony between the North and the South.[41] Although elements of the reconciliation romance are present in the plot that follows Lillie Ravenel's courtship and marriage first to Colonel Carter and then to Edward Colburne, this plotline competes with several others for the reader's attention. One of them is that which follows Colburne's wartime experience. Since the novel's publication in 1867, critics have noted the uneasy relationship between the combat scenes and the romance plot in the novel, arguing that the rather clichéd romance takes away from the realistic descriptions of Civil War combat and army life.[42] What they have not considered, however, is that the experience of the hero, the Union veteran Edward Colburne, creates a narrative trajectory of its own that transcends both the specificity of the camp and combat scenes in the novel as well as his allegorical role in the romance of reunion.

The plotline involving Edward Colburne is a "conversion" narrative in its own right, charting as it does the process he undergoes as he moves from the social status of the civilian to that of the soldier. Colburne's conversion experience echoes that of the heroine Lillie Ravenel as both become infatuated with the seductive figure of Colonel John T. Carter.[43] Where their conversion experiences diverge, however, is in the role Colonel Carter plays within it. Colonel Carter's wooing of Lillie threatens to impede the romantic/political process of her conversion and thereby frustrate the postwar reunion of the nation, but in the case of Edward Colburne it is an essential albeit problematic component of his narrative.

When we first meet Colonel Carter, he is visiting New Boston in an attempt to raise a volunteer regiment. Colburne is fascinated by the contrast between Carter's manhood and that of his hometown. Colonel Carter is tanned, taut, and magnetic, whereas the men of Colburne's acquaintance in the university town of New Boston are pale, limp, and pedantic. The personification of this weak northern manhood is the figure of John Whitewood Jr., the son of a professor at the local university. He is described in the novel as "thin, pale, and almost sallow, with pinched features surmounted by a high and roomy forehead, tall, slender, narrow-chested and fragile in form, shy, silent, and pure as the timidest of girls."[44]

Colburne gravitates to Colonel Carter, who seems to him to represent the essence of masculine identity. Because Colburne wants what Carter currently possesses, it seems inevitable that he will soon become a soldier. The only thing currently stopping him is his sickly mother and lack of faith in his martial abilities. When Colonel Carter asks Colburne if he plans to enter the army, Colburne tells him that he has considered taking a position as quartermaster. Upon hearing this, Carter immediately laughs and calls such a position not only unmilitary but also unmanly. Of course, there is some irony to Carter's stance in this scene, as he will later accept a quartermaster's position in New Orleans as a means of supporting his new wife, Lillie. At this point in the narrative, however, Carter's remarks are primarily a stab at Colburne's sensitive views about northern manhood, particularly his own. Thus, when Carter says to him, "You are a college man, ain't you?—you can learn more in a month than these boors from the militia can in ten years . . . when I get a regiment you shall have a company in it," we know that Colburne's presence in a combat unit is a foregone conclusion.[45] Not long after this scene, Colburne's mother succumbs to her long illness and he enlists as a captain in Colonel Carter's regiment. The new Captain Colburne soon finds himself on a troopship headed for New Orleans and the beginning of his combat experience.

Thomas Fick has already noted, albeit in passing, that the success of Carter's wooing of Colburne depends on the latter's preexisting sense of inadequacy. He also notes that Colburne initially sees in Colonel Carter a potential model for his new manliness. War and soldiering will supposedly provide what the hero currently lacks.[46] Although Fick's analysis of Colburne's relationship to Carter is quite compelling, I disagree with his explanation of Colburne's eventual disillusionment with Carter. In Fick's view, Colburne's disenchantment is associated with Carter's role as the "southern gentleman" in the novel. Because Carter represents a way of life that the war is destined to destroy, it is necessary that Colburne eventually distance himself from his comrade in arms. This interpretation, however, slights the fact that Carter is not only a Virginia Unionist (a fact Fick readily acknowledges) but also a graduate of West Point and an officer in the Regular Army. De Forest takes pains at every turn in the novel to remind us that even though Colonel Carter is commanding a regiment of Volunteers, he is a Regular Army officer. Although the connotations attached to being an officer in the Regular Army are largely lost on the twenty-first-century reader, the average nineteenth-century audience would have made the appropriate connections, seeing in Colonel Carter the practitioner of an outcast profession.

C. Robert Kemble's research on the image of the army officer shows that antebellum Americans held several related while at the same contradictory views of Regular Army officers. Two of the more dominant perspectives were that Regular Army officers possessed the potential of becoming an aristocratic caste that would undermine U.S. egalitarian traditions and also that the Regular Army operated as a school for teaching vice, thereby lowering its officers on the social scale.[47] These negative views toward army officers, examined earlier as part of an investigation of the social perception of the army as a whole, illustrate a much larger cultural phenomenon. Namely, as the historian Durwood Ball notes, "Antebellum Americans had not integrated the professional standing army into their political and social consciousness. They scorned the regular army, and politicians inflamed their prejudice."[48] Confined to the frontier in times of peace, the army was easily forgotten until a war brought it back into focus and resurrected unresolved debates about the nature and purpose of the military in the United States.

Even though De Forest was writing in the postwar period, he freely makes use of the antebellum distinction between Regular soldiers and amateur volunteers in *Miss Ravenel's Conversion*. The Regular Army officer, Colonel Carter, is destroyed as much by his career as he is by his poor behavior. Even Lillie Ravenel sees the fate of her husband as a natural product of his training, saying that "it was West Point which had ruined his noble character; nothing else could account for such a downfall . . . her child should not go there."[49] A hard drinker and gambler, Carter finds himself drawn into marriage with the much purer Lillie. Once ensconced in this domestic haven, the old soldier tries to play the part of husband and father. He accepts a staff position as quartermaster in New Orleans that eventually leads him not only into shady business deals involving smuggled Confederate cotton but also into the arms of his wife's aunt, Madame Larue. Thanks to the complicity of his superiors, Carter's financial malfeasance is never discovered. His personal dalliance is a different story. When Lillie realizes that her husband is a rake, she leaves him, taking their son, and goes to live with her father.

Carter, aware of his domestic incompetence, requests an immediate transfer to a combat unit. He thinks to himself not long before his death that "he had proved himself unfit for family life, unfit for business; but, by (this and that and the other) he could command a brigade and he could fight."[50] Not long after he returns to combat, Colonel Carter dies. His death in battle signifies Carter's postwar irrelevance and thus works to bolster the author's view on the overall superiority of the citizen-soldier. Since Colburne is willing to identify himself as a citizen-soldier rather than as a Regular officer, the author feels confident enough to state that "we need have no fears about the prospects of Colburne... He is the soldier citizen: he could face the flame of battle for his country: he can also earn his own living." However, the novel's happy ending with the marriage of Lillie Ravenel to Edward Colburne is disturbed by the ghost of Colonel Carter.

The now-deceased Regular officer's presence is felt in the final chapter of the narrative not only in the form of the child and widow he has left behind but also in the passing reference to the military rank Colburne has not achieved. As he contemplates his failure to attain promotion in the army, the narrator tells us that, "had he [Colburne] been mustered out of service as a Brigadier-General of volunteers, he might possibly have disdained the small beginnings of a law business, demanded a foreign consulate or home collectorship, and became a state pauper for life."[51] This passage is intended to illustrate the hardy individualism that characterizes citizen-soldiers and makes them successful in both peace and war. But there is something uncanny about the narrative's passing reference to the last brevet rank held by Colonel Carter before his death so close to the novel's "happy" ending. This passing reference suggests that perhaps the sharp distinction between Regulars and Volunteers is not as clear as the author would prefer. Maybe we should be worried about the future of "our hero."

A passage from Chapter 34 shows just how fragile the distinction is between the negative example of manhood created by the author and his hero. Doctor Ravenel visits Captain Colburne, who is on furlough and about to be mustered out of the army. The doctor describes Colburne as "stretched at full length on his bed... his eyes underscored with lines of bluish yellow, his face sallow and features sharpened. The eyes themselves were heavy and dull with the effects of the opium which he had taken to enable him to undergo the day's journey."[52] Doctor Ravenel expresses his concern about the health of his friend, but Colburne consistently dismisses these fears, saying, "I'll be alright in a week or two. All I want is rest. You don't realize how a soldier can pick himself up from an ordinary illness."[53] What the doctor has seen, however, and consequently what the reader has already surmised, is that Colburne's condition is not "an ordinary illness." The narrator admits as much by saying that "he [Colburne] presented the spectacle of a man pretty thoroughly worn out in field service."[54]

Colburne is in fact seriously ill, suffering not from a bullet wound but from a recurrence of the malaria he had previously contracted during the Red River Campaign. Yet he is too stubborn to acknowledge this. He asserts to Doctor Ravenel that he will not only finish the government paperwork required to muster out his company but will also begin searching for a civilian career after a few weeks of rest. One explanation for Colburne's impatience and obstinacy is his manly refusal to be seen as an object of pity. His actions might also be viewed as further evidence of the modesty for which he is known throughout the narrative, keeping his troubles and triumphs to himself. These explanations, however, do not shed light on the vehemence with which Colburne rejects being ill. It is a vehemence that comes close to mimicking the rigors of battle. Combating illness seems to be Colburne's greatest struggle as it reflects his anxiety about his future social role in the postwar nation. De Forest presents Colburne's sickness as a dual reality with both metaphysical and bodily components. Doctor Ravenel, who serves as the unofficial narrator of the novel, tells Colburne at one point, "The Indians die of civilization. So does many a returned soldier. You will have to be careful of yourself for a long time to come."[55]

There is menace as well as sympathy in the civilian doctor's words, but their full import remains unclear. Will Colburne survive the test of civilization (i.e., peacetime life) or fall by the wayside like Colonel Carter? It is no longer obvious to the reader, or perhaps even the author, how or why the citizen-soldier's fate should be different from that of the professional army officer. The reader is thus left with the author's insistence that the difference between these types of soldier exists and is meaningful, while the evidence needed to prove this important distinction is deferred. Action alone will determine the fate of De Forest's citizen-soldier hero as a civilian, but the novel ends before we can view Colburne hard at work building a post-army life. Perhaps reality proved too intractable for De Forest to extend the timeline of his fictional world further into an unknown future, or perhaps he was simply afraid to uncover the answers to the questions he had raised in the novel. Whatever the case may be, the concept of the citizen-soldier in this instance shows itself just as unable as the image of the wounded warrior to explain the postwar relationship of veterans to the civilian population.

The Search for Empathy in Sidney Lanier's *Tiger-Lilies*

There is less of a physical distance between soldiers, civilians, and the battlefield in Sidney Lanier's *Tiger-Lilies*, a southern novel published the same year as *Miss Ravenel's Conversion*. This obviates the need for many of the narrative strategies present in De Forest's novel, such as the soldiers' letters home that bring the war to life for their civilian readers. The proximity of southern civilians to the front becomes vividly apparent in Book 3 of *Tiger-Lilies* as one of the novel's main characters, Flemington, wanders through a section of Petersburg that has been abandoned due to its vulnerability to Union artillery fire. Referred to as "the lower city," this area of Petersburg is within range of the enemy guns, and particularly one the townspeople have nicknamed "Terrible No. 5." This part of town is described as "a cemetery of untenanted graves" where "hobgoblin shells screeched and chattered and made the emptiness hideous."[56] In this instance, the front is just blocks away from where southern civilians live. Although this extremely close proximity to the war was not the case for all southerners, it was rare to find a southern family in the postwar era whose home had not been within easy riding distance of a battlefield. Because of this direct connection to the war and its privations, southern civilians were able to connect emotionally with Confederate soldiers in a way northern civilians could not with Union soldiers.[57]

Despite this camaraderie of suffering, a psychological divide still existed between Confederate veterans and the civilian population. Lanier explains this divide in terms of a distinction between spectatorship of the war and direct participation. Action causes greater pain than spectatorship, according to Lanier, because it creates an illusion of power that is ultimately shattered by defeat. The soldier, motivated by a sense of duty and ideals, is left in the wake of defeat to fumble for a new narrative of personal agency. He is also left to confront the violation of social taboos against acts such as the destruction of property and the taking of human life. Lanier suggests in his novel that the successful resolution of these dilemmas faced by Confederate veterans is only possible through civilian recognition and acceptance of soldiers, one that avoids reference to both duty as well as pity. He imagines a proper form of empathy that will bond former soldiers to civilians in the same way as purified love.

Critics have not customarily viewed *Tiger-Lilies* as a Civil War novel. When it has received critical attention at all, Lanier's novel has been interpreted as an example of "the German prose romance of the late eighteenth and early nineteenth century" that "rhapsodizes endlessly about art . . . [and] seeks rather than shuns incoherence and digression."[58] In Book 1 of the novel, the influence of the German prose romance is obvious at the level of plot, setting, characters, and theme. This portion of the novel takes place at a mountaintop retreat in East Tennessee, improbably known as Thalburg; the only action to transpire between the main characters, besides discussions on art and mortality, is a fight between the rake, John Cranston, and the German immigrant, Paul Rübetsahl. After this fight, we learn that Cranston had earlier seduced a woman named Ottilie in Germany and that Rübetsahl, remembering this event, had come to the defense of Phil Sterling's sister Felix when Cranston had begun to make advances toward her. Lanier's focus, however, seems to change radically at the beginning of Book 2, which is (as some critics note) almost the beginning of an entirely different novel.[59]

The Civil War first enters the narrative at the beginning of Book 2 in the form of "the war flower," which is both the most powerful and at the same time the most curious metaphor in the book.⁶⁰ Lanier spends the entirety of the first chapter of Book 2 describing this "blood-red flower of war," and his development of an otherwise-limited metaphor into something of a conceit suggests that at one point he envisioned this image as the novel's centerpiece. As it stands, the war flower serves primarily as the foil to Thalburg, with the former representing the fallen state of the novel's characters and the latter the Eden from which they have literally descended.⁶¹ Lanier is mourning not simply the death of the antebellum South in this descent from the mountain but also the entry into trauma of Confederate soldiers who will lose in the war both the Eden of their youth and their sense of identity.

The author crystalizes this fall into traumatic experience in the storyline associated with his main character, Philip Sterling. Philip is the son of John Sterling, a southern lawyer who enters the ranks of the aristocracy thanks to an inheritance from one of his wife's relatives. This inheritance allows John to build his mountain retreat, Thalburg, in East Tennessee. Book 1 shows Philip Sterling in his home element, dreaming about time and eternity as he wanders through the Tennessee mountains. When we next see him in Book 2, it is April 1864 and he is a member of a group of Confederate scouts stationed on the south bank of the James River, opposite the Yankee naval base at Hampton Roads. As a "gray-clad scout of the James," Philip Sterling and his friends from Book 1, who are also in his unit, seem merely to continue the carefree and frolicsome lifestyle of their prewar days at Thalburg. Confronting a slave who is fleeing from the Parven plantation, Flemington says, "Halt there, caballero hot with haste and coal-black with speed!"⁶² Flemington's use of language suitable for a Shakespeare play turns the ransacking of the Parven plantation into a scene worthy of a romantic drama. The young men rush off to save Rebecca Parven as knights-errant going to rescue a damsel in distress, an example of the southern cavalier at his best.

Not long after the damsel has been saved, the reader becomes aware that something has radically changed for Lanier between Books I and II of his novel. Sitting in the Parven home for a meal, the narrator comments that "in a battle, as far as concerns the individual combatants, the laws and observances of civilization are abandoned, and primitive barbarism is king *pro tem*. To kill as many as possible;—this, at the actual shock of arms, is the whole duty of man." Furthermore, the narrator notes that the damsel's saviors sit "moody" and "in a half-sullen silence" as Mrs. Parven serves them an "elaborate dinner" to celebrate the occasion.⁶³ Although the ideals themselves have not changed, the setting most certainly has and so have the men.

Scenes like this, and particularly the narrative commentary that accompanies it, provide Lanier's perspective on the change he sees taking place in Confederate soldiers during the war.[64] War lowers men to the status of brutes and destroys the kind of sentiment displayed by the main characters earlier in the novel. The act of killing is just one part of the brutalization that happens to soldiers during war. When killing does occur in the narrative, in most instances it happens as if it were second nature. There is little or no thought about the action before or after.[65] The other half of the brutalization process we see these soldiers undergo is distinct from but related to killing—the development of callousness toward the deaths of others.

In a passage from Chapter 1 in Book 3 we see Cain Smallin, a poor white friend of the Sterling family, cooking biscuits in the trenches near the front at Petersburg.[66] The narrator tells us, rather calmly, that Cain Smallin has unknowingly placed his skillet above a piece of unexploded Union ordinance. Talking among themselves while they wait for their dinner to cook, these men are also looking over letters from their girls back home. Suddenly, "The buried shell . . . exploded. Aubrey, being small, continued to gyrate for some time at varying distances from the centre. Flemington, a long man, rolled longitudinally to an amazing distance, and with dizzy rapidity. Cain Smallin, receiving impetus from his feet upward, described six distinct and beautiful somersaults—six—and a half. The result of the half being that, at the immediate period of stoppage, Smallin's nose was penetrating the earth, and his eyes were sternly fixed upon the same, as if he were upon the point of detecting some agricultural secret of our ancient mother." The last sentence of this passage introduces the gallows humor with which Aubrey will later respond to this scene, when he asks Cain if he is "perusing the 'volume of Nature.'" Furthermore, the overall tone of the passage prepares the reader for the calm manner in which Cain will respond to this potentially fatal explosion. Dusting himself off, Cain asks his friends, who have nearly been blown to smithereens, "Have any of ye seed the skillet?"[67]

These men have apparently become so inured to the potential for sudden death posed by combat that this event warrants no more than a quick dusting off of the pants and a renewed search for dinner. The same attitude of nonchalance toward death is present as Flemington wanders through the abandoned section of Petersburg that lies within easy range of Union artillery. He not only fails to consider the risk to his life of wandering in this dangerous part of town but also feels nothing when a shell crashes into the building he is walking through, burying in rubble two people he hears talking in the room next door. Flemington thinks to himself, "Time is a lens which should be clear. Gorm Smallin was a dust-speck upon it. God had blown him off. Who prays for dust specks?"⁶⁸ Admittedly, one of the victims he hears speaking is a sworn enemy of Flemington's friend, Philip Sterling. Nevertheless, Flemington's reaction to Gorm's death and that of the woman smuggler Jane who accompanies him seems cold because of its complete indifference. He doesn't even bother to see if they are alive. He simply walks away from the house, vaguely troubled at heart, but more for the Sterling family than for the victims buried in the rubble.

Indifference to the demise of others is the product of the survival instinct developed by soldiers in combat to cope with the reality of sudden and unexpected death. Lanier explores this same survival instinct in a very different setting as he illustrates Philip Sterling's experience as a prisoner of war. Sterling is captured by General Benjamin Butler's Union forces, who were attempting to flank Lee's army while Grant attacked the Army of Northern Virginia in the Battle of the Wilderness. Hit in the head by the butt of a musket, Sterling wakes up on the deck of a Union steamer on its way to Fort Monroe. There he is placed in a subterranean prison cell filled mostly with Union soldiers awaiting court-martial or execution.

Lanier's dark sense of humor, which contrasts sharply with his earlier sentimentality and idealism, is heavily in evidence in this scene. Attempting to adjust his eyes to the darkness, Sterling notes a shadow approaching him. This shadowy figure speaks, saying, "Sir . . . permit me to inquire if you intend to remain in this house for some time?" Sterling decides to play along with the scenario of hotelier and guest this shadowy figure has adopted, and says to him, "I must confess, I think it extremely likely." The shadowy figure then leads his guest to a corner of the cell and says to him, "There, Sir! I, myself, having a constitutional aversion to sleeping with the whole Democratic Party, have retired to an inner apartment. But you will find these bricks good bricks, soft bricks as ever you slept on in your life sir. I have tried them." Having led his guest to his "room," the mysterious hotelier disappears back into the shadows, leaving Sterling alone with his thoughts.⁶⁹

Because he is still exhausted from wounds and lack of food, Sterling is too tired to fully contemplate the nature of his situation. However, his observation of his surroundings at Fort Monroe implies disgust at being lumped together with cutthroats, thieves, and deserters. He is defensive of his status as a member of the southern gentry. When Sterling is transferred to a prisoner-of-war camp, the assault on his self-conception intensifies. The narrator comments that "to go into a prison of war is in all respects to be born over." Sterling sees in this POW camp a social order that parodies the one he has known from birth. There are aristocrats and peasants, drones and leaders, but "in the prison-changed behavior of his old army friends [they] met him with smiles that had in them a sort of mournful greasiness. [They] were too busy in devising ways and means to quiet the stomachs and intestines."[70] Sterling notes the changed nature of his former comrades who are now simply bodies attempting to survive on the short rations of the prison camp. He cannot help but wonder how long it will take before he becomes like them, and whether it's worth resisting.

Philip Sterling's crisis in identity advances to a new level when he decides to change names with another prisoner to obtain better sleeping quarters. Someone Sterling had known from better times calls out his name. The narrator never tells us who the man is, but he leads Sterling to the camp bulletin board and finds an advertisement for a potential trade—Sterling's tent in Division 11 for Threepits's tent in Division 3. The man tells him, "All you've got to do is to answer to the euphonious appellation of Threepits, while Mr. T. will respond to the call for Sterling. The corporal [of the guard] won't know the difference. It's a very good thing here to have two names."[71] Given the novel's obsession with names and the reputation those names represent, it seems odd that Sterling would give in so easily. Even a poor white character like Cain Smallin sees the value in a family name.[72] The facility of Sterling's name swapping, however, is made possible the minute he is captured. Powers beyond his control now not only determine his fate but also undermine his once-powerful sense of self, embodied in his family name.

The final scene in which we see Philip Sterling occurs in the last chapter of the novel. It is the first Sunday of April 1865 and, wearied from travel, Sterling is sitting on the edge of a fountain located in the capital grounds in Richmond. The narrator tells us that Sterling "had escaped from prison, had lain in a fever some months at a country-house, had recovered, and late in the afternoon of this day had entered Richmond, emaciated to a skeleton, down-hearted for want of news from home, down-headed for weariness, tattered like an unsuccessful beggar, unnoticing the stir or life in the streets."[73] As the capital burns down all around him and looting and chaos prevail, Sterling sleeps on the edge of the fountain. He is prepared, perhaps, to die within the shadow of the Confederate capital he was duty bound to protect as a soldier and become another victim of the war. While he sleeps, his friends, still in the trenches near Petersburg, decide to desert and go in search of Felix and Ottilie, who are both now in Richmond and are unprotected.

Flemington, Aubrey, Paul Rübetsahl, and Cain Smallin, against all odds, find Felix and Ottilie among the confusion of Richmond. These characters then find themselves drawn to the grounds of the Confederate capital and (violating the

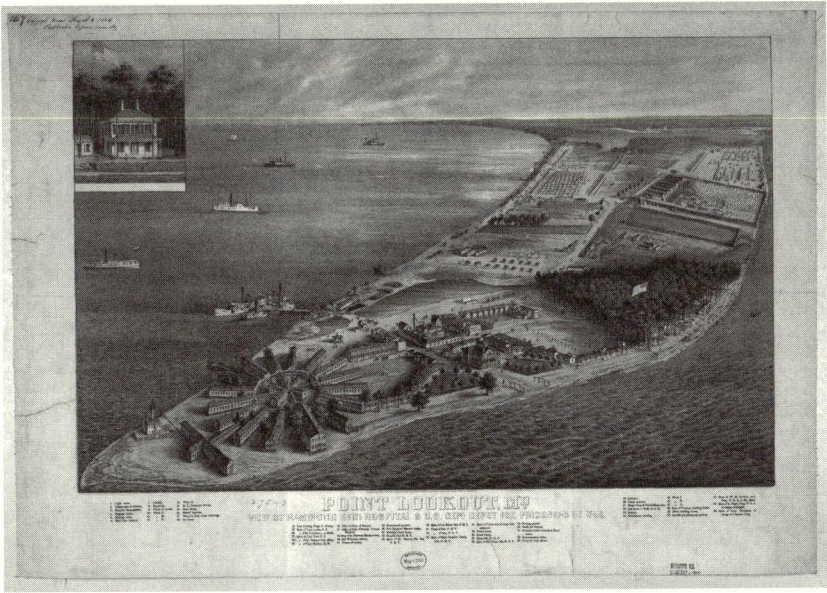

Figure 4. *Point Lookout, MD—View of Hammond General Hospital and U.S. General Depot for Prisoners of War.* Print. March 2, 1864. Library of Congress. Washington, D.C.

laws of probability) end up near the same fountain on which Philip Sterling is sleeping. Even though Sterling initially seems prepared to die alone and be buried as another nameless casualty of the war, when he hears his friends speaking he jumps up in wonder. First he grabs Rübetsahl and then he embraces Ottilie, with whom he has been secretly in love throughout the narrative. Philip Sterling's embrace of his friends and their ability to recognize him restores to Sterling the identity he had lost in the prisoner-of-war camp.

Love is the catalyst for reunion between southern soldiers and civilians at the end of Lanier's novel. He seems to hope that the shared experience of surviving the war will unite southerners regardless of the details of what they have endured. Yet the more realistic moments of the text, such as Lanier's description of Philip Sterling's internment at Point Lookout, make such a view seem overoptimistic. Remembrance of prewar personal relationships and a shared ethos of survival were not enough to trump the corrosive effect of war on identity. To find a pure love that would avoid the pity inherent in the image of the wounded warrior and the moralizing of duty apparent in the concept of the citizen-soldier would require more than Lanier was able to envision in a text written so close to the end of the war. Like De Forest, he could only hope that time would provide the answer to his questions about veteran identity and the future relationship of soldiers to civilians in the postwar nation.

Questions about the fate of returning soldiers became crucial to imagining a resolution to the Civil War. Civilians gravitated toward emotional extremes, seeing veterans as both a potential threat to peacetime society as well as victims of the war. These anxieties did not detract from the civilian belief in the heroism of their armies, but rather indicated a sense that things were different in the relationship between them and those who had served in the war. Civilians wanted to understand these differences and attempted to make them visible in order to regain a sense of agency that had been lost during the war years. Because of this desire, the image of the wounded warrior gained considerable influence in the early postwar years, moving civilians away from the paranoia of the war. This imagery blended familiar elements of antebellum sentimentalism with the early-nineteenth-century figure of the "suffering soldier" that had been used to create a new public memory of Revolutionary War soldiers. In its blending of prewar beliefs and elements of public memory, the image of the wounded warrior reflected a desire among civilians to quickly return to normal relations between themselves and the returning members of their army.

Nonetheless, what helped civilians counter their postwar anxieties about the military and its former soldiers proved unpalatable to many veterans. The act of viewing all former soldiers as victims of the war precluded any kind of future beyond that of spectator, on the one hand, and object of sympathetic care. Veterans responded to the civilian image of the wounded warrior in a variety of ways. One prominent response came from the Connecticut volunteer John William De Forest, who attempted in *Miss Ravenel's Conversion* to restore faith in the prewar concept of the citizen-soldier. He strenuously argued that men who volunteered to defend their homes and communities were different from professional soldiers. These amateur soldiers, he believed, would easily transition from combat to civilian pursuits. Yet his narrative suggests that the distinction between these types of soldiers had been eroded due to their proximity over four years of war. Another response came from the Confederate veteran Sidney Lanier, who struggled to find an emotional space in his novel *Tiger-Lilies* not driven by pity or a sense of duty where civilians and soldiers could be drawn back together by pure love.

The result of all this questioning about civil–military relations in the early postwar years was not greater understanding between soldiers and non-combatants.

Instead, tension and misunderstanding between these groups quietly increased. Veterans found it preferable in the years following the war to focus on their economic future and put the past behind them. They would show through their actions that war had not rendered them unfit for nonmilitary life. Civilians, in turn, found that it was often better to leave veterans to their own devices.

2

Veterans, Artisanal Manhood, and the Quest for Postwar Employment

> Go on writing, and make money; dig your acres, and do the same. What is needed is *work*. Work, then, patiently and bravely, and don't be cast down.
>
> —John Esten Cooke, *The Heir of Gaymount*

White veterans of the northern and southern armies believed that work and the economic advancement it made possible would help quiet civilian fears that war had disabled them, and would also ease the subconscious doubts many former soldiers possessed of combat's effect on their sense of self. They would show through their actions in the workforce that military service did not preclude postwar success. The way veterans understood work, however, was at odds with the changing nature of the American economy in what would come to be known as the Gilded Age. Former soldiers were strongly attached to a prewar model of labor that stressed economic independence, working for oneself rather than as an employee. This image of work and manhood, which many added to their visions of a postwar homecoming, sustained soldiers during the war. Yet this ideal of work and manhood was increasingly impossible to maintain, a fact that becomes readily apparent in the veteran biographies discussed in this chapter as well as the novel *The Heir of Gaymount* by Confederate veteran John Esten Cooke and *Figs and Thistles* by Union veteran Albion Tourgée.

The new postwar economy was gradually becoming national rather than regional in character, and the jobs it produced were for wage laborers rather than independent producers. It was also plagued by strikes along with unpredictable financial booms and busts, which were more frequent than during the antebellum era. Even though economists disagree on what qualifies as a "panic," there is consensus that between the years 1865 and 1900 there were at least four periods of decline in the U.S. economy.¹ One of the worst occurred in 1873 while large numbers of veterans were still attempting to establish financial stability and postwar careers. Of the numerous strikes that occurred in the late-nineteenth-century United States, one of the largest occurred during this same period: in 1877 railroad workers went on strike for several months, eventually compelling President Rutherford B. Hayes to call out the army to disperse the strikers.² Adding to this financial uncertainty and labor turmoil was the disconcerting specter, especially for northern veterans, of rampant government corruption under the presidential administration of former Union general Ulysses S. Grant.³

This confusing and increasingly volatile economy confronted white veterans as a group as they left the army and prepared to enter the ranks of the peacetime workforce. Yet the sheer number of men who enlisted to fight in the Civil War, each with his own unique prewar background and postwar circumstances, makes a "typical" path from the battlefield to a peacetime career nearly impossible to construct. Adding to this difficulty is the fact that veterans were often silent about the details of their postwar lives until decades after the war.⁴ This silence had as much to do with the economic circumstances of veterans in the late 1860s and '70s as it did with the cultural belief that it was preferable to place uncomfortable memories aside.⁵ The need to secure a livelihood to support themselves and their families through the twists and turns of an unpredictable economy left veterans little time to write about the war, let alone their lives following Appomattox. These limitations in the historical record require a nuanced examination of the relationship between veterans, work, and manhood that focuses primarily on general trends and beliefs. Despite the many differences between former soldiers, they shared a conviction that employment should support autonomous manhood. A real man was one who was economically independent. This had been true for veterans before the war and remained just as true at its conclusion.

The Ideal of Artisanal Manhood

Historians have developed a wide variety of terms to describe the prewar view of Americans toward labor that came under siege during the Gilded Age. These have included both the "free labor ideology" and the "myth of the self-made man."⁶ Since both of these terms come heavily freighted with northern connotations, the phrase "artisanal manhood" is used to highlight the similarities between the views on work and manhood held by white veterans of the northern and southern armies. Notwithstanding the obvious differences in their wartime and immediate postwar experiences, these veterans all saw work as an expression of membership in their local communities rather than a sign of status in a larger national marketplace. They also viewed it as a marker of manly independence. A real man, they believed, worked for himself.

To a certain extent, this emphasis on local communities and manly independence is contrary to what we might expect from the survivors of what some historians have called the nation's first "modern" war. Nonetheless, the fact remains that, by and large, former soldiers rejected the corporate model of work and manhood that the technology and logistics of the war had made possible.[7] Instead of seeing themselves as part of a larger organization governed by a rigid bureaucracy, veterans of the war opted to pursue career paths that allowed them to remain autonomous small-scale producers. The reasons for this veteran rejection of what the critic Alan Trachtenberg has called the "incorporation of America" are complex but, in general, tend to revolve around a desire to recapture the prewar lives they had left behind after their enlistment.[8]

Those who had been small-scale farmers and craftsmen before the war sought to return to their trades, while former soldiers who lacked a trade prior to enlistment set out to find employment that fit within the norms of independent manhood they had imbibed in their youth. Both groups of men wanted to believe their lives had merely been interrupted rather than altered by participation in combat. Thus, although many veterans were initially compelled to work for wages after the war, they strove as soon as possible to become their own boss, comforting themselves with the belief that they were apprentices or journeymen steadily working their way up (or back) to the coveted position of master craftsman. This employment position, which included for these veterans career paths not typically associated with the term "craftsman" today, such as the law or general merchandise sales, would allow them to attain a competency that would provide for their families as well as cement their importance in their hometowns.

Civil War veterans were not alone in their desire to live up to the economic independence embodied in the artisanal ideal. Nor were they unique in the growing disillusionment they felt with the massive socioeconomic changes occurring in the United States during the 1870s. However, because veterans had sacrificed so much for their prewar beliefs and placed such a heavy emphasis on economic success as the marker of their successful social integration, changing social conditions caused them much greater dismay. Veterans resolutely refused to turn their backs on the core ideals of their youth, which had led them to war and sustained them in combat's darkest hours.

Since the United States in the late 1860s and throughout much of the 1870s was still largely an agrarian nation, work and artisanal manhood were commonly viewed as being tied to the land. Popular magazines and newspapers featured numerous engravings of the former soldier returning from the war to his family as well as his plow. These images echoed stories that would have been well-known to the nineteenth-century reader—such as that of the Roman general Cincinnatus, who upon the end of the Sabine War returned to the tranquility of his agricultural pursuits, and also the passage from Isaiah that called for the turning of swords into ploughshares.[9]

One of the more famous of these post–Civil War images of the former soldier returning to peacetime agrarian labor is Winslow Homer's *The Veteran in a New Field*, which appeared first as a painting in 1865 and then later was reproduced as a woodcut engraving in *Frank Leslie's Illustrated Newspaper* in July 1867. Appearing the same year as "Our Watering Places—The Empty Sleeve at Newport," examined in the previous chapter, Winslow Homer's *The Veteran in a New Field* illustrates the power that the image of the yeoman farmer continued to hold on the national imagination in the postwar United States. His painting argued for the continuation of the world that its viewers had known, highlighting in graphic form the prewar ideal of independent or artisanal labor and making the case for its role in the reintegration of Civil War veterans.

Homer's painting has as its focus a man with his back turned toward the viewer who is occupied with the task of cutting wheat with a scythe. Without the title, his status as a Civil War veteran is not immediately obvious, as the only other clues pointing to his military service are deftly hidden in the bottom-right corner of the painting. There, if we look closely, we can see a jacket and canteen, obscured by the shadows and nearly buried under a pile of newly cut grain. On the canteen is a cloverleaf insignia, which identifies this solitary reaper as a former member of the Union army.[10] The message of Homer's painting is deceptively simple. It seems to argue that if veterans cast off their past like a worn jacket and get to work, they will soon find themselves acting, thinking, and feeling again like civilians.[11] After all, the man in this image is too busy in his agricultural pursuits to worry about the war.

Yet the war still manages to haunt the image of peacetime labor presented in this painting. Besides the uniform and canteen hiding in the shadows, the scythe the man uses was associated with the grim reaper in American iconography. Furthermore, the labor of harvesting had metaphorical ties to the battlefield, where dying men were commonly described as being "cut down" like grain. Art historian Christopher Kent Wilson notes in his analysis of the painting that, "by the autumn of 1865, it would have been difficult to gaze upon Homer's harvest scene without contemplating the veteran's former life and the deadly harvest he

Figure 5. Winslow Homer. *The Veteran in a New Field*. Oil on canvas. 1865. New York Metropolitan Museum of Art.

had reaped on the fields of war."[12] These traces of the war upset Homer's pastoral scene, reminding the viewer of the bloody war that had only recently ended and battles such as those fought at Gettysburg and Antietam in fields of grain much like the one depicted. Nevertheless Homer suggests through his reference to the well-established artistic iconography of death that the man's previous familiarity with the "fields of war" will ultimately make him all the more successful in peacetime as a harvester in this field of wheat.

Perhaps more curious, however, than Homer's suggestion that cutting down men is a skill ultimately transferable to the cutting of grain is the solitude with which he paints this erstwhile farmer's labor. Throughout most of the nineteenth century, harvesting was a communal activity that called for the hiring of extra hands and elicited the volunteer spirit in neighboring farmers. Given the large amount of grain he has left to cut, one would expect to see other figures in the painting assisting this solitary harvester. Additionally, one might even anticipate catching a glimpse of some farm machinery, such as Cyrus McCormick's popular horse-drawn reaper.[13]

An early review of the painting for *The Nation* commented on what the critic felt was the lack of accuracy in Homer's representation of American agriculture and the American farmer. He quipped that "we are inclined to quarrel with the veteran for having forgotten, in his four years or less of campaigning, that it is with a cradle, and not with a scythe alone, that he should attack standing grain."[14] Twentieth-century analysis of the painting has shown that it was not the veteran who had forgotten the implements of his prewar trade; rather, Homer painted them out. Art historian Mark Simpson notes in his analysis of the image that Homer had originally given the veteran a cradle scythe, a multi-bladed cutting implement that would have allowed him to collect the cut grain into sheaves rather than leaving it in a pile at his feet. At some point in the composition process, however, Homer decided to paint over the extra blades on the scythe, burying the veteran in a pile of grain. This decision on the part of the artist to turn away from strict fidelity to agricultural practices at the time reminds us that the painting is meant to be symbolic. Homer is less interested in the process used to harvest wheat in 1865 than he is in the fate of this representative man. Standing alone in a generic field of grain, the veteran in Homer's composition embodies the thousands of other former soldiers coming home from war and searching for work.

A reviewer of *The Veteran in a New Field* for *Frank Leslie's Illustrated Newspaper* commented on this implied message of the painting. Given the vast numbers of veterans returning home from the army, he argued that "we can well congratulate ourselves upon the manner in which the veterans have returned to their old *fields*, or sought for new ones."[15] Noticing what must surely have been an intended pun on the part of the artist with the word "field," the reviewer further highlights the function of this painting as a statement on the important role of work in the reentry of veterans into civilian life. He also hints in his comments on the painting as the example for an overall vision of American labor. The specific mode of employment in this image or "field" is less important than the attitude with which the task is accomplished.

The veteran is thus left as the solitary figure in this image in order to illustrate the principle of manly independence at the heart of the prewar artisanal ideal. He contains within him all aspects of the production process, which in this case is agricultural. Presumably he has planted the grain and tended to it during the growing process. Now he cuts the grain in preparation for its sale and imminent consumption. The uncomplicated image of labor represented in this painting would have been appealing to a society beginning to encounter the factory and the expansion of national distribution networks made possible by the railroad. It would also have been attractive to veterans looking for signs of continuity in their lives. The ability to succeed in the postwar economy using the values they had espoused prior to the war would mean, as the reviewer for *Frank Leslie's* notes, that former soldiers had left their "sphere of usefulness [only] temporarily to aid the Government in its need."[16] War would then not be a changing force but merely an interruption in their lives.

Civil War Veterans and the Struggle for Artisanal Manhood

Civil War veterans returning home strove, despite often-difficult circumstances, to live up to the ideal of labor embodied in Homer's illustration. Doing so allowed them to ignore warnings of fundamental change to themselves and their world. One interesting example of the struggle this entailed can be found in a pamphlet titled *The Great War Relic*, published by members of the Grand Army of the Republic on behalf of their disabled comrade Charles L. Cummings.[17] Cummings had enlisted as a private in the Twenty-Eighth Michigan during the war and, upon his discharge in June 1866, returned home to Allegan, Michigan. He tells us that after being home a short time he began to feel he "had made a great mistake by going into the army." For not only had he "contracted chronic diarrhoea" in the service of his country, but he had also "missed [his] chance to acquire an education." As a result, "the other boys [in town] had secured the good situations and there was nothing left me but the rough work which I was not fit for."

Cummings explains that he initially struggled to find work of any kind due to his health. At one point he had "secured a situation as an apprentice to learn the machinist trade, but took sick and lost [his] situation."[18] Eventually he went to work for the railroad and was employed by a number of different freight lines before accepting a position as a brakeman for the Toledo, Wabash, and Western Railroad. It was in this position on October 29, 1873, that Cummings experienced a cruel twist of fate. Slipping as he attempted to jump onto a moving boxcar, the wheels of the train rolled over both his legs, crushing them below the knee. Several hundred miles from his hometown, Cummings was taken to a nearby boarding house, where doctors were able to save part of his lower legs but had to amputate his feet. After nearly seven months recuperating, he learned to walk again using crutches.

Cummings's story is unusual when compared to the narratives of most disabled veterans since his injuries were not the result of combat but rather a workplace accident eight years after the war had ended. Nevertheless, he encourages his potential reader with the title of this pamphlet to misunderstand him as a casualty of the Civil War. The narrative soon disabuses readers of this notion, but by the time it is made clear Cummings is the victim of an industrial work accident they have presumably already purchased his pamphlet. Cummings puts his status as a veteran to use, seeing it as a way to increase his earnings. However, he is quick to point out that he is not a beggar but an example of artisanal manhood. Once he learned to walk on crutches, Cummings tells us that the first thing he did was search for some means to obtain a living. He resisted his "friends who wanted to send [him] to the alms house before [he] could learn to help [himself]."[19] This pamphlet containing his life story is simply one of many objects (including pencils and cheap pocket knives) that he attempted to sell on the streets.

Although helping to keep him out of the poorhouse, his sales have often, as he tells us, put him in conflict with the authorities. Not making much money to begin with, Cummings shares with readers that he has been hard-pressed by strict licensing requirements in the towns he passes through. One scene he narrates includes a conversation he once had with a policeman. Cummings says that the "license everywhere [was] from one dollar per day to fifty dollars per day. When I inquired why these prohibitory laws [existed, he told me that] 'it is to protect our merchants who sell the same goods.'" Cummings can only conclude from numerous encounters with the legal system that "a man with $10,000 has a better right to make a living than a man with 1,000 cents."[20]

Despite these obstacles, Cummings persists in his street vending, this time confident that he has an item for sale that is both harder to regulate and even harder to refuse: the life story of a Civil War veteran. Not only does Cummings manipulate the reader with the title of his pamphlet, he also accentuates its appeal as a Civil War narrative to the reader with the frontispiece photo. Initial editions included an image of himself as an aging double amputee on crutches; later editions of the pamphlet replaced this stark realism with a generic lithograph of a Union soldier preparing for battle. Readers might very well refuse the pleas of the injured industrial worker, but they cannot take lightly the claims of a wounded national hero.

Cummings's story shows that disability was not a bar, at least in his mind, to the performance of artisanal manhood. Desiring to remain independent and not rely on others for support, Cummings followed the advice of his friend and fellow Grand Army member George Reed, who reportedly told him that "there [are] one of two things a good American will do when he is busted: he will either write a book or take up a collection."[21] Taking his cue from the growing popularity of books and articles written by Civil War veterans in the late 1870s and early 1880s, Cummings opts for work rather than charity, the "book" instead of the "collection." Through this choice, he demonstrates that he is just as much a man

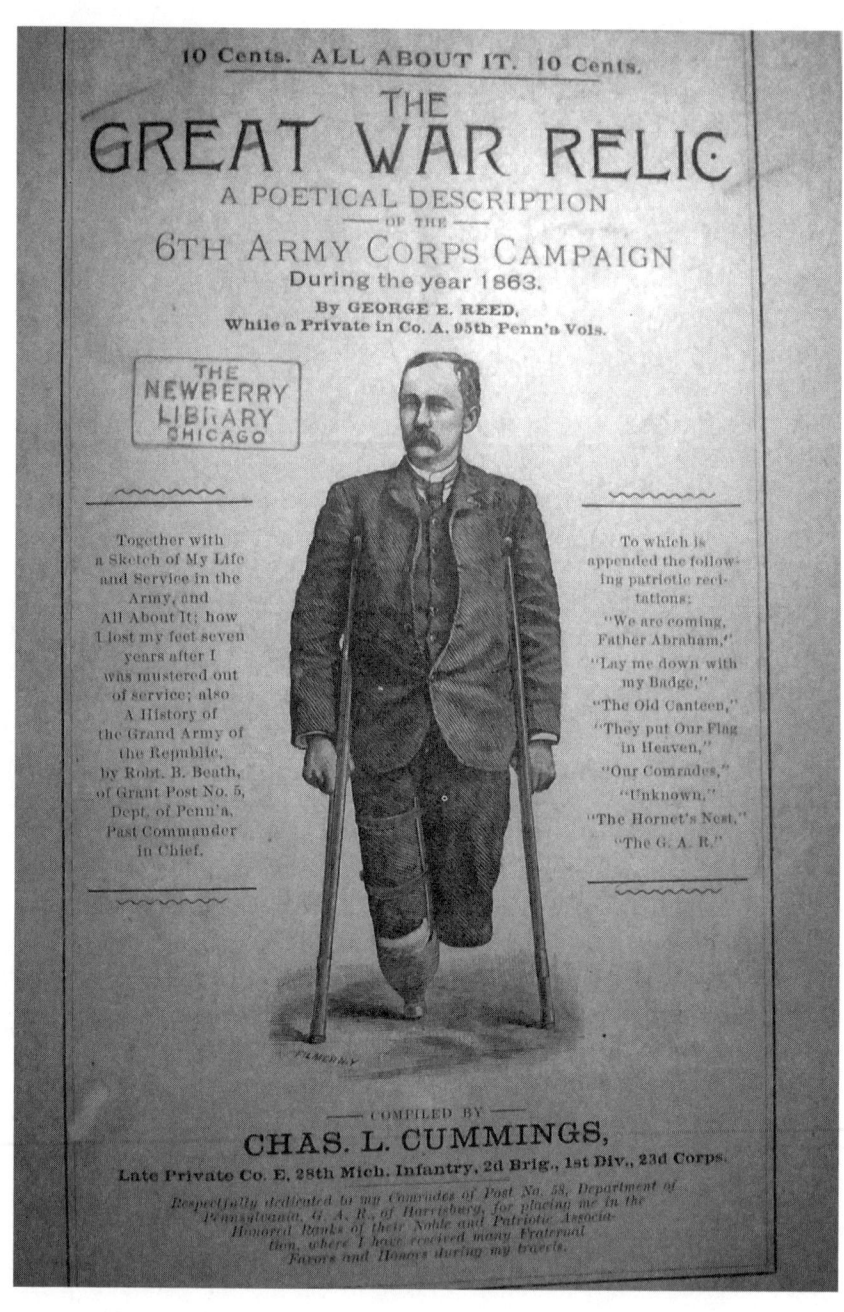

Figure 6. Charles L. Cummings. *The Great War Relic*. Ca. 1885. Photograph by author. Newberry Library. Chicago.

Figure 7. Charles L. Cummings. *The Great War Relic*. Ca. 1888. Photograph by author. Newberry Library. Chicago.

as anyone else, perhaps even more so given his success despite great obstacles. The greatest of these hindrances, according to Cummings, is not even physical disability but a government that is quick to block a man in the pursuit of his trade with needless regulations.

A similar work to that of Cummings was published around the same time by the Confederate veteran John Robson.[22] Titled *How a One Legged Rebel Lives*, Robson's book differs from that of Cummings in the source of the wound that caused the author's amputation. Instead of stemming from an industrial accident, Robson's wound is a direct result of his combat experience as a private in the Fifty-Second Virginia. He tells us that the battlefield of "Malvern Hill will always be a place of painful interest to myself, for there it was the cruel lead forced its way through the bones and flesh of my ankle." Somehow, Robson managed to march on his wounded ankle for the duration of the war. It was not until his return home that he was compelled to have his foot and lower leg amputated. Faced with relentless and excruciating pain, Robson finally went to the doctor. He says, "I found myself, on one bright day in the spring, and a short while after I had returned to my friends from the field of surrender, at full length stretched on a table in the presence of three or four grim disciples of his ancient honor Mr. Aesculapius."[23]

Interestingly enough, despite Robson's legitimate claim to being a wounded war hero, he is far more apologetic than is Cummings at the beginning of his book. In the preface to his narrative, Robson asserts, "Could I find employment in any way, I assure my readers I would not resort to authorship. But I expect many will read my little book and not regret the small sum paid in its purchase." Underneath this modesty, however, lies the same belief in artisanal manhood that inspired Cummings's memoir. Rejecting charity, Robson attempted, through the marketing of his book, to "obtain an amount sufficient to set me up in some business by which I may make my own living."[24]

He illustrates the sincerity of that claim by describing some of the previous business enterprises with which he has been involved. Even though manual labor is not a viable option for Robson, he, at one time, owned "a boarding house on the line of the Chesapeake and Ohio Railroad" and "kept a bar . . . at Rawley Springs, in the county of Rockingham, during the season of 1871." Those businesses were lost, however, due to economic setbacks. In the first instance, it was because of "the suspension of work" by the railroad and "their inability to pay off their laborers, who were my boarders." Left with no income to pay off his debts, Robson was forced to sell his boarding house in order to satisfy his creditors. Financial problems resulted in the failure of his second business as well, but this time Robson admits to setting himself up for failure rather than being taken by surprise. Presented with an investment opportunity to bottle the waters of Rawley Springs, Robson paid a subcontractor to bottle and help distribute this "perfect panacea for all the ills to which human flesh is heir." Looking back on the experience, he concludes that "I was actually and bona fidely bottled [myself], not having to this time got back my advances of five cents per bottle."[25]

Despite his previous setbacks as a proprietor, Robson remained committed to the manly independence of the artisanal ideal. As with Cummings, for Robson his book was a means to an end, a stepping-stone to successful self-employment. This attitude was consistent even among those veterans employed in jobs that could not properly be considered independent crafts or trades, such as that of clerk. In a letter reprinted in the pages of the *Grand Army Journal*, a weekly newspaper published for northern veterans, William Jones, a disabled Confederate veteran from Alabama, tells the United States Pension Office that it had mistaken him for a Union veteran from Massachusetts with the same name. For the last several months, the Pension Office had been sending him this other man's paperwork and compensation. Jones returns all the above materials to the government accompanied by his letter. He asserts in the letter, "I am not a 'pensioner' upon any government. I am now laboring daily, on one leg, to assist in paying pensions to those who shot the other off."[26]

The cruel irony of paying out pensions to northern war veterans, while himself being ineligible to receive one, explains, at least in part, the defiant tone of Jones's letter. Yet Jones seems less incensed by the fact that the man receiving a pension is a Yankee than he does that a man, regardless of his sectional loyalties, would consider receiving a pension in the first place. Despite the fact that he works for the United States government, Jones is still insistent in his belief that he works for himself. He is economically independent and, therefore, a real man.

Because all three of the veterans examined above were amputees, societal perceptions toward the disabled almost certainly played a role in their vocal defense of the artisanal ideal. Nevertheless, their responses were part of a larger reaction by white veterans against the encroaching values and practices of the Gilded Age nation. In a world increasingly dominated by complex systems and markets that led to the expansion of wage labor, former soldiers were quick to defend individual effort and autonomy as well as face-to-face business transactions. Amos Churchill, an able-bodied former lieutenant in the 141st Illinois, was proud of his economic independence, boasting in his biography that "he had never received any assistance from anyone." He was also quick to assert that he had succeeded in his postwar life "by industry and straightforward dealing."[27]

Gad Lowrey, a former lieutenant in the Ninety-Third Illinois, also emphasized the importance of economic independence and personal initiative in matters of employment. He tells us that "after leaving the service, I resided at my old home near Mineral, in Bureau County, Illinois, until September, 1868, at which time, with my family and personal effects, in two covered wagons, I started for Iowa, with the intention of making that state my future home."[28] Once in Iowa, Lowrey attempted to start up a farm, taking advantage of the 1864 changes made to the Homestead Act.[29] He says of his homesteading days, "It was pretty hard work those times, almost as hard as soldiering, for the country was new and had no railroad within thirty miles. I believe my house was the first one built in the township in which I settled."[30] After living on this homestead for ten years, Lowrey moved to Pomeroy, Iowa. At the time of the regimental survey in the 1890s, he was unemployed and resided with relatives about two and half miles from the site of his former home.

In his reply to the questionnaire, Lowrey considered personal failings rather than larger social forces as the main cause of his inability to succeed as a farmer. Were it not for his increasingly ill health—he tells us he is "still suffering from the old trouble contracted while in the army, epilepsy"—and the disinclination of his children towards farming, he suggests he would have probably succeeded in his attempt at economic independence.[31] But the volatility of the U.S. economy in the late 1870s makes the date of Lowrey's decision to leave his homestead highly suggestive. Since even in the best of times homesteading was a precarious way to make a living, the Crisis of 1873 and the Great Railway Strike of 1877 must have been the death knell for whatever hopes Lowrey held for his small farm. He was part of a complex web of personal misfortune aligned with market expansion and instability.

The same was true of former sergeant Elhanon Winters, a veteran of the Thirty-Fourth Illinois. Employed in farming until 1876, Winters left to work as a farm machinery salesman. He held that position in two separate companies, eventually becoming a partner. But in October 1881 he was seriously injured by a fall from a windmill and was not able to work for over a year. Forced to sell his interest in the farm machinery business in order to survive, upon his recovery Winters had to begin his search for employment yet again. This time he took a position as a traveling salesman, which he carried out with some success until 1887, when he suffered a stroke. Incapacitated this time for a year and a half, Winters tried working as a salesman in real estate and insurance, but eventually settled for a less physically demanding position as justice of the peace and pension claims agent.[32]

Some veterans such as Levy Downs sought financial independence and autonomous careers in the southern lands where they once had fought as soldiers. In a letter to one of his sisters, Downs asserts, "I don't know how soon I shall be mustered out but when I am I expect to go to N.C. to live. I have been there since I wrote you before and think I can do better there than in Conn. and as there is nothing in particular to draw me back to Conn. I should go where I can do the best."[33] Downs had served as a lieutenant with the 107th United States Colored Troops (USCT) in eastern North Carolina, where his unit performed security duties associated with the beginning of Reconstruction. After his discharge in November 1866, he went to work as a Freedmen's Bureau clerk in Plymouth, North Carolina, where he had already married a local woman and purchased a house. Downs was placed in charge of processing claims for back pay and bounties due to veterans of the USCT.

Levi Downs made several attempts to succeed in civilian employment after leaving the quasi-military Freedmen's Bureau, including trading in fish, working as collector of customs for Plymouth's port, and finally farming. He confides to his sister Louisa in a letter, "I manage to make a very comfortable living here and get along very well but am growing old fast."[34] Downs tells her that he is weighed down with concerns about fluctuating crop prices, debt, bad weather, and the sickness of his wife and children. When his wife finally died after a long illness in 1880, Downs decided to return to Connecticut to restore his fortunes. He died there in 1883, leaving behind three sons to the care of his relatives.

The diverse life stories of these veterans illustrate the lasting power of the prewar artisanal ideal. Former soldiers refused to let go of their belief in economic independence and personal autonomy as the defining characteristic of true manhood. Their tenacity can be explained in part as longing for a sense of continuity in their lives, but it also sprang from two deep-seated fears. The first was that their failure to succeed at the ideal of artisanal manhood would mark them as social deviants. Many post–Civil War–era civilians assumed that the large number of unemployed "tramps" who moved across country in search of work were former soldiers unable to transition to civilian life. Historian Todd DePastino remarks that this "theory about the origins of the 'tramp nuisance' recurs so frequently in the 1870s that one might fairly call it one of the period's prevailing explanations for why men tramp."[35] The second fear that motivated veterans to tirelessly pursue the ideal of artisanal manhood was a concern that leaving this model of manhood behind would lessen the glory of their service in the war. To no one did it seem to occur that circumstances had changed and that their personal failings alone could not explain their inability to succeed financially.

In this respect, veterans shared the beliefs of the civilian populace that character flaws rather than social forces had created the obstacles that prevented them from fully attaining the pinnacle of manhood and success. Cultural historian Judy Hilkey observes that one of the best-selling success manuals published in the nineteenth century, *Acres of Diamonds* (1870), was the work of a Union veteran.[36] Written by Russell Conwell, a former captain in the Union army who worked as a journalist for the *New York Tribune* and the *Boston Traveler* before being ordained a Baptist minister, *Acres of Diamonds* was part of a genre that argued for the belief that good character rather than worldly riches was the mark of a successful man. Although not all veterans would have agreed with Conwell's definition of success, they nonetheless would have agreed with him on the central role of good character to a man's rise and fall in life. They also would have shared his contention that judicious changes made to a man's character in an attempt to correct his most egregious flaws, would aid in the alleviation and eventual resolution of many of the social and economic ills facing the postwar nation.

The novelists John Esten Cooke and Albion Tourgée share this belief in the efficacy of good character. In Cooke's *The Heir of Gaymount*, the great character flaw of the hero is the idleness he cultivated in his antebellum life, instead of crops. The southern gentleman and Confederate veteran, Edmund Cateret, is shocked into awareness of this crippling personality trait by the experience of defeat, which causes him to reassess his entire life at the beginning of the novel. Gradually accepting his flaws, Cateret sets out to reinvent himself and his region through a reshaping of southern agriculture along northern lines. Although Cateret's actions represent acceptance of the economic view of southern reconstruction, he nonetheless resists northern dominance of southern culture. Cooke has his main character adopt the early republican identity of the natural gentleman as a replacement for the antebellum Virginia cavalier. This allows Cooke to imagine a "New South," reinvented in terms of economy, but essentially unchanged in terms of culture.

Albion Tourgée's *Figs and Thistles* is less interested in specific character flaws than in the source of good character. Tourgée argues that the small-town setting creates good character and therefore must be defended from incursions by urban industrial life. These incursions are represented in the novel by the railroad and the growing government corruption associated with it.[37] The constancy of character found in Tourgée's hero, Markham Churr, is the supposed result of his upbringing in a world of face-to-face interactions. He is steeped in the artisanal values of his antebellum hometown, and becomes their most forceful defender against a growing national economy based on mysterious transactions between impersonal corporations.

Even with the obvious differences in focus of these two narratives, the veteran heroes of both novels are meant to offer hope to the reader that the greed and corruption of the Gilded Age might yet be defeated by the cultivation of good character. This meant embracing and defending the artisanal values of the prewar nation, even if, as in the case of Cooke, those values needed to be reinvented rather than reaffirmed. The alternative, these authors felt, was to accept the inevitable decline of the nation they had fought for, and the emergence of a society that would do justice to neither of the sections that had clashed in the war.

John Esten Cooke: The Return of the Natural Gentleman in *The Heir of Gaymount*

For Confederate veterans like John Esten Cooke, their manhood was stung both by defeat as well as by the massive changes to the social and economic order of the South after the Civil War. Some former Confederate soldiers sought to escape from these changes into a myth that would come to be known as the "Lost Cause," while others directly addressed the postwar conditions of the South, seeking to help in the creation of a New South from the ashes of war.[38] Judged primarily by twentieth- and twenty-first-century critics on the basis of his novel *Surry of Eagle's Nest* and his hagiographic biographies of the Confederate generals Stonewall Jackson and Robert E. Lee, John Esten Cooke has typically been associated with the former group of southern veterans rather than the latter.[39] Although there certainly are elements of chivalry and Lost Cause mythology in Cooke's writings, which proved serviceable to later generations of southerners like his nephew Thomas Nelson Page, the author was not hostile to imagining the possibilities for creating a New South.

In his novel *The Heir of Gaymount*, Cooke embraces the idea that economic development, made possible by northern capital investments, will ultimately heal the wounds of war in southern states like Virginia. His embrace of this ideal, however, is qualified by his desire to save aspects of southern culture and manhood in order to prevent the New South from simply being a clone of the triumphant North. The southern gentleman, according to Cooke, did not need to be replaced but rather reinvented to fit the changed conditions of the South. Ironically, Cooke's reinvention of the southern gentleman to fit a modernizing era involved looking backward to Virginia's colonial past and the early republican figure of the natural gentleman.[40] This allowed Cooke to argue for the propriety of once-leisured upper-class southerners returning to work the land, replacing cash-crop plantations tended by slaves with small-scale produce farms run by southern families that would supply urban markets with fruits and vegetables.

Manual labor in *The Heir of Gaymount* does not degrade the character of the novel's hero, Edmund Cateret, but rather improves it. Before the war, Cateret had been a spendthrift interested primarily in hunting, horse riding, and women. The only son of a distinguished antebellum Virginia family, Edmund's parents had died during an epidemic, and he was sent to live with his Uncle Henry. Edmund is poised to inherit both his family's property as well as that of his uncle, until he enlists in the Confederate army. Uncle Henry, a staunch Unionist, is incensed by his nephew's decision and alters his will at the opening of the war. He leaves Edmund only the crumbling Cateret home and forty acres of land, most of it forest, to which the hero returns at the war's end.

Sitting on the porch of his dilapidated mansion with a former comrade in arms, Guy Hartrigger, Edmund says, "I have a house, and a great park, which came to me in a very singular manner. But you can not eat a house, nor cultivate a lawn." Trained in the ways of the tidewater gentry, Cateret finds himself in the postwar South bereft of money, profession, and social status. He feels superfluous and describes himself as being "like a sword in its scabbard," rusting from lack of use. Making matters worse, he soon discovers he is seriously overdue with his property tax payments and soon to have "his plate and wearing apparel sold within ten days date." Considering his options, Cateret muses that he can "go to Mexico, and join the army there," or perhaps try his luck in some other region of the United States.[41] There is also the possibility of taking out a loan or selling his property outright to the land speculator Tuggmuddle, a former overseer for his father who desperately wants to obtain the Cateret estate.

It is only when his old friend Frank Lance comes to visit that Edmund considers the option of making his living in the South as both a professional writer and a small-scale produce farmer. Frank Lance is a reporter for the fictional northern newspaper *The Bird of Freedom*, and he owes Edmund his life. During the war, Lance had been captured by southern cavalry as a spy and would have been shot or imprisoned were it not for the efforts of Edmund, who gave him a horse and helped him escape back to northern lines. Wanting to return the favor, Lance encourages Edmund to "go on writing, and make money; dig your acres, and do the same. What is needed is *work*." Specifically, Lance recommends "the truck system" to the ruined Virginia aristocrat, writing "sketches" instead of "big volumes," and small-scale, diversified produce farming rather than a cash-crop plantation. Inspired by Lance's optimism, Cateret decides to stay on his estate, declaring, "What I mean to do now is, to give up all such fancies of adding to my estate, to cultivate what I have, and to make this tract of forty acres bring me as much as four hundred or a thousand."[42] Chopping down the beautiful trees in the park that surround his home and digging up the fine lawns, Cateret swiftly turns his family estate into the headquarters of Cateret and Company.

Cooke's willingness to transform an idle but genteel Virginia cavalier into an industrious yeoman farmer seems bewildering at first glance, going against the grain of the author's supposed image as a champion of the Lost Cause and the antebellum plantation ideal. However, Cooke's relationship to the figure of the cavalier, central both to the Lost Cause and the plantation ideal, was much more complex before the war than critics have hitherto noted.[43] Yet the end of the war presented serious obstacles to the author if he desired to continue championing the natural gentleman and the artisanal labor of the yeoman farmer. Foremost among them was the strong attachment of these concepts to the free labor ideology of the victorious North following the war. Espousing the beliefs associated with the artisanal ideal thus involved coming to terms with the sting of defeat. This turn of events touched the author on a very personal level, for, as his biographer John Beaty has argued, "Cateret is plainly Cooke."[44] Although Cooke never enjoyed the antebellum wealth of his fictional hero, he nonetheless struggled like Edmund Cateret with the question of his usefulness as a Confederate veteran to the future of the postwar South. Along with his hero, the author was attempting to reinvent himself and, by doing so, to re-create his war-torn state.

At least in *The Heir of Gaymount*, the adoption of certain northern values does not appear to be an insurmountable obstacle to the hero's success. What really seems to stand in the way of Cateret's full adoption of the New South Cooke is trying to create in the novel is the figure of Tuggmuddle. His Dickensian name automatically marks him as a villain in the narrative, but the significance of his villainy is more complicated than the reader might at first suppose. As an overseer turned land speculator, Tuggmuddle is eager to lend money to his former employers. He knows that most of them will never recover the fortunes they lost during the war, and he anticipates the foreclosure and subsequent seizure of their property. Tuggmuddle thus appears at first glance to be nothing more than the stock figure of a poor white villain that would be a staple of southern literature well into the twentieth century.[45] His role in *The Heir of Gaymount*, however, is closer to that of the greedy bankers in Hamlin Garland's local-color tales about Midwestern farmers than to the traditional role of the poor white scoundrel.

Tuggmuddle's allegiance is not to a class or a political creed but rather to money. He is a man who profits from the labor of others, making money by lending it, and thus represents the antithesis of the artisanal ideal. Tuggmuddle, moreover, embodies the contradictions of the economic path to success that victorious northerners encouraged the defeated South to pursue. The economic independence championed by the artisanal ideal, of which free labor was simply a variant, was increasingly impossible to attain in the North, where figures like Tuggmuddle abounded. Recognizing that the path to prosperity championed by optimistic northerners like the fictional newspaper writer Frank Lance was in reality a scam, Cooke initiates a dramatic swerve in the direction of the plot toward the end of the novel.

Throughout much of the narrative, Edmund manages to stay free from any debts to Tuggmuddle. But when it becomes known that the usurious lender is close to foreclosing on the property of his sweetheart Annie Vawter's father, Cateret borrows money from Tuggmuddle to pay off their debts, using his land as collateral. He is convinced that the profits from his truck farming, along with the occasional pieces of writing on the Civil War he publishes, will help him pay off this loan. However, now married to Annie Vawter, and the father of a small child, Cateret finds himself close to eviction from his home.

Rather than allow this to happen, the author intervenes in the narrative with the heavy-handed plot device of buried treasure. One day while sitting in his study, Edmund discovers a piece of paper written in some sort of code. He determines that the seemingly random series of letters and numbers must lead to some cache of riches; after considerable effort, he manages to crack the code. What Edmund uncovers is a chest buried in the yard by his long-dead father. In this chest are not only money and jewelry but also a copy of a will leaving him the entire Gaymount estate, which includes the land currently owned by his cousin Arthur Botleigh. By selling off some of the land he has inherited, Edmund is able to free himself from the clutches of Tuggmuddle. Furthermore, Tuggmuddle is ruined because Arthur Botleigh no longer possesses the collateral he put down for his loan, making it impossible to repay.

At the end of the novel, the land speculator is defeated and Edmund is a gentleman again, but this message is problematic, as it undercuts the entire midsection of the narrative. Suddenly the manual labor of the artisanal farmer no longer seems as noble. The natural gentleman becomes overshadowed by the southern gentleman Cooke at first seemed eager to replace. Furthermore, the sharp contrast between the literary realism of the portrayal of Edmund's attempts at "scientific" agriculture and the hackneyed discovery of buried treasure at the end are striking.⁴⁶ The author appears to have been blindsided by the revelation that the agents of reconstruction were giving southern people old economic advice that no longer matched working conditions in the North. Dismayed by this discovery, Cooke instinctively returns to the world he knows—that of the antebellum South.

Regrettably, *The Heir of Gaymount* was Cooke's only real attempt to imagine a new postwar South. His later narratives retreated further into Virginia's past rather than considering its present and future. Nevertheless, this uncharacteristic novel illustrates that future critics of Cooke's work should pay closer attention to his entire body of writing, rather than a select number of his novels and biographical sketches. It also shows that Cooke did not remain a consistent and unchanging advocate of the Old South ideal, with its plantations and cavaliers. Even in those works where he seems most engaged in mythology, Cooke was interested in the evolution of southern culture and identity. He was limited, however, by his origins.

Cooke himself admitted as much in a comment on the growing popularity of realist fiction, saying, "Mr. Howells and the other realists have crowded me out of popular regard as a novelist, and have brought the kind of fiction I write into general disfavor. They see, as I do, that fiction should faithfully reflect life, and they obey the law, while I cannot. I was born too soon, and am now too old to learn my trade anew."⁴⁷ Written not long before his death, these comments serve as a fitting epitaph for Cooke, who strove all his life to find a useable past. They also hint in the phrase "learn my trade anew" at the many levels of difficulty facing Confederate veterans like Cooke on their journey back to civilian life. Confederate veterans shared with former soldiers in the Union army the desire for economic independence, but the specifics of how they understood the ideal of artisanal manhood was of necessity different due to the existence of slavery. With slavery now gone, southern veterans, burdened by the stigma of defeat, were left a series of unpalatable options. They could stay true to the past and become irrelevant, existing like Edmund Cateret at the end of *The Heir of Gaymount* in a space outside of time, or compromise with the present, risking the loss of their southern identity in the web of expanding national commerce.

Albion Winegar Tourgée and the Corporate Jeremiad

Despite his association with the victorious armies of the North, the Union veteran Albion Tourgée shared the Confederate veteran Cooke's concern about the status of former soldiers in the postwar economy. Believing that he had fought not only to free the slaves but also to defend the ideals of artisanal labor, Tourgée committed himself to writing about the dangers of the corporate economy emerging in the 1870s. He hoped that by calling the attention of his readers to the perilous detour the nation had taken since the end of the war, American society might yet return to the virtuous path of artisanal manhood and the values of the small communities from which such manhood emerged.

Critics have missed this message in part because, like Cooke, Tourgée's body of writing has been interpreted based on only a handful of his works. Examining primarily *A Fool's Errand* and *Bricks Without Straw*, an image of Tourgée has been created as the quintessential "carpetbagger" and champion of African American civil rights. Although Tourgée was interested in the problem of race relations in the postwar South, *Figs and Thistles* demonstrates that he was engrossed by a wider variety of issues than those that concerned Reconstruction.[48] In this novel, Tourgée turns his gaze on the North, which had begun to change dramatically thanks to the rise of the corporation and the transportation revolution unleashed by the railroad, even as it was busy rebuilding the South in its own image. Conceiving the book as a "corporate jeremiad," the author urges his readers to return to prewar artisanal values of labor and manhood in order to save the nation, before it is too late, from the growing scourge of government corruption and corporate greed.[49]

Now almost completely forgotten by critics, *Figs and Thistles* was envisioned as the first novel in a trilogy that included *A Fool's Errand* and *Bricks Without Straw*. These works appeared in the literary market in rapid secession, each bearing the year 1879 as its date of initial publication. Recognizing that no one group or issue could be blamed for the failure of southern Reconstruction, the author distributes blame judiciously in each of his three novels. The most famous work of this trilogy, *A Fool's Errand*, examined the role of southern racism and the South's stubborn resistance to what Tourgée believed were the forces of progress introduced into the region by northern reformers such as himself. *Bricks Without Straw* illustrated the long-term effects of slavery on the black community in the South and addressed the pressing need for education in order for the population of former slaves to have a chance at upward social mobility. *Figs and Thistles*, in contrast to both of these southern-focused novels, examined what the author felt was the northern betrayal of the Civil War legacy.

Tourgée turned in a number of directions in *Figs and Thistles* to explain the thornier issue of northern culpability in the failure of Reconstruction. The first was toward the emergence of big businesses such as the railroad, which would come to be known as "corporations." The second was in the direction of the national government, which had been enticed by corporate lobbyists to forget the needs of its small-town constituents. These two forces together, Tourgée argued, assured that his task as a southern reformer would be a "fool's errand" from the start. Since the values he was preaching to the South increasingly lacked firm footing in his home state of Ohio, they had little chance of gaining a lasting hold in the post-slavery South.

Considering the novel's reformist message, it is not surprising that *Figs and Thistles* follows the narrative style of the jeremiad. The author calls on his readers, who were more than likely small-town northerners, to return to their origins. In particular, he reminds them of the value and continued relevance of the artisanal ideal, which stressed economic independence and face-to-face business transactions. To demonstrate the value and relevance of this prewar ideal of labor and manhood, Tourgée creates the fictional character Markham Churr. Born in the northeastern corner of Ohio, Markham, like Edmund Cateret in *The Heir of Gaymount*, is orphaned at an early age. Left in the care of an indifferent guardian, his maternal grandfather Deacon Andrus, Churr gravitates toward a number of surrogate fathers. The first is the yeoman farmer Curtis Fields, who offers him the love and attention denied in the Andrus home. The second is the hide tanner Albert Morrey, whom Churr meets in the small town of Rexville after having run away from home.

Both Morrey and Fields help Markham pay for his schooling at the Rexville academy and then later assist him in being admitted to college in upstate New York. Not only does Churr begin his educational journey in Rexville, but there he also is initiated into romantic life. During his time at the Rexville academy, Markham meets his future wife, the farmer's daughter Lizzie Harper. He pledges to marry her upon his graduation from college and establishment in the legal profession. Thus, when he finally receives his law degree and passes the Ohio state bar, Markham moves back to Rexville and prepares for the day he will have the money to marry Lizzie and start a home of his own.

At this point in the narrative, the hero might easily fade into obscurity were it not for the catalyst of a bank robbery that occurs in the nearby town of Aychitula. Curious to discover more about this event than the papers can tell him, Churr travels to the scene of the crime. The addition of this element to the story speeds up the plot and introduces Churr to the third and most influential surrogate father he encounters in the novel, Boaz Woodley. When Markham and Woodley meet at the bank, of which Woodley is the main shareholder and president, the older man decides to hire him as a private investigator. From the beginning it is clear that Woodley is interested less in Markham's ability as a detective than in his potential to be the old man's protégé. Woodley plays an ever-larger role in the life of Markham Churr, using his political influence to steer the life course of his surrogate son.

One instance of Woodley's growing influence in Markham's life occurs not long after the outbreak of the Civil War, which follows closely on the heels of the bank robbery. Churr had initially enlisted in the Union army as a private, but he was sent home after the First Battle of Bull Run with a serious wound. Upon his convalescence, Churr discovers that Woodley has obtained for him the rank of lieutenant colonel in a volunteer regiment Woodley had raised.[50] Woodley soon thereafter resigns his command of the regiment, making the onetime private its commanding officer.

Leading his men in the battles of Stones River and Chickamauga, Colonel Churr is preparing for the siege of Atlanta when he learns he has been promoted to the rank of brigadier general. However, this is not the end of his meteoric rise to power. Churr suddenly finds himself, thanks again to Woodley's influence, nominated to be the Republican candidate for his congressional district in the House of Representatives. Torn between his desire to finish fighting the war with his unit and the latest opportunity for advancement offered him by Woodley, Markham is ultimately swayed by his surrogate father's claim that "the fighting—the heavy fighting—is about over" and that "the chances are more than ten to one that the star on your shoulder will never see its fellow."[51] Agreeing with Woodley that further promotion for him in the army seems unlikely and that he would be of greater use in the Congress, General Churr takes his seat in the House of Representatives and abruptly becomes Congressman Churr.

Although his rapid rise is presented by the narrative as indicative of the hero's commitment to hard work and manly independence, the fact remains that Markham owes his social position almost entirely to Boaz Woodley. Without the intervention of this father figure, Churr's social advancement would most certainly have been limited in scope, perhaps amounting to a captainship in a regiment by the war's end and a successful small-town law practice. Catapulted to national power in a short span of time, the hero seemingly has done little to attain his social position other than know the right people and show up where he is told.

This contradiction comes back to haunt the narrative's main character at the end of the war. Just as Markham Churr has reached the pinnacle of his success in the 1870s, Woodley has reached something of a nadir in his career. Having installed his protégé safely in the ranks of the social elite, Woodley appears to have little left to accomplish. Restless and casting around for something to employ him, Churr unwittingly provides his mentor with both a new outlet for his energies as well as the poison that will nearly destroy their relationship. The narrator tells us that "as chairman of numerous committees and sub-committees, he [i.e., Churr] had submitted many reports which had great weight in shaping important legislation."[52] A bill appears in Churr's committee that involves a charter for the T.C.R. Co., or Trans Continental Railroad. Since Woodley has extensive experience, not only with business matters but also with railways, Churr asks him to investigate the company in order to help him decide whether it is worthy of a corporate charter.

As Woodley investigates the T.C.R. Co., he increasingly becomes obsessed with the idea of the enterprise, which is the largest and most audacious business venture Woodley has ever observed. Eventually he buys enough stock in the T.C.R. Co. to become its president, and then purchases shares on behalf of his protégé. Woodley assumes that Markham will continue to faithfully follow the will of his "father" and vote on behalf of the corporate charter and loan guarantees for the T.C.R. Co. Should he do so, Woodley anticipates a dramatic rise in stock prices that will benefit both the "father" and his "son." Congressman Churr, however, belatedly proves his independence by resisting the pressure exerted by his mentor and voting against the bill. Enraged by this sudden insubordination, Woodley leaks to the press Congressman Churr's ownership of stock in the railroad he had voted against.[53]

Woodley's transformation from loving mentor to greedy corporate capitalist is meant to be shocking. However, a final plot twist is intended to resolve the issue of corruption in this seemingly solid example of artisanal manhood. Attempting to ruin Markham financially as well as politically, Woodley files a lawsuit against him for the full sum of the investments he has made on behalf of his onetime protégé. Because Churr and Woodley are no longer on speaking terms, Markham's wife, Lizzie, goes to plead for her husband. She takes with her a piece of paper she discovered earlier in the narrative. This tattered newspaper article shows that Boaz Woodley does not really exist. He is, in fact, Basil Woodson, a fugitive from justice in Massachusetts wanted for stealing from and then killing the merchant he was apprenticed to as a young man. Lizzie threatens to expose Woodley, and through this act manages to save her husband financially.

The reader is encouraged to see Woodley's fall into the morass of corporate greed as the result of a personal flaw rather than as a sign of the northern antebellum community's preexisting vulnerability. The author believed that good character could be found in Union veterans like Markham Churr who, in contrast to Boaz Woodley, remains a figure of immovable rectitude when faced with the temptations of the corporate lobby. The author is confident that men like Congressman Churr will continue to defend the vision of the nation as an artisanal republic in the legislative chamber just as they did on the battlefield.

Perhaps because of his claims that Union veterans were the rightful defenders of the artisanal ideal in the face of government corruption and the rise of the corporation, the publishers of Tourgée's novel marketed later editions as a fictionalized biography of presidential candidate James Garfield.[54] They added a frontispiece showing Garfield in his Union general's uniform humbly accepting the mantle of civilian political power.[55] Moreover, advertisements for the book, one of which is printed on the last page of a post-1879 edition, give the novel a telling subtitle not chosen by the author: "A Typical American Career."

Reader interest in *Figs and Thistles* as a possible fictionalized biography of Garfield remained strong throughout the 1880 election. That interest only intensified when Garfield became president and then was assassinated by the anarchist Charles Guiteau after a mere four months in office.[56] An article published in the July 21, 1881, edition of the *Chicago Daily Inter-Ocean* remarked on the boost that an assumed connection to Garfield's life and death had on the novel's sales, saying, "The publishers of Judge Tourgée's book, *Figs and Thistles*, have shown themselves very clever in taking advantage of the national interest in everything that pertains to the Garfield family."[57] Whether Tourgée intended his readers to make the connection between the fictional life of Markham Churr and the life of James Garfield is not clear, but the ease with which it was made suggests the popularity of the story he was telling—one that argued, like the late-nineteenth-century success manual, that "individual virtue, far from moribund in the competitive new age of industry, was what young men who wanted to succeed needed most."[58]

What Tourgée added to this equation, however, was a sense of urgency. In *Figs and Thistles* the author called for the mobilization of former soldiers and civilians in defense of the ideals associated with the small-town community. Together they could stop the infection of corporate life corrupting the nation, by voting for upright political representatives like the fictional Union veteran Markham Churr who would stand up to lobbyists and resist the temptations of patronage in the ever-expanding national government. By resisting the encroachment of the corporation on the values of artisanal manhood and small-town life, Tourgée hoped to prevent the Civil War veteran from turning into a historical curiosity. Like John Esten Cooke, Tourgée worried that, if the changes he saw taking place in the United States during the 1870s were allowed to proceed unchecked, the soldiers who had taken part in the war would inhabit a society in which they had no place. In a corporate world, these exemplars of antebellum artisanal values would be outmoded, like the single-bladed scythe used by the veteran in Homer's painting. Young men and machines would take their place and leave them little to do but watch in confusion, frustration, and awe.

Over time, the hope espoused in narratives such as those written by Cooke and Tourgée was replaced with a sense of futility and loss. Powerless to check the social and economic changes taking place all around them and unwilling to swerve from their antebellum beliefs, a significant number of veterans turned to the past for comfort and meaning. Former soldiers could not remember their prewar lives, however, without encountering the painful memories of those they had killed or seen cut down on the field of battle. These traumatic visions interrupted their idyllic vision of the past, setting up a wall between their lives before and after the war. Trading a painful present for an equally painful past, Civil War veterans discovered through the realm of memory they were different from the rest of American society. The nation had moved on while they had not, and former soldiers decided to interpret this change as a fall from grace. Increasingly, men who had fought in the war saw themselves as members of an elect society that held firm to the values of the true America, and from this belief they fashioned for themselves a new identity—that of "the veteran."

3 Narrating Traumatic Experience in Civil War Memoir

Of reminiscences there is no end. I have a vast store of them laid up, wherewith to wile away the tedious years of my anecdotage—whenever it shall please Heaven to make me old.

—AMBROSE BIERCE, "A Sole Survivor"

The 1880s ended a period Civil War scholars have referred to as one of "quiescence" or "hibernation" for white veterans' narratives. Whereas only a handful of memoirs and personal narratives related to the war had been published in the late 1860s and 1870s, a flood of white veteran writing from both the North and South now appeared in books, newspapers, and magazines.[1] Although there are a number of explanations for this shift from silence to vocality, the timing of this explosion in veteran-authored war memoir seems tied to the struggles of veterans to achieve independence in the postwar economy. Former soldiers began to turn to an idealized vision of the Civil War and the decade that had preceded it, as an alternative to the materialistic character of the Gilded Age. In doing so, they engaged in a nostalgic activity to which many civilians were also drawn. The territory of memory, however, was a far more contested terrain for veterans than it was for civilians. Alongside the pleasant memories of their prewar youth and the camaraderie of the Civil War camp, former soldiers encountered less savory aspects of their past that had remained buried for nearly fifteen years. These visions of death and suffering, and of guilt at having violated strictly established social norms and mores, threatened to both overshadow their idyllic image of the past as well as harm their health and sanity.

A few veteran reminiscences stand out from the large number of memoirs and personal narratives written during this period. Union General William Tecumseh Sherman's *Memoirs*, Confederate Private Sam Watkins's personal narrative *Company Aytch*, and a series of short stories and sketches written by Union lieutenant turned fiction writer Ambrose Bierce were chosen for analysis due to the richness of their language and the depth of their insight. In contrast to the matter-of-fact reports present in many Civil War narratives, the works written by these authors expose the emotional complexity of memory for former soldiers. They show how scenes of war shook the preexisting worldviews of each writer without necessarily replacing them with new ones. Sherman's *Memoirs* present a "hard-boiled" surface to the reader that only partially conceals the author's concern about how his harsh actions as a military commander during the war have set him apart from peacetime society. In his personal narrative *Company Aytch*, Watkins also worries about how his actions have set him apart, but he addresses feelings of separateness in religious terms rather than through the eyes of a seemingly jaded "realist." Bierce's short stories and autobiographical sketches of the war, in contrast to both, seem to revel in the distance between the veteran author and the civilian populace, even as he tries to understand the forces that caused this gap in experience.

Real differences exist between these texts in narrative form and tone. Nonetheless, the language of each veteran's war reminiscence reveals a distance that he believed had opened between him and the civilian population. These authors sensed instinctively that war had changed them irrevocably, and they struggled to explain those changes in a conscious way. They ultimately discovered that reconnecting themselves to the general populace was impossible. Only a comrade who had lived through many of the same traumas and struggles in combat and camp could understand the transformative experience of war. This quasi-mystical experience became crystallized for them in one word—"veteran."

Trauma and the Civil War Veteran

Since the end of the Vietnam War, there has been a resurgence of interest in the subject of combat trauma in the United States.[2] This plethora of research, however, was not systematically applied to the study of the Civil War until the publication of Eric Dean's groundbreaking *Shook over Hell*. Dean examines reported cases of posttraumatic stress disorder (PTSD) in Vietnam veterans alongside the medical records of Indiana Civil War veterans committed to the state asylum. He found a similarity between the symptoms described by the doctors and family members of Civil war veterans committed to the state asylum and the diagnostic criteria currently associated with PTSD. Veterans from both wars, Dean asserts, "continued to suffer from the aftereffects of the war and, along with their families, often lived in a kind of private hell involving physical pain, the torment of fear, and memories of killing and death."[3] This led him to suggest that while the terminology applied to combat trauma might change with each generation, the underlying problem remained the same.

Eric Dean's research has proved controversial among Civil War scholars. Even though combat trauma is frequently referred to in relation to the war, it is treated as out of place in reference to the Civil War.[4] This is due in no small part to the unfortunate association of combat trauma, PTSD, and the Vietnam War.[5] Scholars of the Civil War era have been reluctant to openly discuss the issue of veteran trauma—not simply because doing so would impose contemporary concepts on a much earlier period, but because it would imply a connection between the "bad war" that was Vietnam and the "good war" that was fought in the 1860s between the North and South.[6] What this debate overlooks, however, is that Americans in the late nineteenth century had terms and concepts of their own to describe combat trauma. Instead of calling it PTSD, they referred to it as "irritable heart," "melancholy," or "nostalgia." By using these nineteenth-century medical terms as guides, it is possible to track the post–Civil War conception of combat trauma along with its common forms of treatment.

Nineteenth-century medicine in the United States varied wildly in its quality and the specifics of its treatment regimens. Nonetheless, there was a consensus among physicians that illness must have a physical cause. Trauma was thus primarily understood in its pre-psychological sense as the body's response to a blow or shock. Cardiologist J. M. Da Costa began with this assumption when he examined hundreds of Union soldiers sent to him at Turner's Lane Hospital in Philadelphia. Da Costa observed in the majority of his patients a rapid heartbeat. Moreover, he noticed that this condition was frequently accompanied by other physical symptoms, such as diarrhea or fever as well as sharp stabbing pains in the chest. Believing these symptoms to be related, Da Costa coined a new term for the condition: "irritable heart."

In the paper that eventually resulted from his examinations of over three hundred patients suffering from the condition during the war, Da Costa concluded that irritable heart was primarily the result of the emotional and physical strains of the combat experience, what he termed "hard field service." Under this rubric were included forced marches, excessive exposure to the sun and rain, poor diet and sanitation, and "active movements in the face of an enemy." Looking at the relationship between actual fighting and the condition, Da Costa noted, "I could find but extremely few instances in which a wound had even seemed to be the starting point."[7] The full experience of war—not just the fighting—seemed to him the major contributing factor to the condition. Once those stresses were removed, Da Costa concluded, most soldiers quickly recovered. Those who did not, according to Da Costa, typically had underlying cardiac health issues that preceded the emergence of irritable heart.

Because it related to the bodily impact of the combat experience on soldiers, irritable heart was most prominent as a medical diagnosis in the early years following the war. Da Costa's research, however, could not adequately account for the sudden emergence of comparable symptoms in veterans who were decades removed from the war and its battlefields. To address such late-onset symptoms, the diagnosis of "melancholy" or "nostalgia" was applied.[8] Unlike irritable heart, melancholy and nostalgia did not rely on physical causation to explain the onset of symptoms in patients. Memory itself was the problem, specifically obsessive memories. The French psychiatrist Pierre Janet was just beginning to conduct studies on the origin and mechanism of these types of memories in the 1880s at the Salpêtrière Hospital in Paris.[9] Yet late-nineteenth-century American physicians, by and large, limited themselves to the treatment of these memories without greatly concerning themselves with their etiology. Treatments for melancholy and nostalgia were varied, but typically involved physical exertion and mental diversions that would refocus patients' attention back to the demands of the present and help them forget the unnecessary and hurtful memories of the past.

Documents associated with soldiers' homes and state asylums offer us a glimpse into the specific treatment regimens used by doctors in the Civil War era to help veterans forget the traumas of war. Soldiers' homes were initially created to care for war amputees and other classes of veterans unable to care for themselves, but later expanded to include a wide variety of disabilities including melancholy and nostalgia.[10] In an advertisement for the Missouri soldiers' home, printed in the *Confederate Veteran* magazine, some of the activities and diversions listed include a reading room, chapel, billiard room, and 362 acres of land where veterans could raise their own food.[11] State asylums, which were not intended to treat veterans alone, took a different approach. Dean notes in his examination of policies at the Indiana state asylum that "veterans participated in recreation and dances and engaged in work, which could entail kitchen duty, farm labor, or chores on the ward; if they could be trusted, they were given liberty to roam the three-hundred-acre grounds of the asylum." In addition to these forms of diversion, veterans were given "a wide array of drugs." These included purgatives "to free the body of noxious agents," tonics to "build up strength," and sedatives to calm down "disturbed or manic patients."[12]

Regardless of degree, late-nineteenth-century medicine's approach to treating melancholy and nostalgia involved letting go of the past. This went against the inclination of most Civil War veterans, who felt a complex relationship to their wartime memories. Veterans possessed a sometimes perverse will to remember that manifested itself in the profusion of stories they told about the war. Before the last battle had even ended, large numbers of soldiers were already attempting to make sense of their wartime experiences, documenting in their diaries, letters, and journals the horrendous sights, sounds, and smells of combat. They also wrote postwar memoirs about these same events decades after the war, sometimes based on their earlier accounts. The majority of these writings would not be published until well after the death of the authors, but their abundance suggests the crucial role played by written narratives in the process of explaining and resolving the psychic wounds of war.

The Relationship Between Trauma and Narrative

The clear therapeutic value of narrative for Civil War veterans who were suffering from melancholy or nostalgia goes against the paradigm that dominates contemporary theories of trauma. Based on the scientific research conducted by neurobiologist Bessel van der Kolk and popularized by literary critic Cathy Caruth, this theory claims that trauma is "an event that is experienced too soon, too unexpectedly, to be fully known and is therefore not available to consciousness until it imposes itself again, repeatedly, in the nightmares and repetitive actions of the survivor."[13] Because trauma is remembered differently from ordinary memory, Caruth and van der Kolk assert that it can only be relived, and that it cannot be represented through traditional means of narration.[14]

Ruth Leys has carefully examined the problems inherent in this theory of traumatic experience. Chief among them is its naïve perspective toward narrative representation. No method of communication, even the performative, can exactly re-create the original experience. All methods of reproduction are simulacra. In addition, Leys is deeply critical of the neurobiological theories on which Caruth bases her claims about trauma and the new methods of storytelling it necessitates. She states, "I am dismayed by the low quality of van der Kolk's scientific work . . . there are slippages and inconsistencies in his arguments about the literal nature of traumatic memory, arguments that are inadequately supported by the empirical evidence he adduces." Leys calls for a greater degree of skepticism toward van der Kolk's work, which has yet to prove in the lab that traumatic memory cannot be represented, and she chastises humanists like Caruth for accepting his work at face value.[15]

Although her critique has not yet managed to unseat van der Kolk and Caruth's dominance within trauma studies, Ley's research has opened the door to greater skepticism of the ruling paradigm in the field. This allows scholars interested in the relationship between trauma and existing narrative forms a chance to explore those connections rather than assume that such links don't exist. In the case of the Civil War, it allows scholars to review the extensive body of life writing composed during the war and published in great volume during the 1880s for signs of combat trauma and the ways veterans of the conflict sought to reconcile that trauma with their postwar lives through narrative. What becomes apparent in the writings of William Tecumseh Sherman, Sam Watkins, and Ambrose Bierce is that combat trauma ruptures each author's worldview—their conception of the norms and mores that govern their lives and communities. The structure offered by the existing narrative forms of life writing (i.e., the memoir, sketch, and personal narrative) and the short story provide them ways to potentially heal those ruptures and make sense of what they have survived.

Clinical psychologist James W. Pennebaker has noticed this strategy being employed by contemporary patients recovering from trauma, saying, "The formation of a narrative is critical and is an indicator of good mental and physical health." Especially vital for individuals who have experienced traumatic events is the ability to create coherence in that narrative. As Pennebaker notes, "To the degree that the event is unresolved, we will think, dream, obsess, and talk about it for days, weeks, or years." Once a coherent account of the traumatic event is produced, one that incorporates it into the life of the traumatized subject in the present, it "allows us to forget or, perhaps a better phrase, move beyond the experience."[16] The problem with Pennebaker's perspective on narrative healing when applied to Civil War memoir is that some veteran memoirs, such as those by Ambrose Bierce, show no interest in "moving beyond the experience," but choose instead to hold onto the "authentic" horror of the original event.

In "What I Saw of Shiloh," Bierce laments that he "recall[s] with difficulty the danger and death and horrors of the time, and without effort all that is gracious and picturesque."[17] His war narratives tend to have a circular or repetitive quality, with the same event returning in a dizzying variety of guises. Just as frustrating for the reader, this repetitive manner of storytelling is commonly paired with intense demands on their emotions. An early reviewer of Bierce's short story collection *Tales of Soldiers and Civilians* (printed in England as *In the Midst of Life*) noted, "We read of nothing [in Bierce's stories] but the minutest details of bodily and mental pain. The details are given with the sort of power one sees in a Russian battle-piece, and will repel more readers than they attract."[18] Other Civil War memoirs, such as those by Sherman and Sam Watkins, attempt to move beyond the horrors of war to achieve psychic closure, but find in those experiences much good mixed in with the bad. These authors had a sense that what they experienced in the war had made them the men they were at the time of writing. Letting go of the past, therefore, also involved letting go of themselves. They felt just as ambivalent about letting go as they did about holding on to the horrors of war.

In her study of trauma, narrative, and community, American Studies scholar Kalí Tal observes that traumatic memories are often contradictory. On one level these memories expose the conflicting attitudes of a survivor toward his experience, and on another they reveal contradictions in the existing social order. Together these contradictions manifest the ways "traumatic experience catalyzes a transformation of meaning in the signs individuals use to represent their experiences."[19] To those who have crossed the threshold of trauma, simple words and the concepts that underlie them no longer mean what they once did. As traumatized subjects realize the discrepancy between their conception of the world and that of the non-traumatized, they increasingly separate themselves from the supposed "outsiders." Speaking primarily to one another in a language whose meaning is premised on a shared experience, those who have survived a traumatic event consolidate over time into new subcommunities that revolve around not only a shared language and worldview but also a strong sense of superiority. When taken to its logical extreme, this process of group consolidation carries within it the potential for society's disintegration.[20]

Because such societal disintegration did not occur in the aftermath of the Civil War, most scholars of the postwar period have not accepted the full implication of veterans' claims to cultural superiority in their writings. Consequently, rather than see in these statements signs of friction between soldiers and civilians in the post–Civil War era, they have tended to follow the lead of historian David Blight in interpreting Civil War veteran claims to cultural prominence as yet another manifestation of the impulse among white citizens to reconcile their political differences at the expense of the black population. Underneath these much-louder struggles of race relations and sectional animosity, however, were signs that a shift in veteran self-identity that had been incubating since the end of the war was finally coming to fruition during the 1880s.

In a speech to a New Hampshire Grand Army of the Republic post in 1884, the Union veteran and future Supreme Court Justice Oliver Wendell Holmes claimed that Civil War veterans had been "set apart by [their] experience" and that their "hearts were touched with fire."[21] Echoing the language of the New Testament where the Holy Spirit descends upon the Apostles as tongues of fire, Holmes captures in his statement an ontological shift brought about by surviving combat. The speaker and those listening to him see themselves as literally new men born from out of the traumatic experience of war.

Historian Gerald Linderman notes that civilians "granted public recognition" to what men like Holmes were feeling, and that veteran "estrangement [was] elevated to a civic virtue."[22] Although it placated veterans to a certain extent, public recognition in the form of pensions, parades, and monuments was less an attempt to accept veterans and their experience and more of an attempt to reframe the ambivalent personal narratives of Civil War veterans into a form compatible with the postwar nation's image of itself. This attempt to reshape veteran narratives, or in Tal's terms to "mythologize" them, is most clearly visible in the work of editors like those at *Century* magazine, who sought through their "Battles and Leaders" series to make the combat experiences of veterans intelligible to a civilian readership and at the same time demonstrate to veterans that they were not substantially different from the general population.

When the editor of the series, Robert Johnson, met with one of its most famous veteran contributors, Ulysses S. Grant, who had agreed to write an article on the Battle of Shiloh, Johnson wanted to help him "realize the requirements of a popular publication on the war." This included both the choice of topic as well as the language used to describe it, which should sound like "a talk ... he would make to friends after dinner."[23] In his role as translator and cultural mediator, Johnson was trying to suggest that the differences between veterans and civilians were negligible when compared to the enormity of the crisis they had survived together.

Veterans struggled, with or without the help of editorial mediation, to articulate what had happened to them during the often-traumatic experiences of combat. At the same time, civilian readers felt intimidated by the way veteran narratives assaulted deeply held assumptions about not only the Civil War but also the overall meaning and purpose of their world. This tug of war between the needs of former soldiers and the narrative expectations of a civilian audience is apparent to varying degrees in the writings of Sherman, Watkins, and Bierce. Moreover, each author seems aware of this conundrum and it shapes these narratives in visible ways. This makes their writings ideal objects of study in the attempt to understand not only combat trauma in the Civil War era but also the larger issue of reintegration of which trauma is a part.

Sherman's *Memoirs* reveal an inner turmoil beneath his tough narrative and carefully crafted public persona. This agitation was due in part to the contradictions of his wartime experience as a leader of men, which compelled him to order his armies to fight once-close friends from the old army and burn the property of families with whom he spent many pleasant evenings during his military service in the antebellum South. He also felt unease about leading to their death thousands of soldiers who looked up to him as "Uncle Billy." Sherman's inner turmoil appears at unexpected moments in the *Memoir* and seems to upset the authorial intention of the sections in which these thunderbolts of emotion appear. Writing around his reactions to troubling events in the narrative, Sherman exposes a range of responses. These suggest a continuum of trauma, since what he feels is clearly stronger than simple guilt or remorse but at the same time weaker than what might typically be considered worthy of the name "combat trauma."

Sam Watkins's personal narrative, *Company Aytch*, reveals a different inner struggle that is closer to our conception of how combat-related trauma should appear. Having served as a frontline soldier, this former Confederate private attempted to reconcile in his war stories the transgressions he committed against social norms and mores during the war with the religious beliefs ostensibly shared by his hometown readers. Watkins's attempt to use these supposedly shared values of religion to obtain closure ultimately fails. This is due largely to the corrosive influence of his war experiences on his prewar systems of belief. Much of what he has survived simply cannot be explained using the conventional language of justice and morality.

The short stories and sketches of Ambrose Bierce represent something of a closed circle. They illustrate an author struggling not to articulate or reconcile his war experiences to a civilian audience, but to explain to himself the change in identity made possible by war. Repetitive and obsessed with sensory details, Bierce's writings come closest to challenging the relationship between narrative and trauma. But instead of rejecting narrative altogether, each story seems to search for a new way of telling what happens in combat, pushing the limits of existing narrative to find a new form of expression. His shift between fiction and nonfiction war narratives also provides useful insights into the limits of life writing as a way to comprehend war and the potential of fictional forms to describe the visceral experience of combat.

Each of these three authors takes a different approach to writing about the war, depending largely on the degree of their trauma. Sherman's relatively mild suffering leads him to create a fairly conventional war memoir that occasionally exposes raw emotions the author presumably did not intend to share with his readers. Watkins's personal narrative displays a greater degree of trauma, with numerous stories that often reveal more than the author intended. However, Watkins still manages to maintain a modicum of control over his tales as he applies morals to the events experienced after the storm of emotions has passed. Bierce is the most alienated of the writers considered. His stories show a greater affinity for the dead than the living, and suggest that he is unable to successfully adjust to a nation at peace. By analyzing these authors together, we are able to view the full spectrum of traumatic experience and better understand the relation of trauma to narrative forms. It also becomes clear that as different as these authors are, each felt that the war they had survived was not simply *an event* in their lives but *the event*, a transformative experience that had shaped everything that would follow.

"War Is All Hell": Sherman's Hard-Boiled Reminiscences

Generals have typically been viewed as exempt from combat trauma. To a certain extent, this is the result of our collective understanding of combat trauma, which is derived from the experiences of frontline soldiers and has been applied without much success to the commanders leading those men. Leaders of armies experience a different kind of suffering in the aftermath of war. On the surface it might appear to be solely self-aggrandizing, as many memoirs written by generals are simply interested in defending the decisions made during their campaigns. Nevertheless, the writings of some commanding officers aim at more than simply protecting their legacy. They are attempting to come to terms with the complex emotions they feel at having set in motion events that caused suffering and death for thousands of soldiers and civilians. Through looking at the experiences of these leaders of armies, it is possible to reconceptualize trauma as a continuum that moves between two poles: the first is the phenomenon of simple remorse or regret; the second, the complete breakdown of the emotional self that is exemplified in many instances of PTSD.

Nowhere is this complexity of emotion more apparent than in the *Memoirs* of Union General William Tecumseh Sherman. The first edition of Sherman's *Memoirs* was composed in the 1870s in St. Louis during a period of self-imposed exile from Washington, D.C. At the time, Sherman was commanding general of the U.S. Army, but his position had largely become symbolic due to political wrangling for power between the president, Congress, and the secretary of war.[24] Hating politics and with no real duties to perform, Sherman decided to spend his time surveying his more glorious past. As with most military memoirs, Sherman was concerned with bolstering his reputation as a leader of armies. He specifically sought to answer charges that his marches through Georgia and South Carolina reflected his inability to engage and defeat an opposing army. Supporters of General George Henry Thomas, including H. V. Boynton, were particularly critical of Sherman on this issue, feeling that he left Thomas to do the hard work of defeating Hood's army in Tennessee while Sherman took a leisurely walk through undefended enemy territory in Georgia.[25] Sherman also sought to answer charges that he had violated the rules of war in his destruction of southern property and treatment of civilians. This aspect of his memoirs was directly related to charges made about the general in 1861 that he was "crazy," a sobriquet that continued to haunt Sherman long after the war had ended.[26]

Publishing his memoirs when and in the manner he did was an audacious move. Many of the characters involved in his narrative were still alive and equally eager to protect their wartime reputations. Scandal erupted soon after the book's publication by D. Appleton and Company in 1875. The *St. Louis Globe-Democrat* observed that the memoirs were guilty of "injustice to the living and to the dead," and that they contained "too numerous instances in which the General uses his office of Author to defame others and exalt himself." The publication of Sherman's *Memoirs* also seemed to fulfill the *San Francisco Daily Evening Bulletin*'s prediction that his narrative would serve as catalyst for "an outburst of war literature."[27] Soon a "battle of the books" between former Union and Confederate generals began through letters and competing memoirs. At the head of the columns assaulting Sherman was Union veteran H. V. Boynton.

Boynton had served as an officer in the Army of the Cumberland during the war and was brevetted to the rank of brigadier general after being wounded at the Battle of Missionary Ridge.[28] In December 1864 he became the Washington correspondent for the *Cincinnati Gazette*, a position he still held in 1875. Not long after Sherman's book appeared in print, portions of which had already been circulated in newspapers across the nation to boost sales, Boynton published *Sherman's Historical Raid: The Memoirs in the Light of the Record—A Review Based on Records from the War Department*. Boynton's book was a point-by-point refutation of Sherman's that the general might have easily ignored. However, the mere idea that a newspaperman had more access to the war records and the "real story" of the Atlanta campaign than did the man who commanded those forces and now was in charge of the entire federal army galled Sherman. He began a proxy war against Boynton through the newspapers that finally ended in Boynton filing charges on January 28, 1880, with Secretary of War Alex Ramsey, asking that Sherman be court-martialed for conduct unbecoming an officer.[29] Secretary Ramsey referred Boynton to the civil court system and suggested he file a libel suit against Sherman. Boynton declined to take his feud with Sherman any further and thus the matter was dropped.

Sherman's lengthy feud with Boynton is an excellent example of the impulsiveness of character that nearly all Sherman's biographers have noted. Although it is tempting to attribute the cause of Sherman's feud with Boynton exclusively to this trait, there are other factors that better help us understand both Sherman's reasons for publishing his *Memoirs* and the reception they initially received. In his introduction to the Penguin edition of Sherman's *Memoirs*, Michael Fellman notes that Sherman testified to a claims commission in 1872 that he was "trying to get to the bottom of the issue of culpability for various extreme war measures."[30] Furthermore, he notes that Sherman denied from the very beginning that his men had burned Columbia, South Carolina, or that he had ordered the vandalism carried out by his "bummers." Sherman had to have been aware of his reputation as a "monster" and the epitome of a new form of "modern" war. He notes in his *Memoirs* that southern civilians "had invented such ghostlike stories of our prowess in Georgia, that they were scared by their own inventions."[31] At the time of his campaign he relished that power, but in the postwar years Sherman was anxious to present himself to southerners as a friend. His *Memoirs* were meant, among other things, to answer charges that he had engaged in barbarities during the war and to reaffirm that every action he took was meant to hasten the end of the war and the reunification of the nation.

Sherman is most assiduous in his self-defense in the chapters that follow the capture of Atlanta. He tells us, "I was resolved to make Atlanta a pure military garrison or depot, with no civil population to influence military measures." Aware that this action might seem harsh to some readers, he refers back to prior experiences in towns such as Memphis and Vicksburg, where allowing the civilian population to stay led to greater suffering for them and placed an undue burden on the army who had to "guard and protect the interests of a hostile population." Rather than defend against guerila attacks from Atlanta's population, Sherman decided to send civilians away, "giving to each the option to go south or north, as their interests or feelings dictated." His concern that his actions be viewed as justified was apparently not limited to the postwar readership of his *Memoirs*, as he also includes an excerpt from a letter written to Army Chief of Staff General Halleck on September 4, 1864. He tells Halleck, "If the people raise a howl against my barbarity and cruelty, I will answer that war is war, and not popularity-seeking. If they want peace, they and their relatives must stop the war."[32]

Sherman would use a similar logic to defend his later actions during the march through Georgia and Carolina. Southerners were to blame for the destruction. All they had to do was stop the war and his army would cease its punitive actions. Not surprisingly, southerners were not convinced. In one of the more colorful sections of the *Memoirs*, Sherman includes an exchange of letters between himself and the Confederate General John Bell Hood that touches on Sherman's forced evacuation of the city. Sherman initiates this conversation by sending Hood a request that he "assist in conveying them [i.e., the citizens of Atlanta] south." To this request Hood replies, "I do not consider that I have any alternative in this matter." Not content to end his commentary with this simple statement of fact, Hood adds near the end, "And now, sir, permit me to say that the unprecedented measure you propose transcends, in studied and ingenious cruelty, all acts ever before brought to my attention in the dark history of war. In the name of God and humanity, I protest."

Sherman responds to Hood's letter with a copy of his orders to allow transfer of Atlanta's civilians through Union lines to a location where Confederate forces can take over their transport south. He then goes on to castigate Hood, asserting that his actions are "not unprecedented," as "General Johnston himself very wisely and properly removed the families all the way from Dalton down." Sherman also takes issue with Hood's invocation of God, saying, "If we must be enemies, let us be men, and fight it out as we propose to do, and not deal in such hypocritical appeals to God and humanity." Hood replies to Sherman's letter by stating emphatically, "I see nothing in your communication which induces me to modify the language of condemnation with which I characterized your order." He affirms that "I must decline to accept your statements in reference to your kindness toward the people of Atlanta, and your willingness to sacrifice everything for the peace and honor of the South, and refuse to be governed by your decision in regard to matters between myself, my country, and my God."[33] Sherman sends one more letter to Hood, but it is only to signal that their conversation is now at an end. Thus concluded the battle of letters between Sherman and Hood that followed the military assault on Atlanta.

Sherman's discontinuance of his correspondence with Hood suggests not only that both writers have come to an ideological impasse—as he puts it, "This discussion by two soldiers is out of place, and profitless"—but also that Sherman feels he has scored the argumentative victory desired in that exchange. Nonetheless, he still seems to find it necessary to further defend his actions in Atlanta, as he includes both the letter he sent to the mayor of Atlanta and General Halleck's response to Sherman's earlier letter describing his plans to evacuate the city. Halleck tells Sherman, "The course which you have pursued in removing rebel families from Atlanta is fully approved by the War Department." He then vents his frustration to his subordinate that "we have tried three years of conciliation and kindness without any reciprocation." It is now time, Halleck contends, "that we apply to our inexorable foes the severe rules of war." Sherman's inclusion of these letters not only justifies his actions in relation to the civilian population of Atlanta, but also sets the stage for the chapters covering his march through Georgia and the Carolinas. He wants us to see that the punitive measures he applies to the South are not the product of a madman's brain, but rather are reflective of the Union government's new policy toward those states still in open rebellion.[34]

In November 1864, Sherman sets off on his march to the sea. He begins this section of his narrative by affirming the admiration his soldiers have for him, as he quotes one saying as they left Atlanta, "Uncle Billy, I guess Grant is waiting for us in Richmond!" Sherman approves of the exuberance of the officers and enlisted men, what he calls their "devil may care" attitude, but he also expresses his concern that "success would be accepted as a matter of course, whereas, should we fail, this 'march' would be adjudged the wild adventure of a crazy fool." Sherman is also quick to note in this key portion of his memoir that from the very beginning he pointed out the difference to his men between "foraging" and wanton robbery and destruction. The general sees a soldier pass with a ham stuck on his bayonet, a jug of molasses under his arm, and a honeycomb in his hand. Somewhat shocked to see his commander, the soldier replies between bites of the honeycomb, "Forage liberally on the country," quoting back Sherman's orders to the army prior to the start of the march. Sherman tells us, "I reproved the man, explained that foraging must be limited to the regular parties properly detailed."

It is doubtful that Sherman's reprimand had much effect on this soldier. He all but concedes his lack of control over the foraging parties when he states, "No doubt, many acts of pillage, robbery, and violence, were committed by these parties of foragers, usually called 'bummers' . . . [but] foraging in some shape was necessary."[35] Again, in this passage Sherman seeks to avoid responsibility for the actions he has set in motion. This time the supply necessities of an army in the field serve as his explanation.

Since it was impossible for him to provide an army of this size with traditional rations so far from his supply depots in Tennessee, foraging was needed to feed his men. Moreover, if that foraging happened to undermine southern morale, in Sherman's eyes the justification for it was even greater. Meeting light resistance, Sherman cut a swath of devastation through Georgia. In doing so, he enacted sentiments he had expressed to his oldest daughter, Minnie, earlier that year. Sherman's biographer John Marszalek sums up those feelings as follows: "Destruction of property was better than taking lives, especially when those lives be-

Figure 8. F. O. C. Darley. *Sherman's March to the Sea*. Lithograph. Ca. 1883. Library of Congress. Washington, D.C.

longed to friends."[36] Having served in Florida, South Carolina, and Georgia before the war, many of the people he would now encounter were friends. Sherman was determined to show them tough love in order to end the war swiftly.

When his army finally entered Savannah, Sherman decided not to evacuate the town as he had in Atlanta. At first glance this might seem contradictory, but he contends that his decision was perfectly in line with the psychological war he was waging in the South. Sherman tells us, "There were about twenty thousand inhabitants in Savannah, all of whom had participated more or less in the war, and had no special claims to our favor, but I regarded war as rapidly drawing to a close; and it was becoming a political question as to what was to be done with the people of the South." He gave the citizens of Savannah a choice to either "remain or join their friends in Charleston or Augusta." Sherman tells us, "The great bulk of the inhabitants chose to remain in Savannah." To reward their decision to stay and remain peaceable, Sherman restrained his army's conduct towards those civilians and restored trade in Savannah. He also says he "issued stores from our own stock of supplies" to those who were too destitute to purchase foodstuffs.[37]

Preparing to move north through the Carolinas, Sherman includes another letter from Halleck to justify his subsequent actions. Halleck says somewhat cold-bloodedly, "Should you capture Charleston, I hope that by *some accident* the place may be destroyed, and, if a little salt should be sown upon its site, it may prevent the growth of future crops of nullification and secession." Although Sherman does not march on Charleston, choosing instead to move toward Columbia, South Carolina, his men unleash their fury on the state where secession was perceived to have been born and the Civil War thus begun. But again Sherman desires his readers to understand that there were reasonable limits to the damage his men would inflict on southern civilians. This was "hard war," to be sure, but not "total war" as it was understood in his day or, for that matter, our own.[38] Referring to the burning of Columbia, Sherman says, "Many of the people thought that this fire was deliberately planned and executed. This is not true. It was accidental, and in my judgment began with the cotton which General Hampton's men had set fire to on leaving the city."[39] Once more Sherman deflects blame from himself onto others, this time the Confederate cavalry officer Wade Hampton. He suggests that he would have been satisfied with destroying only "public" property belonging to the Confederate government but that Hampton's carelessness led to a greater loss of property and potentially greater loss of life.

By now the pattern of the argument in Sherman's narrative is clear. Other forces are responsible for causing the events that Sherman simply guides to their natural conclusion. This perspective on his participation in the war is markedly similar to the one Grant will take in his later *Personal Memoirs*, which begin with the statement "'Man Proposes and God Disposes.' There are but few important events in the affairs of men brought about by their own choice."[40] One might easily be tempted to view this pattern of deflection and self-justification as proof that the critics of Sherman's *Memoirs* were right. Sherman's motivation for this narrative technique, however, is far more complicated than his critics (then and now) have acknowledged. Even though he did not experience trauma to the degree we will soon see reflected in the works of Watkins and Bierce, Sherman has nonetheless left traces in his memoir that suggest the war has significantly changed his perception of himself and his world, a trait that the psychologist Ronnie Janoff-Bulman has identified as the core element of trauma. Most notably the war has shaken Sherman's understanding of friendship.

In the *Memoirs* we see represented not simply the reluctance to kill friends referenced in Sherman's letter to his daughter Minnie, but a silent reflection on the fact that in some cases he has already done so.⁴¹ During the Siege of Vicksburg, Sherman discovers that "the family of a Mr. Wilkinson, of New Orleans, was 'refugeeing' at a house near by." He rides to the house and encounters the daughters of "General Wilkinson, of Louisiana." Their mother, they tell him, is away at Parson Fox's house. Sherman rides off to Fox's home and discovers Mrs. Wilkinson. He introduces himself, asking "if she had a son who had been a cadet at Alexandria when General Sherman was superintendent." To his query, Mrs. Wilkinson replies that the boy is inside the besieged town of Vicksburg. Sherman tells us, "I then asked about her husband, whom I had known." Mrs. Wilkinson suddenly bursts into tears and cries out, "You killed him at Bull Run, where he was fighting for his country!"⁴² Sherman immediately denies having personally killed his friend, missing the widow's point. Sherman is culpable not as an individual but as a representative of the enemy. War has, in Mrs. Wilkinson's eyes, shattered the bonds of friendship that predated its commencement.

Sherman refuses to recognize this break and attempts to prove himself a friend to Mrs. Wilkinson and her family even as he leads a campaign that may result in the death of her son inside the besieged town. He provides her with a pass through the Union lines into Vicksburg. Sherman appears proud of his magnanimous action on behalf of Mrs. Wilkinson, but is nonetheless disturbed by his encounter. It is a not so subtle reminder of whom he is fighting. Through the lens of time, the now-famous general is able to rationalize this death in his memoir. Yet the fact remains that many of those he has killed—directly or indirectly—have faces and names he remembers from his prewar life. Searching for those people in the midst of war, Sherman discovers the unpleasant fact that the world has changed and he has changed with it. Traveling through Charleston after the surrender of Johnston's army, Sherman tells us, "I inquired for many of my old friends, but they were dead or gone." The general asserts that "Charleston deserved the fate that befell her," but his hard-boiled assertion merely serves as a screen to hide his emotions at the awful scourge that had turned friends into enemies and enemies into corpses.⁴³

Challenged Communal Ties in Sam Watkins's *Company Aytch*

Generals faced obvious social constraints as they wrote their war reminiscences. Due to their celebrity status in the postwar nation, men like Sherman were careful to craft the perfect image of themselves for the reading public. They were also restricted by the genre conventions of the military memoir, which historically had been used to defend strategic and tactical decisions made by army leaders during a particular war.⁴⁴ Although "Civil War memoir" is often used as a generic marker that encompasses all veteran writing about the war, memoirs were understood in the nineteenth century as an upper-class genre. They were book-length publications that offered, in contrast to the related genre of biography, a snapshot into the actions of a great man taking part in a historic event. Personal narratives, in contrast, were a lower-class genre that included such disparate forms as slave narrative, captivity narratives, and conversion narratives. Often they were written as continuous life stories, but it was also common for them to be broken up into shorter sketches or vignettes illustrating humorous or educational moments in the author's life.⁴⁵ The personal narrative genre was more conducive to the display of candid emotions and actions. Moreover, the lower social status of the genre's authors removed the pressure felt by writers of memoirs to present a coherent public image to their readers.

The primary limit to self-expression in the personal narrative came from an authorial desire to protect any local or group-specific social standing they might have achieved. This limitation of the personal narrative is clearly visible in Sam Watkins's *Company Aytch: A Side Show of the Big Show*, which demonstrates how much of a challenge that task could be. Comprising a series of seemingly disconnected sketches, Watkins's narrative represents an attempt to restore the system of beliefs he possessed before the war. With his combat experience having challenged his confidence in such fundamental concepts as courage, chivalry, and the sanctity of human life, Watkins tried in his sketches to reconcile the things he had seen with the interpretations of those events that were offered by the postwar community he inhabited. But as he narrates his traumatic memories of the war, they show a stubborn resistance to this reconciliation. Watkins eventually discovers that his goals of narrating traumatic memory and of reconciling it to communal values, which are primarily religious in nature, are incompatible. Struggling to remain true to his experiences and still retain his ties to his home and community, Watkins is gradually forced to conclude that his sense of self has irrevocably changed—and with it his understanding of the nature of community.

Company Aytch began as a series of articles published in Watkins's hometown Tennessee newspaper, the *Columbia Herald*, during the years 1881 and 1882. These articles were later published in book form by the Cumberland Presbyterian Publishing House of Nashville.⁴⁶ On the surface, *Company Aytch* makes a claim to plain storytelling and homespun artlessness, but it demonstrates in both its title and its form an indebtedness to two previously existing genres. The first is the regimental history, which ostensibly provides the overall structure of the book. Watkins follows throughout the narrative the wartime fate of his comrades in Company H of the First Tennessee, ending with the unit's surrender. The second genre Watkins borrows from is the tall tale.[47] Each chapter of the personal narrative comprises self-contained stories that are offered as part of a series of semi-humorous incidents in the life of a Confederate private. These incidents are presented as "a sideshow of the bigshow," and are to be understood, as Watkins reminds us, not as history but simply as the adventures of an ordinary man caught up amid an extraordinary war.

The content of these adventures is quite diverse, but Watkins's sketches tend to break down into three main types: the first involve a battlefield view of engagements fought by the Army of the Tennessee, the second describes the sufferings of average soldiers living in army camps, and the third examines the gap between military language and logic and what Watkins sees as "common sense." In all three types of sketch, he begins with the intention of telling an amusing anecdote, but his original plan falls apart as Watkins becomes immersed in the events of traumatic memory. After confronting the reader with powerful visions of unremitting suffering, Watkins is then compelled to explain these scenes using religious language and imagery or to dismiss them to the best of his ability.

A passage from Chapter 14 of *Company Aytch* illustrates the first type of sketch. Recalling his participation in the Battle of Jonesboro, Watkins imagines a conversation taking place between the army commander, General Hood, and his subordinates. Punning on the military term *feint*, which refers to a diversion made by one unit to hide the movements of another, he attempts to show the foolishness of the men leading him and his comrades into battle. The corps commander, General Cleburne, says to Hood, "I have feinted, feinted, and feinted, until I can't feint any longer." To this Hood replies, "If you can't feint any longer, you had better flee, fight, or *faint*" (my emphasis). Not content to point out the incompetence of his own army's commanders, Watkins then lampoons the commander of the opposing army, bringing back in this chapter the recurring character of "Mynheer Dutchman." Mynheer Dutchman is a fictional Union commander who represents the author's belief that most of the Union army was made up of foreign hirelings. Preparing for the battle, Mynheer Dutchman says to his adversaries, "Vel I ish peen von leetle pit hungry dish morning, und I yust gobble you up for mein lunch pefore tinner dime. Dot ish der kind of mans vot I bees!"

As these wise fools prepare to move their pawns on the chessboard, Watkins shifts his view from the hypothetical conversations taking place back at the command post to the events happening on the front line. He tells us, "Lieutenant John Whittaker . . . and myself were sitting down eating breakfast out of the same tin plate. We were sopping gravy out with some cold corn bread." This mundane and almost domestic scene is interrupted by artillery fire. Captain Flournoy shouts, "Look out, Sam; look! Look!" and as he turns his head, Watkins narrowly avoids being killed by a cannon ball. Watkins says, "I turned my head, and in turning, the cannon ball knocked my hat off, and striking Lieutenant Whittaker full in the side of the head, carried away the whole of the skull part, leaving only the face. His brains fell in the plate from which we were sopping, and his head fell in my lap, deluging my face and clothes with his blood."

In the passage above, Watkins's tone abruptly changes. Earlier in the sketch, it was humorous and sarcastic, reflected by his choice of language in the hypothetical conversation between commanders. Here the language is descriptive and comes upon the reader as suddenly as the cannon ball falling in Watkins's camp, but it is curiously flat in tone. There is little or no emotion in the depiction of the event, and in its aftermath, the emotional response by the dead man's comrades seems inappropriate. Once the body is removed, Captain Flournoy jokes with Watkins on the narrowness of his own escape, saying, "One tenth of an inch more would have cooked your goose." Whittaker is then quickly buried and the men resume what they were doing, eating and resting before resuming the battle.

Perhaps because he recognizes the impropriety of his unit's response at the time of Lieutenant Whittaker's death, Watkins engages in a lengthy interpretation of the event after the fact. Invoking his community's religious and patriotic sympathies, Watkins says, "He died for his country. His soul is with his God. He gave his all for the country he loved, and may he rest in peace under the shade of the tree where he is buried . . . while the gentle breezes play about the brave boy's grave."[48] Presumably telling his reader more than he intended, Watkins's later interpretation of Lieutenant Whittaker's death only highlights, instead of resolving, the discrepancy between the values of the combat zone and those of his hometown. It is a perfect example of the intrusive and potentially divisive nature of traumatic memory.

Interestingly enough, some of the most divisive memories in Watkins's narrative occur far from the battlefield. Among the second type of sketch that appears in the book, stories relating to the suffering of soldiers in camp, is one titled "Y's You Got My Hog?" Joining two other hungry privates on a "raid" looking for food, Watkins enters the house of "an old lady and her sick and widowed daughter." The old woman prepares a meal for Watkins and his companion, telling them that her husband and all three of her sons have been killed while serving in the Confederate army. Little does she know that while she feeds these hungry soldiers, a third man is in the barn slaughtering the old woman's pig. Watkins begins to feel guilt at his part in this raid, but by the time he decides to back out it is too late. The hog has been killed and his companions are in the process of carrying it back to camp.

Soon the old woman discovers the death of her hog. Watkins tells us, "On looking back I saw the old lady coming and screaming at the top of her voice, 'You got my hog! You got my hog!'" Discomforted by his behavior, Watkins concludes, "We had the hog, and had to make the most of it, even if we did ruin a needy and destitute family." As if in punishment for that thought, the men arrive at the river not long after their raid only to discover that the canoe they used to cross the river has floated away. While Watkins waits in the dark with one of his comrades, another floats across the river on a wooden gate to retrieve the canoe. All three of them then return to camp with their plunder. Watkins confesses to the reader, "The hog was cooked, but I did not eat a piece of it. I felt that I had rather starve, and I believe that it would have choked me to death if I had attempted it."[49] Given the numerous anecdotes in Watkins's personal narrative related to his unit's constant hunger and their nonchalant attitude toward foraging, this claim seems suspect. Unable to retrieve the humorous tone of a story that he now seems to regret sharing with his readers, Watkins spends the rest of the sketch reframing his actions in moral terms.

Watkins is affected by his attempt at foraging in "Y's You Got My Hog?" in a way that is markedly different from his manner in "Death of Lieutenant Whittaker." Unlike the earlier sketch, where he appears to be fully absorbed in the recollection of the event, here he remains conscious enough of the gap between now and then that he feels more acutely the need to explain his actions. Driven by hunger and the numerous other privations and indignities of life in the army camps, Watkins illustrates how he and his comrades reverted to an instinctive and animallike existence. Although he uses the war as justification for his acceptance of this ethos, he is nonetheless eager to confess his sin and thereby reaffirm his decency—and through it demonstrate his humanity. Watkins tells us that he returned to the old woman's home, paying her for the hog and providing her with wood and water to last several days. His final words in the sketch supply the link between his avowed penitence then and his upright course of living after the war: "I have never in my life made a raid upon anybody else."[50]

As different as the scene involving the theft of the hog is from Lieutenant Whittaker's death, they both challenge communal norms and mores in intensely evocative ways. In *Shattered Assumptions*, psychologist Janoff-Bulman argues that trauma is an assault on both the individual psyche as well as the values of a given community. She defines trauma as "times when one's guiding 'paradigms'—one's fundamental assumptions—are seriously challenged and an intense psychological crisis is induced."[51] Recovery must therefore involve an attempt to repair the individual psyche, sociological beliefs, and interpersonal relations at the same time. All of Watkins's sketches attempt these highly complex psychic repairs but ultimately founder on his lack of faith in the efficacy of prewar values and beliefs. War has, in Watkins's view, corrupted society at all levels, leaving him little firm ground on which to stand. Even language has been contaminated by war, as military logic supplants common sense.

This corruption of language by war is vividly exemplified in the story "Hanging Two Spies," which is an example of the third type of sketch found in *Company Aytch*. Hearing through the ranks that two enemy spies have been captured and are soon to be hanged, Watkins says, "I wanted to see a Yankee spy hung. I wouldn't mind that. I would like to see him agonize." Taught through both training and continuous privation to hate the enemy, Watkins hopes to gain pleasure from watching the suffering and death of these spies." His hopes are soon disappointed, however, as he "saw two little boys . . . but did not see the Yankees that I had been looking for." When these boys are led up to the scaffold, Watkins suddenly realizes in horror that they are in fact the spies he had heard about. Watching these boys/spies being hanged, Watkins can only say, "I was appalled; I was horrified; nay, more, I was sick at heart."[52] This sickness of heart carries over from the moment of the event to that of the much later narration, and, to a certain extent, comes to define *Company Aytch* as a whole. Watkins remains puzzled at how civilized society can allow itself so easily to accept the logic of war and then just as easily believe that life can resume the same as it was before. His personal narrative shows a gradual awakening to the persistent difference between what he has experienced and civilian interpretations of that experience. It is hard not to wonder if he felt he was reconciling himself with the wrong community. Perhaps only other veterans could understand what this "poor old Rebel webfoot private" had survived.[53]

Ambrose Bierce's Witness to War

Ambrose Bierce seemed to embrace the gulf of experience that separated him as a veteran from the civilian population, rather than attempting to reconcile that gap like Sherman and Watkins. Soldiers and civilians are mutually exclusive categories in Bierce's worldview. For although he makes halfhearted attempts to communicate with them, civilians are largely excluded from the possibility of comprehending the traumatic memories the author narrates. In Bierce's works, comprehension depends on a body of experience, most of it related to combat, that civilians by definition are denied. The presence of stories like "An Occurrence at Owl Creek Bridge" and "Chickamauga" in the "Soldiers" section of Bierce's famous collection of short stories, *Tales of Soldiers and Civilians*, ironically offers this perspective further support, as it is only through crossing the line from civilian–spectator to soldier–participant that Peyton Farquhar or the deaf–mute child are able to comprehend the events they are caught up in.[54]

One need not comprehend the traumatic memories he narrates, however, to feel the pain of Bierce's tales. This frustrating dynamic, in which endless displays of misery and death are presented to a civilian reader who is then denied entry into Bierce's inner sanctum of meaning, gives us a new way of understanding the author's long-standing reputation as "bitter Bierce."[55] It also helps explain why, when read as a whole, Bierce's stories are not only "monotonous" (as an early critic noted) but also relentless in their mode of expression. More interested in uncovering for himself the truth of war than generating either empathy or understanding, Bierce exhibits toward war the zealotry of the religious acolyte seeking oneness with his god. In his passion, he demonstrates a belief in the transformative power of war, which has baptized him into a new identity.

The author's commitment to re-creating the truth of the quasi-religious combat experience is noticeable in one of his earliest pieces of writing on the Civil War, "What I Saw of Shiloh."[56] This autobiographical sketch is one of the most rewritten pieces in Bierce's body of work, appearing in three different periodicals before being included in his collected writings.[57] However, Bierce made no significant revisions to either the core events or the narrative style of this tale, opting only to make each subsequent version slightly longer than the previous one. It is as if the author believes that, through the accretion of detail alone, the transformative nature of the experience of Shiloh can be known and understood. The story, consequently, remains more of a list than a narrative in the true sense of the word.

By way of explanation for the fragmented nature of his "narrative," Bierce tells the reader, "The incidents related necessarily group themselves about my own personality as a center." These "incidents" include his seemingly random remembrance of a woman, with a baby and "a small ivory-handled pistol" in her hand, joining his unit as it crosses the river to join the battle on the second day. Blended with this fleeting recollection are images of war such as "the forest seemed all at once to flame up and disappear with a crash like that of a great wave upon the beach—a crash that expired in hot hissings, and the sickening 'spat' of lead against flesh." There are also scenes of life in camp, as Bierce tells us of "the tall,

Figure 9. War Department. Office of the Chief of Engineers. *Sketch of the Battle Field of Shiloh Showing the Disposition of the Troops Under the Command of Major General D. C. Buell on the 6th and 7th of April 1862.* Map. April 19, 1862. U.S. National Archives and Records Administration. Washington, D.C.

blue smoke of camp-fires ascending . . . [and] the ghost of an odor from pines that canopy the ambuscade. I feel upon my cheek the morning mist that shrouds the hostile camp unaware of its doom, and my blood stirs at the ringing rifle-shot of the solitary sentinel."[58]

Bierce's identity as a participant in the event is supposed to provide the connecting thread to the "incidents" described in the story. Yet, despite his participation in the Battle of Shiloh, the narrator admits that it remains "unknown" to him, a "wonderland." The author thus continues to write about this occurrence, expanding on his list of details as part of an ongoing quest for meaning. He was cognizant, however, of the limited ability of language to express truthfully the events of war such as Shiloh, and was deeply distrustful of the narrative forms available to convey that experience. Conventional war narratives were, in Bierce's view, attempts to tell civilian readers what they wanted and expected to hear about battle. Furthermore, he felt that veteran self-interest, which included the desire to appear as a hero in the eyes of the home community, often caused writers to force interpretations on events that were flimsy and unwarranted. As Bierce noted with his characteristic sarcasm in "The Devil's Dictionary," truth for most of society was "an ingenious compound of desirability and appearance."[59]

Bierce's critique of this process of forced coherence is at its most ruthless in the short story "Jupiter Doke, Brigadier-General." Published in 1885 at the height of veteran writing about the Civil War, this story is easy to see as a parody of a typical "Battles and Leaders" tale. Although Bierce might have initially envisioned this story as a caricature of Grant, the narrative focuses more on the distorting power of language than the characters that use it, most of whom remain undeveloped in the tale.[60] In Doke's case, this distortion results from the play on the analogies between military and political ways of speaking. Sounding more like a ward boss than a commanding officer, he refers to the enemy in his official reports as if he were involved in a political rather than a military campaign, calling them "the militant Democrats on the other side of the river."[61] Doke's indiscriminate blending of the language of politics with that of war makes the unreliability of his observations obvious. He is more concerned that he appear a hero in the eyes of the public than he is with preparing for military operations.

The military campaign described in the story, which culminates with the Battle of Distilleryville, is conceived of by the high command as a suicide mission. By sending Doke's undermanned unit into a region swarming with enemy partisans, his superiors hope to get him killed and relieve themselves of an incompetent leader. When he manages to survive, primarily through dumb luck, Doke's superiors decide to publicly praise him. They not only grant him a promotion but even pass a congressional resolution thanking him. Doke takes full advantage of this situation and writes an account for the fictional Illinois newspaper *The Maverick*. Responding to this account of the battle, the newspaper editors state, "Verily, truth is stranger than fiction and the pen is mightier than the sword. When by the graphic power of the art preservative of all arts we are brought face to face with such glorious events as these . . . [by] the Great Captain who made the history as well as wrote [about it]."[62]

Passages like this not only accentuate the irony of the tale, by reminding readers of the tremendous gap between what is going on and how the participants explain those events, but also serve to undermine the reader's faith in the first-person accounts that, taken together, make up the historical archive. In "Jupiter-Doke, Brigadier General," Bierce has chosen to construct a fictional narrative out of imagined excerpts from letters, diaries, and official documents. By doing so, he implies that, far from being objective, the archive is "made up of outright lies, selective omissions, and, at best, statements that take full advantage of the ability of military language to drain the unfortunate character from what it describes."[63]

The only source that Bierce seems to trust from the fictional archive he constructs in this tale is the "statement" of Hannibal Alcazar Peyton. Peyton is a slave from Jayhawk, Kentucky, who has been pressed into service as an aide-de-camp for General Doke. His statement, which appears after the congressional resolution of thanks passed to honor Doke's heroism at the Battle of Distilleryville, reveals that the general's supposed victory was actually made possible by his cowardice. Peyton wakes Doke up in the night to alert him to what he believes is the sound of approaching enemy forces. Fearing capture, Doke flees to the rear of the army, triggering a mule stampede. This stampede ultimately wins the battle for the Union cause by blocking a Confederate advance. What makes this explanation seem plausible to Bierce is that it does not rely on simple causation. The ending of "Jupiter-Doke" thus places the story of Distilleryville not within the heroic tradition imagined by *The Maverick*, but instead within a long line of Bierce tales that demonstrate war's resistance to the traditional modes of narration founded on the relationship of cause to effect.

Among these Bierce tales are stories such as "One of the Missing" and "The Affair at Coulter's Notch." In the first of these stories, Private Jerome Serling is sent to scout enemy positions. While viewing the Confederate army retreat from inside an old barn, a stray artillery shell fired by a bored enemy officer hits the building, trapping him under a beam. Convinced that no one will ever find him, Private Serling eventually dies of fright. His brother, a lieutenant leading a scouting patrol, then finds Jerome's corpse a few hours later but is unable to recognize it. Looking at the "yellowish white" face of his brother's body, he simply says, "Dead a week." In the second of these tales, a Union artillery officer, Captain Coulter, is ordered to shell a house. We discover at the end of this tale that the officer, while zealous in his military duty, has been shelling his own home and has killed his wife and child. Creating a strange allusion to the image of the Virgin Mary holding the body of the crucified Jesus, Bierce has the colonel of the regiment observe a scene where "the dead woman clasped in her arms a dead babe. Both were clasped in the arms of the man [i.e., Captain Coulter]."[64]

Unlike the bewildering and somewhat overwhelming list that appears in his nonfiction account of the Battle of Shiloh, the recurring technique of his short fiction attempts to use the ending of his stories to shock readers out of the lull created by their own narrative expectations. The author intends this shock as a means of opening a window into the truth of the combat experience. Yet once this window is opened, it reveals the same dilemma that the author encountered at the conclusion of "What I Saw of Shiloh." The combat experience seems to resist existing modes of narration and demands a new approach toward its explanation.

In his short story "A Resumed Identity," Bierce moves away from attempts to recall memory through conscious effort, instead exploring the narrative potential of reliving memory in a manner similar to hypnosis or what we might call today "flashback."[65] At the beginning of this story the reader is placed in an unknown landscape, with a man who never receives a name. We are consequently just as confused at the beginning of the narrative as the main character, who "looked curiously about him on all sides, as one who among familiar surroundings is unable to determine his exact place and part in the scheme of things." As both the reader and the protagonist attempt to orient themselves to this uncanny setting, we are together taken aback by the sudden appearance of "a group of horsemen riding to the north [and] behind them men afoot, marching in column, with dimly gleaming rifles aslant above their shoulders."[66]

Here our experience as readers begins to diverge from that of the unnamed man. Although the reader remains perplexed about the setting, the protagonist is simply puzzled by the silence with which these soldiers move. He is also convinced that the men he observes advancing are a threat to his personal safety. The man has provided the missing context to his experience—he is on a battlefield and the silent column is either the advancing enemy or the retreating ranks of his own army. Concerned that he might be captured, the man then follows what he believes to be the path of his army. Searching for his unit, he wanders about in fields that exhibit to the reader no outward signs of war.

After several hours, he comes upon a doctor, Dr. Stilling Malson of Murfreesboro, Tennessee. Dr. Malson is the first character in the story to be specifically identified, and his presence further shifts the narrative perspective in the tale. For the first time, we receive some description of the external appearance of the protagonist. Dr. Malson describes his initial encounter with the man in the following terms: "A man approached him from the roadside and saluted in the military fashion, with a movement of the right hand to the hat-brim. But the hat was not a military hat, the man was not in uniform and had not a martial bearing." The doctor questions the man about who he is and where he is going. The man tells him, "I am a lieutenant, of the staff of General Hazen ... of the Federal Army. Kindly tell me what has happened here. Where are the armies? Which has won the battle?" Without answering any of the man's questions, the doctor asks several more questions of his own, including one involving the supposed "lieutenant's" lack of a uniform. To this query the man/lieutenant replies, "I—I don't quite understand."[67] Frustrated by the doctor's inability to tell him anything about the battle or the direction of the Union army's advance, the protagonist again rushes off into the fields, leaving the doctor sitting on his horse, still trying to decipher this encounter.

This moment of contact between the doctor and the unnamed man illustrates the substantial gap in their experience of both space and time. Standing in the same setting, these characters are participants in parallel universes that touch but do not intersect. The doctor, guided by the "objective time" represented by clocks and calendars, is confused by the appearance of a non-martial figure acting like a soldier on the site of a former battle. The man, guided by his individual experience of the passage of time—or "subjective time"—is confused by the doctor's lack of awareness that a battle is currently taking place all around him.[68] Despite the experiential divide between them, the man's encounter with the doctor seems to have unsettled his assurance of his perceptions. Stopping to rest for a moment, the man decides, for some reason, to look at his hands. He notes in surprise that they are "lean and withered. He lifted both hands to his face. It was seamed and furrowed; he could trace the lines with the tips of his fingers." As yet unaware of "objective time," the man exclaims to himself, "How strange!—a mere bullet-stroke and a brief unconsciousness should not make one a physical wreck."

Confronted with physical evidence that seems to contradict not only his understanding of the previous events of the day but also his self-conception, the man concludes, "I must have been a long time in hospital. No wonder that fellow thought me an escaped lunatic. He was wrong; I am only an escaped patient." What the man soon discovers is that he is both right and wrong. He has been in a hospital for a long time, but not for the gunshot wound he believes he has received in battle. No longer twenty-three and a lieutenant in the Union army, he is in fact an old man, a veteran who has escaped (presumably) from a soldiers' home and has been wandering about on the site of one of his former battlefields.

This flash of recognition finally comes to the man with the help of both an inscription and a pool of water. The inscription is on a stone monument placed inside a small cemetery. Inscribed on that monument are the following words:

Hazen's Brigade
To
The Memory of Its Soldiers
Who fell at
Stone River, Dec. 31, 1862

Not long after reading this inscription, he sees his reflection in a pool of water, and the pieces of the puzzle all fall into place. Or at least they appear to. For Bierce ends the story abruptly at this point with the man's death. The only clues we are offered about the significance of this final scene come in the "terrible cry" of the man and the comment by the narrator that the man then "yielded up the life that had spanned another life."[69]

The first of these clues, the protagonist's "terrible cry," suggests a moment of recognition. But it remains unclear what exactly has been revealed. From the second clue, the narrator's brief comment on the protagonist's death, the reader is led to believe that the man has experienced a form of double-consciousness: he has been living two lives simultaneously.[70] Even though the significance of the

Figure 10. *Hazen Brigade Monument*. Photograph. Stones River National Battlefield Website. Photo Gallery: Monuments and Markers. National Park Service Washington, D.C.

man's death after this moment of revelation remains mysterious, it seems likely that awareness of his state of double-consciousness constitutes what is revealed to the protagonist before his death. Moreover, the death of the man following this revelation implies that any attempt to reconcile these two halves of his personality is not only futile but also fatal. Bierce thus implies that death has finally supplied the meaning that eluded the veteran in his attempts to narrate the combat experience. Where the reader might be tempted to see a tragedy, Bierce suggests a moment of transcendence. The veteran has at last returned home.

The war narratives of Sherman, Watkins, and Bierce illustrate that Civil War service was not merely an episode in veterans' lives. Writing to make sense of the traumas of war that had left them divided internally between their past and present selves, these veterans discovered they had been fundamentally changed by the war. Lacking the therapeutic language generated by the twentieth- and twenty-first-century study of trauma, they understood these changes in largely religious terms. Like the experience of sudden conversion, they felt that only those who had lived through the combat experience could fully understand who and what they had become. They were new men born from the ashes of war.

The emergence of a new and distinct veteran identity along with the belief of some veterans that civilians were to be alternately humored, pitied, or simply held at arm's length, opened up a permanent divide between civilians and former soldiers. In the last decades of the nineteenth century, civilians were thereafter compelled to speak in an oblique manner about veterans and the veterans' experience. Young men of the white middle classes like Stephen Crane would engage in an indirect mode of narration that mixed public praise for veterans with a more private resentment and annoyance at their stranglehold on American manhood. The younger generation pondered in hushed tones what might constitute the natural limits of gratitude, and sought for ways around the exclusionary claims of the nation's aging war heroes. Desperately desiring to become men themselves, the rising generation sought opportunities to undermine the pretensions of Civil War veterans, all the while waiting for an opportunity to find a war of their own.

4 The Glorious Burden of the Aging Civil War Veteran

> The youth had been taught that a man became another thing in a battle. He saw his salvation in such a change.
>
> —STEPHEN CRANE, *The Red Badge of Courage*

By the 1890s, the ranks of Civil War veterans in the North and South had begun to thin. This led remaining veterans to become ever more protective of their war. For not only had the war given them a new sense of self, it also gave them a privileged social status. The defensiveness of these aging veterans posed a serious problem for the middle-class white men of the younger generation, regardless of whether they were sons of veterans. Like Henry Fleming, the protagonist in Stephen Crane's novel *The Red Badge of Courage*, these men coming of age in the decades after the Civil War had been taught from birth that "war makes men." Consequently, they longed for a chance to prove their own manhood on the battlefield. The aspirations of this rising generation, however, butted against veteran claims that they had fought the last real war in American history. To the younger generation these claims suggested that the path to true manhood was no longer available, even though society argued that such a rite of passage was necessary for full citizenship. This contradictory message placed the nation's young men in an uncomfortable situation, one in which they were asked to live out their own manhood as custodians of the previous generation's legacy.

As a result of this contradictory message, tension developed between the veterans of the Civil War and the middle-class white males of the younger generation. Yet this tension has received little critical interest from scholars studying gender relations in the late nineteenth century. Historian Kristin Hoganson makes a partial attempt at such an examination. She outlines the conflicted role of Civil War veterans in the jingoist movement that sparked the wars in Cuba and the Philippines, but ultimately she overemphasizes the amity between those in the younger generation who clamored for war and the nation's aging war veterans.[1] The majority of studies on the topic of manhood in the Gilded Age, however, focus not on the conflicts within the middle-class white male ideal, but on outsiders such as black men, immigrants, white women, and the working class who provoked the perceived "crisis" in masculinity that marked the last decades of the nineteenth century. Or they examine the myriad ways middle-class white men attempted to regain what they saw as their eroding power.[2]

The focus of these diverse studies on the external forces that supposedly provoked the gender crisis of the 1890s obscures the problem posed by the imminent transfer of power between the aging Civil War generation and the generation that had come of age since the war's conclusion. With the close of the war, it had become normal to "demand political rights based on [military] service."[3] Civil War veterans, in many instances based solely on their military service, had occupied positions of actual and symbolic male authority in the nation for more than thirty years. Of the seven U.S. presidents between the years 1869 and 1901, only one, Grover Cleveland, had not served in the Union army. To men lacking this war-born sense of authority, it was not at all clear who would assume power when the last of the Civil War generation had passed away.

Stephen Crane's *The Red Badge of Courage* provides a prominent example of the dynamics of this tense transfer of power between the members of the rising generation and the aging population of Civil War veterans in the 1890s. Faced with the burden of the veteran-saturated cultural climate of that decade, in which old soldiers argued both for the compensation of literal pension debts as well as for the debt of gratitude they felt the younger generation owed them, Crane initiated in his writing a battle for the title of "real" American man. Placing the novel within this context of its production provides us a new way of reading what is arguably the best-known piece of literature ever written about the Civil War. This reading goes beyond seeing the novel as either a precursor to modern war fiction or an homage to the Civil War generation. Instead, we can see Crane's narrative as the contradictory product of a transitional age, a work that exhaustively re-creates the experience of Civil War combat only to undercut it. This interpretation thus exposes the narrative's role as a marker for the final stage of Civil War veteran reintegration. Old soldiers had begun to move from memory into history, but they would not fade away without a fight.

Veteran Pensions: A Financial Burden of War

Prior to examining Crane's response to the burdensome legacy of the Civil War veteran, it is first necessary to review the process whereby former soldiers became perceived as a burden to the nation. One place to track this process is in public discussions of the financial burden many civilians felt veterans placed on the United States through their application for pensions. Before the Civil War, veteran pensions were limited to the severely disabled. Veterans were required to prove that their injuries not only prevented them from working to support themselves and their families, but also that these injuries were a direct result of combat. In lieu of pensions, most veterans in the early-nineteenth-century United States received land grants or small monetary bounties. There were also a limited number of soldiers' homes available where disabled veterans who might not qualify for a pension could apply to live. After the Civil War, the pension-eligibility requirement that soldiers prove their injuries directly related to combat remained in effect. Land and monetary bounties also continued to be the preferred method of rewarding former soldiers economically for their service, while soldiers' homes struggled to expand to meet the new demands placed on them by an ever-increasing number of disabled veterans.[4]

Due to the political pressure applied by veterans' groups such as the Grand Army of the Republic and the growing requests of disabled former soldiers for government assistance, a wide variety of pension-reform plans were debated in Congress during the late 1880s. The two dominant plans under consideration were the "service pension plan" and the "dependent pension plan." The first of these, which was ultimately rejected, would have offered pensions to any soldier who served in the Union army for at least ninety days, and after their death to their wives and dependents. The second offered pensions only to former Union soldiers who were unable to work, regardless of the origin or date of disability, and to their dependents upon their death. On June 27, 1890, after years of acrimonious debate, the second of these pension plans was passed by both houses of Congress. Confederate soldiers, even those who had served in the United States army before the war, remained ineligible for these federal benefits. They were left to rely on whatever assistance their home states could provide. Even though the Dependent Pension Act did very little directly for southern veterans, it would nonetheless influence how the states interpreted eligibility for Civil War pensions thereafter. Old age and illnesses acquired long after the war, rather than just battle-related injuries, would now make a former soldier eligible to receive government aid.[5]

The Dependent Pension Act was a lightning rod for public debate. Although many public figures believed that no price was too high to pay to show the nation's gratitude toward its veterans, many feared that expanding pension eligibility rules opened the door to civilian profiteers who could easily manipulate Americans' gratitude for their aging war heroes. These fears were the subject of numerous editorials, including one noteworthy piece that appeared on the front page of the *Philadelphia Times* on March 21, 1891. The editorial stated with some force that "the time is past when self-proclaimed demagogic leaders of the Grand Army can command the confidence of the public to shield robbery in the name of the soldier or the soldier's orphan, and a thief must be stamped as a thief regardless of the uniform he has worn."[6] To use the word "thief" in the same sentence as the word "soldier," especially on the newspaper's front page, would seem to be an instance of editorial suicide. Yet the authors adroitly avoid such criticism by construing their argument as a call to arms for civilians and veterans alike. The editors castigate the villainous pension agents and the corrupt leadership of the Grand Army of the Republic, who were, in their view, taking advantage of hapless war heroes.

This call for reader solidarity was a form of narrative indirection that allowed the writer to engage in a subtle critique of the financial burden imposed by veterans on the nation without appearing to directly attack them as greedy. Another example of this narrative indirection can be found in a *New York Times* editorial commenting on the proposed special enumeration of Civil War veterans and their widows for the Eleventh United States Census. The author exclaims at the beginning of his piece, "What a treasure will be this volume when it gets in the hands of the pension agents!"[7] Again, the primary image evoked in the editorial is of profiteers taking advantage of the nation's gratitude toward its Civil War heroes. The *Times* editors position themselves as disinterested protectors of the veterans' legacy, under assault by con men, and at the same time as advocates for responsible national spending.

This manner of speaking, which subtly criticized the financial strain veterans placed on the nation without appearing unduly censorious, reflects the reality that by the 1890s society at large viewed the Civil War veteran as a white elephant, a costly gift or glorious burden imposed on the backs of the rising generation.[8] The time was ripe for a change in the way both the war and its veterans were depicted and understood, but that change would need to be achieved in a delicate manner. Former Civil War soldiers still enjoyed considerable social prestige; any overt criticism of them, even in the name of fiscal responsibility, would have drawn fierce attacks. The *New York Tribune*'s publisher, Whitelaw Reid, a staunch

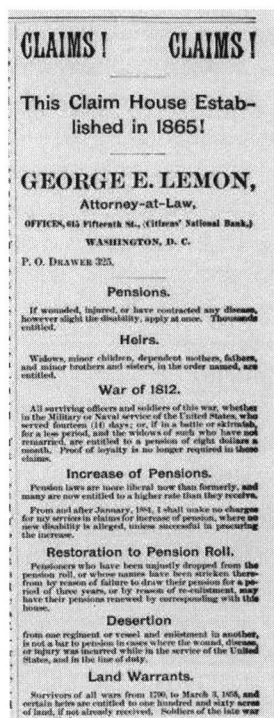

Figure 11. George E. Lemon. "Pension Advertisement." September 24, 1881. *National Tribune*.

Republican and candidate for vice president in 1892, discovered this when he reminded readers that pension expansion should be carefully limited to those veterans who actually needed the financial support. Reid claimed in a July 7 editorial titled "Time to Halt" that "the measure of proper expenditure has been reached, if indeed it has not been passed already. There is no active demand, on the part of the veterans of the Union, for sums exceeding those already appropriated, and those veterans are sensible enough to know that appropriations exceeding half the entire revenue of the Government, to the benefit of a small fraction of the people, might quickly cause the collapse of the whole system for lack of popular approval and support." Following the appearance of this article, the *Daily News* of Denver reported that "a Washington Pension publication threatened to read the New York *Tribune* out of the Republican Party."[9] Apparently even hinting that some veterans who received pensions didn't need them was cause enough to draw severe criticism from the powerful "soldier vote" caucus.

Indirect forms of narration appeared in newspaper editorials during the pension debates of the late 1880s and early 1890s primarily as a strategy to circumvent public criticism that civilian editors like Reid were disrespecting the heroes of the Civil War. Its emergence as a stylistic technique was also a sign, however, that the Civil War had begun to shift from the realm of memory to that of history. Arguments that were ostensibly about fiscal responsibility had in fact more to do with the cultural relevance of the Civil War and its survivors to a generation that had not lived through the conflict.

The distinction between living memory and history is the subject of analysis for French historian Pierre Nora, who notes that "memory is a perpetually actual phenomenon, a bond tying us to the eternal present; history is a representation of the past."[10] Nora's conception of memory is similar to what we might consider tradition, which offers rituals to reaffirm for a society the importance of past events to the present generation. History, as Nora understands it, is a collection of objects needing skilled interpretation to make sense.

In the late-nineteenth-century United States, such a distinction between memory and history was evident in the symbolism attached to the Decoration Day parade, which celebrated the sacrifice of northern soldiers killed in Civil War battles, versus the symbolism associated with Civil War monuments. During the 1890s, Civil War monument construction advanced at a dramatic pace. By the end of the century, as art historian Kirk Savage notes, nearly every town in the United States, North and South, had a statue dedicated to the Civil War soldier.[11] These monuments offered reassurance to veterans that their sacrifices would not be forgotten, but they also assured members of the rising generation that the rites of gratitude they were engaged in would not last forever. Whereas a parade suggested an ongoing duty of the younger generations to promote the legacy of their elders, the monument implied fulfillment of that duty.

A poem appearing in the May 30, 1897, issue of the Democratic newspaper the *Galveston News* serves as an example of the younger generation's desire to move away from the memory associated with Decoration Day parades to the history embodied in the Civil War monument. This poem appears at the beginning of a Decoration Day article titled "More Than Half Are Dead," which addresses the high mortality rate of aging Civil War veterans. The writer begins by evoking the noise of battle alongside the din of the Decoration Day parade. He refers to the "Great Captains, with their guns and drums." These noises, the writer asserts, will only "disturb our judgment for the hour." Not necessarily referring to a specific duration of time for the parade, the author is instead suggesting the end of an era. With the death of veterans, their era of noise, which has "disturbed our judgment," is almost over. In its place is a "silence" that comes "at last." Now that the readers of the poem are freed from the distraction of the "Great Captain's" noise, they can focus on the concerns of the moment rather than the rituals of the past embodied in the Decoration Day parade. To replace this time-consuming ritual, the author champions "their [i.e. Civil War veterans'] fame." The anonymous author asserts that this object will soon stand "like a tower" that "Children shall behold."[12] The writer of this poem seems to anxiously await the moment when the statue will finally supplant the ritual of the parade, which will mean the acts of gratitude will be complete.

Because the *Galveston News* was solidly Democratic in its politics and was owned at the time by a Confederate veteran, A. H. Belo, we could simply ascribe the poem's tone to lingering southern bitterness toward a holiday celebrating the northern dead. However, the theme of rapid veteran mortality was nearly universal in U.S. newspapers published during the 1890s. It was assumed that Civil War veterans were dying at such a rapid pace that soon the only veterans of the war available for civilians to see would be the statues placed in cemeteries and town squares. To those public writers concerned with the financial burden veterans were placing on a "grateful" nation, this trend seemed oddly comforting. That is likely why the theme of rapid veteran mortality frequently appeared alongside discussions surrounding the rising cost of veterans' pensions.

Examining the results of the 1890 United States Census, however, we see that this belief in rapid veteran mortality was mistaken. The special enumeration of Civil War soldiers and their widows included in the Eleventh Census indicates that 1,466,093 Union and Confederate veterans were alive in the 1890s. Membership records kept by the Grand Army of the Republic also indicate a gradual decline rather than a sudden demise, as their membership mortality rate rose from 1.33 percent in 1890 to 2.35 percent in 1897.[13] A gradual decline of Civil War veterans rather than a more dramatic rate of mortality would clearly present a troubling reality to the nation as it prepared to enter a new century. For one thing, pension costs would continue to rise far into the foreseeable future. Even more devastating, however, to middle-class white men coming of age in the postwar nation was the reality that the Civil War generation would continue to dominate American culture—and through it, the ideals of American manhood—for a long time to come.

The Cultural Burden of the Civil War Veteran

Veterans groups like the Grand Army of the Republic were responsible not simply for increases in economic compensation to Civil War veterans but also for steering cultural norms concerning manhood, and with it, the models of proper citizenship. Commander in Chief of the Grand Army of the Republic John Palmer addressed these links between manhood, citizenship, and service in the Union army during his opening remarks at the group's twenty-sixth national reunion in 1892: "We were citizens before we became soldiers and volunteered at the call of an imperiled Nation, that we might fulfill the highest duties of citizenship, and the lessons we learned amidst the storm of battle have made us more mindful of our duties as citizens."[14] The idea that soldiering was "the highest duty of citizenship" was widespread in the 1890s, thanks in large part to veterans and their organizations. Moreover, this development occurred despite claims in the newspapers about the financial cost to the government of maintaining former soldiers with military pensions. Arguments about what the nation literally owed its veterans had become inextricably linked to discussions about what the younger generation owed its elders in terms of reverence and remembrance.

This symbolic debt is vividly illustrated in an engraving titled "The Veteran's Memories" that accompanies another Decoration Day article in the May 30, 1897, edition of the *Galveston News*. The image presents on the left-hand side a young soldier, wide-eyed and open-mouthed, running into battle. On the right-hand side is an old man talking to a child who is leaning on his knee. The old man is presumably an aged version of the young man at the left, with one side of the frame representing the present and the other the past. Notice, however, that the young man is significantly larger than his older self, and that his bayonet is pointed toward the old man's non-amputated leg. The youthful figure thus not only dominates the frame, but also seems to violate the strict division of the present (on the left) from the past (located on the right). Although the young soldier appears to be apprehensive, he also takes on something of a menacing aspect. He seems to run out of the picture, toward the reader. But it remains unclear who the enemy is in this re-created scene. All we are aware of is that the image at the left is designed to illustrate for the viewer the memories that the elderly veteran is seemingly imparting to the child.

Despite the fact that the aged veteran's reminiscences are presented as an amusing tale, since the child listens with wide eyes and open mouth, there is also a hint that they contain a certain degree of menace. This threat is suggested both by the stance of the soldier to the left and by the explosion that seems to be taking place in the background of the picture. The explosion is yet another example of the past crossing over to the other side of the frame and intruding on the present. It could easily be interpreted as just another part of the old man's tale, perhaps a cannon ball exploding on the battlefield, but it more closely resembles the appearance of a comet or meteor crashing into a planet or, perhaps, an eclipse.

Figure 12. G. Kauffman. "The Veteran's Memories." Engraving. May 30, 1897. *Galveston News*.

Whatever the veteran is telling this child, the image suggests, will affect his life for a long time to come. It will overshadow the boy's own reminiscences, tingeing them with the colors of the old man's past.

Bearing in mind the influence of the veteran's memories on this young boy, it is worth noting that the old man's son is missing from this image, as it is hard to imagine this young child as being his direct progeny. Perhaps he is at work, or more than likely he is tired of hearing his father's stories. Either way, his absence reminds us of the predicament faced by members of the generation in between that of the old man and what is probably his grandson. This in-between generation of young men was told that war made men and that the highest aspiration of a citizen should be the desire to be a soldier. Yet, at the same time, they were told that the Civil War had been the last real war, which left them little option but to keep alive the memory of their fathers' heroism without experiencing heroism and praise of their own.[15] This unpleasant dilemma adds a new significance to the son's absence in the engraving, as he seems both literally and figuratively "out of the picture."

The experience faced by members of the in-between generation—of being out of the picture and eclipsed by their fathers' deeds—is further illustrated in the remarks of Grand Army commander George Merrill. During the sixteenth national reunion, Merrill stated, "No one, not even our sons, can appreciate the memories of camp and march, of bivouac and battle, as those who were participants therein; the scenes of the great struggle can never be to them what they were to us."[16] Merrill's comments were occasioned by ongoing discussions about whether the sons of Union veterans should be allowed a more active role in the organization than simply being caretakers of their fathers' memories. Merrill argued, and the majority agreed with him, that it was better for the organization to cease to exist rather than expand the role of veterans' sons.

Southern veterans' groups were less emphatic on this score, but they still maintained a distinction between those who had actually experienced combat and those who only had knowledge of it through reading or listening to soldiers' tales. Duke Goodman noted with some concern in a letter to the *Confederate Veteran* magazine, "I find in many portions of the state that the UCV [United Confederate Veterans] camps are amalgamating with the masses and holding reunions; the masses are fast overshadowing these camps. The day is not far distant when, if this is kept up, these camps will lose their identity."[17] "Amalgamate" is clearly a loaded word in the postbellum nation, bearing within it southern connotations of racial impurity. In the context of Goodman's statement, however, it had more to do with issues of veteran identity and control over the legacy of the war that had made them. Veterans would continue to manage the active remembrance of the war, while sons and grandsons would learn to become the respectful stewards of this legacy.

Intergenerational Struggle in *The Red Badge of Courage*

The exclusionary rhetoric of Civil War veterans, which claimed that war made men but then denied young men a chance to find manhood through a war of their own, provides us with a new way to understand the quintessential work of Civil War fiction—Stephen Crane's *The Red Badge of Courage*. Traditionally, literary critics have ignored the novel's roots in 1890s American culture and instead have tried to insert it into the context of 1863 and the Battle of Chancellorsville, or have seen it as a sign of the emerging trend of twentieth-century modernism represented by Hemingway and the "Lost Generation" following the First World

War.[18] When we see *The Red Badge of Courage* as part of the veteran-saturated cultural discourses of the last decade of the nineteenth century, it becomes clear that the novel represents a struggle between middle-class white young men and the lingering power of their cultural "fathers," the veterans of the Civil War. In *The Red Badge of Courage*, Crane hopes to imaginatively re-create the combat experience of Civil War veterans in order to find a way to supersede them.

To fully understand the process Crane went through to transcend the Civil War veterans' legacy, we must begin with the question of origins. Crane had no direct ties to Civil War veterans through his immediate relatives, and it does not appear that he spoke to veterans of the war prior to writing his novel.[19] Nonetheless, at the time Crane was living in the New York/New Jersey area there were 109,748 Union veterans living in the region and 997 Confederate veterans. Grand Army of the Republic records also indicate a strong member presence in both states, with 117 posts in New Jersey and 647 in New York.[20] Surrounded by veterans, it seems probable that Crane would have heard their tales and observed the cultural authority these tales provided them.

Crane was also familiar with the mechanics of soldiering from his brief sojourn at the quasi-military academy Claverack College. He enrolled there in January 1888 with the intention of eventually attending West Point. Class photos show a young Crane as a member of the school drill team, dressed in a blue Civil War–style uniform and carrying a musket. Although it is not possible to fully surmise his older brother William's intentions, we know he encouraged Stephen to withdraw from Claverack in the spring of 1890. William is reported to have told his younger brother that joining the army was a bad idea, since "the United States was unlikely to fight a war during Stephen's lifetime"; consequently, he "persuaded him to attend a civilian college rather than West Point."[21] Stephen reluctantly accepted his brother's advice and soon enrolled at Lafayette College as an engineering student.

Without overstating the role of Crane's biography in the creation of the novel, these events from the author's early life are the place we must begin if we are to understand the origins of *The Red Badge of Courage*. Crane's experience comes not just from the veterans he may have spoken to or from what he might have read, but also from the world he lived in. This world was one of mixed messages for young men like Crane. Union veteran Lew Wallace alludes to this problem in an address to the Grand Army of the Republic's thirty-first national reunion: "I have heard men say that the coming generation is not equal to the generation which is passing away. I have heard say they were too much given to bicycling and foot-ball and golf, and the like. Comrades, I differ with them. Those are the exercises that make men. I see a game of football and the thought, in my mind, is not as to the result of the game, but as to the courage and the muscle that is called out. That is the making of the man."[22] The former general, long before American philosopher and psychologist William James's call for a "moral equivalent of war," was attempting to provide a substitute for war's power to create manhood. He was also calling for a truce that would alleviate the strain in intergenerational relations he saw escalating to the point of conflict in American society during the 1890s. Men like Crane, however, were not interested in substituting football for war. College sports were in his mind too closely associated with the enforced adolescence he was trying to escape.[23]

Only war itself would suffice for Crane, but he first needed to analyze the source of the Civil War veterans' power. Then he could search for ways to assume their mantle of martial prowess and American manhood. This goal required the author to adopt a stance of both competition and identification with the main character in his novel, the Civil War veteran Henry Fleming.[24] Crane is constantly probing for a way to undermine Henry Fleming without damaging the social position he occupies. He wants to understand through Henry's experience just how war makes men. This is after all the central message that Crane's culture has consistently communicated to its white middle-class male youth, and it is a message that appears directly in the novel itself. In Chapter 3, as Henry's unit is moving in preparation for combat, the narrator tells us, "The youth had been taught that a man became another thing in battle. He saw his salvation in such a change."[25] The majority of critics assume that the "salvation" referred to in this passage involves issues of heroism versus cowardice on the battlefield, but instead it represents a genuine curiosity on the part of the author toward the supposed man-making power of war.[26] He wants what Henry possesses and yearns to understand the mechanism that made Civil War veterans like him into cultural icons.

Because these veterans were still a powerful force in American life, Crane must have known he had to move forward carefully in his attempt to dethrone the heroes of what was then America's "greatest generation." This is where the author's experience in journalism proved invaluable. In contrast to *Maggie* and Crane's other Bowery tales, concerning which it has become commonplace to look at how his journalism influenced his fiction, it is rare for critics to consider *The Red Badge of Courage* alongside Crane's newspaper writings. One reason for this omission is that the bulk of Crane's war reporting appeared after the novel's publication. But if we expand our notion of "war reporting" to include Decoration Day pieces and tributes to Civil War veterans, we can see the ways *The Red*

Badge of Courage is indebted to Crane's early journalism, supplying him with examples of the language and imagery necessary to address the highly contentious relationship during the 1890s between the younger generation and veterans of the Civil War.

In his role as a newspaper writer, Crane would undoubtedly have read many of the Decoration Day articles published in the New York and New Jersey region, which seemed to offer the expected praise of veterans but hinted at the exhaustion of both the writer and the reader with the topic. Moreover, as a special contributor to the *New York Tribune*, Stephen Crane would have undoubtedly seen the numerous articles in that publication that were cautiously critical of pension expansion. There is also a reason to believe that the author may have entered the public conversation on Civil War veterans with the publication of a Decoration Day article of his own. In a letter written to Hamlin Garland on May 9, 1894, Crane says, "I wrote a decoration day thing for the *Press* which aroused them [i.e. Crane's editors at the newspaper] to enthusiasm. They said, in about a minute though, [sic] that I was firing over the heads of the soldiers."[27]

Thomas Gullason and Daniel Hoffman both claimed in the 1950s to have uncovered the Decoration Day piece Crane refers to in this letter. Gullason argued that it was an anonymous article published in the *New York Press* in May 1894 titled "Veterans' Ranks Thinner by a Year." This piece, although unsigned, bears a striking similarity in language to Crane's other writing. It also fits the time frame and the newspaper mentioned in Crane's letter to Garland. The other possible candidate for this Decoration Day piece was a handwritten article titled "The Gratitude of a Nation," unpublished in Crane's lifetime, which the critic Daniel Hoffman found in Columbia University's Stephen Crane Papers.[28] Both pieces illustrate the author's attempt to work through his frustration at the cultural dominance veterans held over American manhood, and they serve as precursors to the indirect language Crane would utilize in *The Red Badge of Courage*.

"Veterans' Ranks Thinner by a Year" begins by asserting a complex web of emotional and intellectual connections between the writer and his readership: "As a holiday, Decoration Day was probably never so joyously observed. As a day of memories, it was probably never so fraught with sadness. To the rising generation it meant a revel of sports and pastimes; to the fading generation it was a sharp reminder that the fires of the last bivouac were growing bright in the deepening twilight; to the lusty generation that stands between, it was a mixture of both."[29] Although the adverb "probably" creates a degree of uncertainty about the author's pronouncements, the following lines resolve some of that uncertainty by showing that the meaning of this Decoration Day parade differs depending on whom you ask. For the younger generation, boys similar in age to the one pictured in the engraving "The Veteran's Memories," Decoration Day is one spent in the pursuit of "sports and pastimes." In contrast to the games of these boys are the "bivouacs" of the older generation, which somberly recall the danger and sacrifice of the past. Situated in the middle are the members of what the article calls "the lusty generation that stands between." These are young men or adolescents on the cusp of full maturation. The author seems to identify with them the most, and the rest of the article mixes the tones of sadness and joy spectators from this in-between generation feel as they look upon the now-elderly veterans who are not just taking part in a march "in memory of the dead" but seem to be marching toward death themselves.

There is something about these men the author relates to. The elderly veterans in this parade highlight for him the stark contrast, made visible in the engraving examined earlier in the chapter, between these onetime soldiers now and then. Once like him, lusty and strong, these veterans are now feeble and unsteady. The process of their aging poses the conundrum of how and why they are still objects of cultural veneration. Ultimately, the parade raises more questions than it answers, and leaves the observer from the in-between generation with a lingering taste of bitterness in his mouth. That bitterness comes out near the end of the article, where he says, "This particular Old Guard not only never surrenders, but apparently never grows old."[30] We know from the author's description of the parade as a procession of the elderly that the word "apparently" is meant to sound false to the reader, expressing the viewer's frustration with his own situation.

These men are, in his opinion, unreasonable for not retiring and making way for lusty young men like himself, but his own desires are judged by society as being inappropriate. His longing for the mantle of real manhood seems to be at odds with a sense of filial piety. Realizing that the men who dominate the norms of American masculinity are, in reality, now pitiable old men, the writer feels unable to place himself in a position of superiority toward them. To do so would seem both to the author and to his audience not only unwarranted but also unkind. As he views this slow march with no apparent end in sight and contemplates yet another one at the same time next year, the author is compelled to consider the limits of gratitude: when will it be his turn to be venerated by the community as a man?

The concept of gratitude, rather than the ritual of a parade, is the starting point of the other Decoration Day piece, unpublished during Crane's lifetime, "The Gratitude of a Nation."[31] Crane begins the article by saying that "Gratitude, the sense of obligation, often comes very late to the mind of the world. It is the habit of humanity to forget her heroes, her well-doers, until they have passed on beyond the sound of earthly voices. It has almost become a great truth that the man who achieves an extraordinary benefit for the race shall go to death without the particular appreciation of his fellows."[32] The narrator seems to present a fairly straightforward critique of the younger generation's lack of a proper sense of obligation to its forefathers, the Civil War veterans who "are disappearing" each day along with the glorious past those heroes represent. Furthermore, the narrator's exhortations appear to call on his youthful readers to change the error of their ways, and to "struggle to defeat this ironical law of fate" whereby the younger generation forgets the deeds of its elders and thus loses sight of its obligation to the past. The highly exaggerated tone of the piece, however, suggests less the classic jeremiad than the veiled accusation that the older generation has somehow failed the younger one. In phrases such as "stars shot from guns would not hinder their devotion to the flag," the tenor of the language hints that the older generation's excessive calls for devotion to the legacy of the fathers have condemned the sons to a state of perpetual youth.[33] Gratitude thus becomes a one-sided phenomenon, as the sons are expected to keep their father's memory alive but the fathers appear to have no responsibility to allow for the maturation of their sons.

In each of these Decoration Day articles, the highly charged message of the author is skillfully masked by the indirection of its language, which causes the reader to consistently ask not only the meaning of each pronouncement but also who is speaking. Crane will take a similar narrative approach in *The Red Badge of Courage*. Through a subtle blending of voices, the author explores the conflicted relationship between himself and his main character, Henry Fleming. As the author examines how war makes men, the careful reader becomes aware of slippages in the text, moments where Crane begins to express his own frustrations through the words of his protagonist. These moments are more obvious in the manuscript edition of the novel, which Henry Binder published in 1982, but they can also be found in the Appleton text, the standard edition of the novel published in 1895.[34]

One such moment appears in the Appleton text when Henry looks upon the dead and dying on the battlefield and expresses his resentment toward them. He calls their supposed marks of honor "stolen" crowns and "sham" "robes of glorious memories."[35] Envy toward the dead and dying, described here as members of an elite club, makes Henry seem petty and small-minded. This in turn creates a disjunction in the reader's mind between the image of the Civil War veteran as a cultural icon and the actual men who fought in the war. The author then seizes on that moment of disjunction to ask a leading question—what makes the young men back *then* superior to the ones living *now*? They, too, Crane suggests, coveted a place in the pantheon of real American men and did not necessarily follow the rules of social propriety in order to achieve it. As long as the author remains cloaked in the persona of Henry Fleming, Henry appears to be the one espousing such views, and he alone is viewed in a negative light. Such indirection thus allows the author to speak his mind with impunity. The dead and dying in this scene, consequently, become not the bodies lying on the Chancellorsville battlefield, viewed by a rationalizing Private Fleming. Instead, they represent the exclusive fraternity of war veterans, circa 1895, who have robbed the youth, Stephen Crane, of his own "robes of glorious memories."

This slippage between the author's voice and that of his main character is far more obvious in the manuscript edition of the novel, which lacks the subtlety of the text published by Appleton. In the discarded version of Chapter 12, there is a passage where Henry Fleming muses on his failure to rationalize his behavior on the battlefield:

> When he had erected a vindicating structure of great principles, it was the calm toes of tradition that kicked it all down about his ears. He immediately antagonized then this devotion to the by-gone; this universal adoration of the past. From the bitter pinnacle of his wisdom he saw that mankind not only worshipped the gods of the ashes but that the gods of the ashes were worshipped because they were the gods of the ashes. He perceived with anger the present state of affairs in its bearing upon his case. And he resolved to reform it all.[36]

Henry concludes that the burdens of tradition and the reverence of the past, what he calls "the gods of the ashes," are to blame for his actions. They are blocking his passage from the status of a "youth" to that of a "man." Yet, within the context of this scene, it is not at all clear that there are any traditions holding him down. The only way this passage gains significance is if we consider that it is not Henry Fleming who is speaking here, but Stephen Crane. The author reveals fairly openly his frustration with the bombastic claims of the previous generation, the "by-gone" "gods of the ashes," who stand in the way of him achieving martial glory. Only by sweeping them away can the final steps toward maturation be achieved and the youth, at last, become a man.

In his eagerness to wrest away from the Civil War veteran his cultural status and power, Crane has seriously underestimated his opponent. Just as the veteran will not reveal the secrets of his manhood without a struggle, so, too, will he refuse to simply vanish like ashes in the wind. In a passage from Chapter 5 of the Appleton text, the seeming ubiquity of the veterans' power becomes apparent. While far more muted in tone and subtle in its indirection than the earlier one cited from the manuscript, this scene exhibits much of the same ferocity and frustration toward the Civil War veterans' legacy. As Henry is waiting for the Confederate advance, he thinks to himself:

> of the village street at home before the arrival of the circus parade on a day in the spring. He remembered how he had stood, a small, thrillful boy, prepared to follow the dingy lady upon the white horse, or the band in its faded chariot. He saw the yellow road, the lines of expectant people, and the sober houses. He particularly remembered an old fellow who used to sit upon a cracker box in front of the store and feign to despise such exhibition. A thousand details of color and form surged in his mind. The old fellow upon the cracker box appeared in middle prominence.[37]

Crane's placing of this scene before the beginning of the major battle in the narrative is an instance of foreshadowing. Henry's progress through the story will mimic his experience of viewing the circus as a child. Initial excitement at "going to see the elephant" (a standard phrase used during the Civil War to refer to experiencing combat) will give way to disillusion, which the youth will eventually attempt to purge from his consciousness by the novel's end.

Neither Henry nor the circus players, however, are key figures in this scene. That honor belongs to the old man on the cracker box, who is described as sitting in "middle prominence" and pretending to despise the events unfolding before him. The prominence of this old man, who appears to stand in for the members of the generation prior to Henry's, represents an additional level of foreshadowing. The scornful presence of the old man deflates the youth's moment of anticipation. Even as he awaits the approach of battle and his chance to become a man, his memories are already dominated by the presence of a scornful older generation. This seemingly insignificant passage thus marks the failure of the author's attempt to transcend the Civil War veterans' legacy through the process of imaginative reconstruction. It would seem that in the ongoing struggle between the author and his creation, the Civil War veteran Henry Fleming has won. The younger generation will not be allowed knowledge of the mysterious power whereby war makes men. Nor will it be permitted membership in the elite fraternity of American warriors.

Ironically, given the author's intent, the novel ultimately strengthened rather than detracted from the legacy of the Civil War veteran. Responses from the nineteenth-century readership of the novel confirm this view since, with a few exceptions, *The Red Badge of Courage* was understood as a fairly straightforward tribute to the Civil War veteran rather than a critique. Crane's publishers encouraged this interpretation, and used the author's status as a youth who could write about war without ever having experienced it to market the book. Crane voiced his frustration at this turn of events in a letter to Curtis Brown, saying, "I hear the damned book '*The Red Badge of Courage*' is doing very well in England."[38] Although he appreciated the notoriety his novel had gained him, there was something faintly ridiculous about being praised for the wrong reason. Crane had hoped to become famous for unlocking the secret of the Civil War veterans' fame and passing it on to young men such as himself. Instead, he had simply reaffirmed the fame of the prior generation and endeared himself to them for his supposed praise. The author had clearly been too subtle in his use of language, but his options were limited. He could either risk offending living veterans through a more direct narrative approach or risk misunderstanding through the use of indirect language. He had chosen the latter and was reaping the result.

One of the few readers who understood the novel the way Crane intended and left a record of his response was the former Union general and Chicago publishing executive Alexander C. McClurg. In a review published in the April 11, 1896, issue of the magazine *The Dial*, McClurg called the book "the vain imaginings of a young man born long since that war, a piece of intended realism based entirely on unreality." His strongly worded evaluation of the book unfortunately masks the otherwise-perceptive reading of the novel that follows. McClurg correctly notes that the book is critical of Civil War veterans, calling it "a vicious satire." He also notices that Henry Fleming is intended as an antihero, what he calls "an ignorant and stupid country lad, who, without a spark of patriotic feeling, or even of soldierly ambition, has enlisted in the army from no definite motive that the reader can discover, unless it be that other boys are doing so."[39] In a social climate where Civil War veterans still appeared as godlike figures, Crane must have counted himself lucky that McClurg was one of the few veterans to take offense at the novel, even as he experienced frustration that he had not attained his original goal.

Crane left little commentary on the composition process of *The Red Badge of Courage*, and what he did write was unclear. Nonetheless, the novel's publication history does offer us some clues about the compromises necessary to publish a book expressing resentment toward the Civil War generation's stranglehold on

American manhood. When in 1894 he was unable to find a publisher for his manuscript, Crane sold an abridged version of the novel (approximately fifteen thousand words) to Irving Bacheller for syndicated publication in the newspapers.[40] Encouraged by the responses of newspaper readers, Crane brought clippings from the novel's syndicated version to Appleton's acquisitions editor, Ripley Hitchcock. These clippings convinced Hitchcock to consider the novel for publication, but what he saw was not innovation but rather the continuation of an already-successful narrative strategy.

The version of *The Red Badge of Courage* that appeared in the newspapers was, in fact, close to the "Battles and Leaders" tales Crane had once criticized. According to his friend the painter Corwin Knapp Linson, Crane exclaimed, after reading several works from this popular war series, "I wonder that some of those fellows don't tell how they felt in those scraps! They spout eternally of what they did, but they are as emotionless as rocks."[41] The syndicated version of *The Red Badge of Courage*, like the "Battles and Leaders" tales, focuses primarily on Henry Fleming's actions during the battle. The author largely removes the passages, criticized by McClurg, where we see the highly personal ways in which Henry experiences combat.

Although this change in itself is significant, the greatest variation between the syndicated version of the narrative and its book forms (both the manuscript and the Appleton text) is the addition of camaraderie to the novel. Throughout the newspaper version of the story, Henry is an integral part of his regiment, and this alters a wide variety of events and relationships in the novel, including Henry's bond with Wilson. In the book-length version of the narrative, Henry and Wilson are presented as rivals. The syndicated version of the story completely erases this rivalry, especially by omitting Wilson's giving Henry his death letter and Henry's later contemplation about whether to use that letter as blackmail against his "friend." In the newspaper version, Henry and Wilson instead become pals who undergo the experience of combat together, and both feel elated near the narrative's end when they can bask in the praise of their officers: "Several men came hurrying up. Their faces expressed a bringing of great news. 'Oh, Flem, yeh jest oughta heard!' cried one eagerly." What these unnamed comrades want Henry to have heard is then reported as the praise of the brigade's colonel, who says, "They deserve t' be major generals." Hearing this, Henry and Wilson are "flushed from thrills of pleasure" and "They exchanged a secret glance of joy and congratulation. They speedily forgot many things. The past held no pictures of error and disappointment. They were very happy."[42]

"They" is intentionally repeated near the end of this shortened version of the narrative to remind the reader that this was not just Henry's experience but that of his whole unit (including Wilson). "They" become men together, and the consequence is a narrative far more conventional and considerably less critical of Civil War veterans than the one the author initially envisioned. That Crane was not happy with the syndicated version of his war story, which was cut to meet the space demands of the newspaper editors to whom it was sent, is evident in the letter that accompanied the newspaper clippings he sent to the Appleton editor, Ripley Hitchcock: "Dear Mr. Hitchcock: This is the war story in its syndicate form—that is to say, much smaller and to my mind much worse than its original form."[43] Hitchcock, however, was sufficiently pleased with what he had seen to ask the young author for a copy of his full manuscript.

A War of One's Own

Although we do not know Hitchcock's response after reading the complete narrative, it is possible to surmise through a comparison of the first published book-length edition to the manuscript that both Crane and his editor recognized that the manuscript's lack of subtlety would hinder the novel's success. Crane, therefore, made cuts to the manuscript for the same reason he allowed them to be made to the newspaper version of the story—he wanted his work published. Equally important, however, was the author's realization that there was little reason at this point to reveal his hand. By the time his book saw widespread publication Crane still believed that war made men, yet he had given up on the idea that this transformative process could be imaginatively re-created; instead, actual participation in the experience of war was the initiation needed to belong to the warrior's elite fraternity. This change in perspective is evident in the sequel to *The Red Badge of Courage*, Crane's short story "The Veteran," which was originally published in August 1896 in *McClure's* magazine and then reprinted in the short story collection *The Little Regiment*. "The Veteran" marks the end of Crane's contest with the Civil War veteran Henry Fleming for entry into the ranks of an older generation of warriors. It also serves as a rejoinder to the public's misguided reception of the novel.

The story opens with a scene that seems to embody the kind of postwar life that the youthful Henry imagined for himself in *The Red Badge of Courage*, which is summed up in a passage from Chapter 15 of the novel: "He could see himself in a room of warm tints telling tales to listeners. He could exhibit laurels. They were insignificant; still, in a district where laurels were infrequent, they might shine. He saw his gaping audience picturing him as the central figure in blazing scenes."[44] Now, as an old man in the short story "The Veteran," Henry sits in the grocery store of his small hometown, sharing with his townsmen his "gilded images of memory." But there is an interesting twist to Henry's behavior in "The Veteran" that makes it hard to read the story as "a daydream from within the context of the novel."[45] Henry decides in "The Veteran" to tell the truth. He describes in this short story events that are already familiar to anyone who has read the novel. But he adds to them the admission that he ran away from his first battle. He says, "I thought they were all shooting at me . . . and it seemed so damned unreasonable, you know. I wanted to explain to 'em what an almighty good fellow I was. But I couldn't explain. So I run!"

For the reader of *The Red Badge* who is frustrated by Henry's rationalizations of his behavior, his honesty in old age must seem like vindication—a sign that he has finally matured. That is what makes the scenes that follow so odd, appearing like punishment rather than appreciation of the old man's honesty. After Henry has finished telling his story, his grandson, Little Jim, walks up to him and asks, "Grandpa—now—was that true what you was telling those men . . . about your running." Henry replies to his grandson, "Why, yes, that was true enough, Jimmie. It was my first fight, and there was an awful lot of noise, you know." Jimmie walks away from his grandfather in disgust after he receives this reply, and we are told that "his stout boyish idealism was injured."[46]

From the above scene, the story then jumps abruptly to nighttime at the Fleming family's homestead. The entire family is awakened by cries of "fire, fire!" Henry quickly gets dressed and goes outside to find his barn engulfed in flames. He rushes into the burning barn seven times to save the animals from the fire. His final sortie into the barn is to save two colts, but, this last time, Henry fails in his mission. The roof collapses and kills him. To die in a barn fire would seem to be an incredibly commonplace ending for a war hero. It also seems a bit heavy-handed to have Henry die saving the very type of animal he and Little Jim discuss in the last moments of the opening scene at the grocery store. Before Little Jim storms off in a huff, Henry asks his grandson, "Sickles' colt is going for a drink. Don't you wish you owned Sickles' colt Jimmy?" Jimmy's sullen reply to his grandfather's question is "He ain't as nice as our'n."[47]

The colt, a young male horse, appears in this scene as a symbol for a specific vision of manhood—the conflicted space of adolescence, filled with "storm and stress."[48] Furthermore, Crane's use of the name Sickles in reference to that colt, a name that Stephen Crane must have known would conjure up for his readers an image of the former Civil War general Daniel Sickles, connects that vision of adolescent manhood to the controlling presence of the Civil War generation.[49] Jimmy's response, therefore, sounds like the younger generation's rejection of what its elders have to offer by settling instead for what is "our'n" rather than what belongs to men like Sickles. The subsequent death of this same type of horse in the later scene (along with Henry) hints at the consequences of the older generation's stranglehold on the life of its "colts." One side must give way in this struggle or both will ultimately die. Henry Fleming has lived past his moment. It is time for him to leave the stage.

This reading is supported by Crane's description of the moment of Henry's death: "When the roof fell in, a great funnel of smoke swarmed toward the sky, as if the old man's mighty spirit, released from its body—a little bottle—had swelled like the genie of a fable. The smoke was tinted rose-hue from the flames, and perhaps the unutterable midnights of the universe will have no power to daunt the color of this soul."[50] Although Crane's use of the genie-in-a-bottle imagery in this scene conjures up a romantic and highly conventional death scene, this "rose-hued" smoke only distracts us from what is left in the wake of the barn fire: ashes. Regardless of the fate of Henry's soul—or as Crane refers to it here, its "color"—Henry's body is now dust and ashes. He has become in this scene, in fact, the very "god of the ashes" that the young Henry Fleming was raging against in the manuscript edition of *The Red Badge of Courage*. The difference is that here, after the old man's honesty, his status as a god, and thereby his potential to form a lasting tradition, has been undermined. As the story tells us, what most astounds Little Jim is that "this idol, of its own will, should so totter."[51] Since the godlike veteran has tottered from his pedestal, there seems little chance that this "god of the ashes" will rise.

Henry's death represents for the author a moment of closure. In the years following the publication of *The Red Badge of Courage* and "The Veteran," Crane searched for a war of his own rather than reliving the war experiences of a prior generation. In articles like "Marines Signaling Under Fire at Guantanamo" and "*The Red Badge of Courage* Was His Wig-Wag Flag," Crane reshaped the part of newspaper reporter into that of war correspondent. In the process, he positioned himself as somewhere in social status between the professional writer and the soldier. This change allowed him to both observe and experience combat without enlisting, something his chronically poor health made impossible.

Crane illustrates the unique position of the war correspondent in a scene from "Marines Signaling Under Fire." As a war correspondent, he places himself in a role similar to that of the marine signalman. The difference is that he "signals" his readers back home about what the war in Cuba is like, whereas the signalman communicates with the warships in the bay for artillery support. What Crane communicates to those readers, however, and what he himself seems to discover about war, remain distinct. The critic Bill Brown has argued that in scenes such as this the author has become "both spectator and spectacle . . . [while he] witnesses a war in motion." To a certain extent this is true, since Crane demonstrates in "Marine Signalmen Under Fire" that, as Brown notes, "observation itself can be intoxicating."[52] Nonetheless, Crane sees himself not as a "spectacle" or a "witness" in this scene, but as a participant in what he describes.

The author tells us, "It was great joy to lie in the trench with the four signalmen." He shares with them the danger of their assignment as "the bullets began to snap, snap, snap . . . [and] the woods began to crackle like burning straw." The war correspondent feels strongly connected to these marines, and, regardless of whether the feeling is mutual, this sentiment affects the writer's language. In phrases such as "one felt like a leaf in this booming chaos," Crane captures the sensory experience of war, which goes beyond merely seeing the events of battle. He also illustrates in his description of war's "theatricality" his growing love for the experience of combat, which includes not only being fired on by the enemy, but also fraternal bonding over shared adversity: "Grimy yellow face looked into grimy yellow face, and grinned with weary satisfaction. Coffee!"[53]

The great change from the language of *The Red Badge of Courage* to that of Crane's war correspondence and his later war novels such as *Active Service* has been shocking to generations of critics accustomed to seeing Crane as ambivalent toward war. Whereas his earlier writing seemed to capture the un-heroic and un-lovely nature of combat, the author in "Marines Signaling Under Fire" appears enamored with the battlefield experience. This shift in tone was, however, far from being abnormal, as it followed naturally from Crane's initial questions about Civil War veterans. All along, Crane had not objected to war, but rather to the previous generations' monopoly over it—and with that monopoly their stranglehold over the cultural conceptions of American manhood. Consequently, we can see here in the affectionate language of Crane's war reporting the transcendence the author had hoped for in his earlier fiction. The "gods of the ashes" have finally been laid to rest on a battlefield in Cuba.

Crane was not the only member of his generation to have had this transcendent experience of the Spanish–American War. The May 28, 1899, edition of the *New Orleans Daily Picayune* approached the issue of transcendence with the bold claim that the Decoration Day parade to be held that year would be the last: "May 30, 1899, means a public good-bye to the veterans of the civil war, the passing into a memory of the fine old fighters and a welcome to the newer army that whipped Spain in such grand style." Even though the editorial asserted that this eclipse of one group of veterans by another "is being done in the very best of spirits," they were quick to point out what they believed were the overblown claims of the earlier generation of warriors, saying at one point, "The old fellows affect to regard the beating we gave Spain as mere child's play in comparison with the battles between the blue and the grey; they love to talk grandiloquently."[54] The goodwill between these groups of veterans is made possible by the present generation's ability to dismiss their fathers' claims to heroism. Having experienced war as it is, these young men can now claim their place as true citizens while at the same time tolerating their fathers' stories as the ramblings of irritable old men.

This attitude is reflected in the engraving that accompanies the article. Subtitled "An American Goddess Between Veterans of Two Wars" the scene is suggestive of a wedding ceremony. On the left stands an elderly Civil War veteran and on the right a youthful veteran of the recent Spanish–American War. Between them stands a woman, dressed in the modern style. She is holding onto the arm of the elderly Civil War veteran, the same arm with which he holds his cane. As we look at the young man, we can see he is presenting his arm to the young lady. It seems as if a father is giving away his daughter to his new son-in-law, but the addition of the flag bunting in the background and the laurel wreathes the woman carries suggests that this is no ordinary wedding. The young lady in fact seems intended to represent the nation, Lady Liberty or Columbia. The wedding thus becomes a metaphor for the transfer of power between men of two different generations. Giving up his charge, the Civil War veteran turns the nation over to her new protector, the veteran of the Spanish–American War.

This image reflects a popular perception among Americans at the turn of the century that the Spanish–American War had finally broken the monopoly of the Civil War and its veterans over American life, showing that the rising generation was just as capable of fulfilling "the highest duty of citizenship." However, the old man was not as willing to give up his charge as the image above might have us believe. Many Civil War veterans pressed Columbia even closer to their breasts in the period leading up to the Spanish–American War and reasserted their claims to superiority in the one area of life that had come to define them.

The March 16, 1898, issue of the *New York Times*, reprints under the title "New York Veterans Ready" a letter written by Colonel Albert D. Shaw of the Watertown, New York, post of the Grand Army of the Republic. Shaw addresses President William McKinley, himself a veteran of the Union army, and offered the services of his ten-thousand-man GAR post in the event of hostilities between

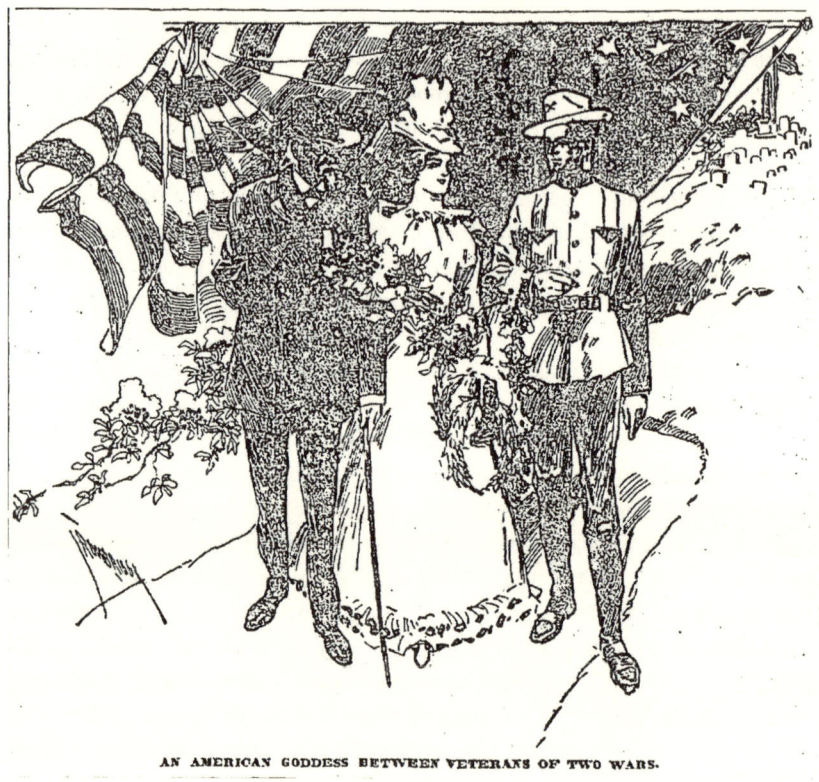

AN AMERICAN GODDESS BETWEEN VETERANS OF TWO WARS.

Figure 13. "An American Goddess Between Veterans of Two Wars." Engraving. May 28, 1899. *New Orleans Daily Picayune*.

the United States and Spain. The paper does not record what response, if any, Colonel Shaw received from the president, but subsequent editorials are quick to point out that any talk of these aging warriors fighting in Cuba was ridiculous. This sentiment was expressed by an unnamed staff member at the War Department, who is quoted in the March 25, 1898, issue of the *Times* as saying:

> The next war, whether it be fought next year or ten years from now, will be fought by young men who have had no military experience. There has been a great deal said and published about the veterans of the late war forming the nucleus of the army that some of us expect to invade Cuba or defend our own coasts; but as a matter of fact, most of these veterans are barred from service.

In the first place, they are too old; and, in the second place, they are drawing pensions because of disability. Either of these conditions would disqualify them from military service.⁵⁵

The comments of this government official must have been particularly devastating to veterans of the Civil War, as he attempted to take away from them the last area of their lives where they felt useful to the republic. Spurred by perceived insults such as these, many Civil War veterans risked forfeiture of their pensions in order to reenlist. Despite their age and infirmity, they were unwilling to concede their authority in the realm of war. Civil War combat had made them into an elite fraternity and they were determined to protect it from upstarts and pretenders, including their own sons.

Revealing the tensions that existed between an aging population of Civil War veterans and the rising generation of middle-class white males in the last decade of the nineteenth century modifies our understanding of the role the Spanish–American War played in the cultural life of the nation. Young men of this new generation had been brought up on the memories of Civil War veterans. These memories taught them that war makes men. It was the defining event that made one a worthy citizen of the republic and fitted one for active involvement in political life. At the same time, however, they were taught they could never live up to the standards of their fathers. This contradiction set the stage in the 1890s for a struggle between sons and fathers in which one generation would be compelled to cede cultural authority in order for the other to rise to full manhood. This struggle created Stephen Crane's fame as a writer, but it was a fame bought at a high cost—the overshadowing of the rest of his career by the legacy of one novel.

5 Racial Uplift and the Figure of the Black Soldier

> The part enacted by the Negro soldier in the war of the Rebellion is the romance of North American history. It was midnight and noonday without a space between. No one in this era of fraternity and Christian civilization will grudge the Negro soldier these simple annals of his trials and triumphs in a holy struggle for human liberty.
>
> —GEORGE WASHINGTON WILLIAMS, *A History of the Negro Troops*

White veterans spent nearly twenty years attempting to understand their war service, eventually coming to the conclusion that combat had changed their identity. Many African American veterans, in contrast, understood military service as leading to a change in identity from the moment of enlistment. After the passage of the Emancipation Proclamation finally allowed slaves to don the uniform of the Union army, they considered themselves free men even if they had come from slave states still in the Union (e.g., Kentucky). Moreover, in some instances, the families of these newly enrolled black soldiers were able to live free by virtue of their enlistment.[1] Black men who were already free and living in the North also experienced a change in their sense of self upon joining the army, but the contrast was not as dramatic as it was for former slaves. Military service offered free black men in northern cities the tantalizing possibility that race prejudice might be transcended. There was a legitimate hope among antebellum freemen that the full rights of citizenship were finally within their grasp.[2]

Once in the army, however, freemen and former slaves soon realized that feeling like new men was not the same as being recognized by society as such. They confronted in the ranks a stubborn race barrier that manifested itself in the Union army's decision to keep black troops in segregated units led by white officers.[3] These units, moreover, often served in support roles rather than combat assignments, and received poor quality equipment as well as unequal pay and bounties.[4] These wartime injustices foreshadowed the difficulties that black men, regardless of whether they had fought in the war, would encounter in the decades following the Civil War. Nonetheless, serving in the Union army and thereby demonstrating a willingness to die for the survival of the nation, did provide a powerful image that black men used to their advantage in the years immediately following the war.

During the era of Reconstruction, black veterans were highly vocal about their wartime service. They used this social prominence to great effect in order to improve the living conditions of African Americans in general.[5] This status, however, was short-lived. In the last two decades of the nineteenth century, black men who had served in the northern army rapidly faded from public consciousness. We might easily ascribe this decline in stature to the deteriorating condition of race relations in what came to be known as the "Jim Crow" era. Another explanation for why African American veterans seemed to lose their voice even as white veterans found theirs, through memoirs and personal narratives, is the lack of access to publication venues along with the lower incomes and literacy rates of black men.

These accounts are persuasive but overlook the equally important factor of the growing tension within the black community surrounding the subject of military service in the Civil War. African Americans in the Jim Crow era faced a dilemma as they sought a way to celebrate their heroes while at the same time searching for new role models to build a strong black middle-class and thereby "uplift" the race. Black soldiers conjured up images of violence that seemed to support white claims that black males were primitives. Additionally, at a time when unity was desperately needed, the memory of soldiers' military service exposed past humiliations associated with northern racism during the war and class divisions that continued to plague the black community.

"Freedom's soldiers" appeared to have lost their relevance to a new generation of African Americans, who were living at a low point in race relations in the United States. Leading figures in the black community, like the writers Paul Laurence Dunbar and Francis Ellen Watkins Harper, sought ways to separate the ideals for which black men had fought from the army uniform they had worn. These ideals could then be associated with middle-class black professionals such as doctors, lawyers, teachers, and ministers.

African American veterans, already slighted by the white memorialization of the war, now felt themselves abandoned by their own race. Black union veterans George Washington Williams and Joseph Wilson attempted to counteract this trend. Their histories of African American military service in the Civil War memorialize the soldierly attributes of the black male at a time when most of the nation would have preferred to forget. Reaching back into the distant past of the race, with Williams going back as far as the dynasties of ancient Egypt and Wilson to black patriots like Crispus Attucks in the Revolutionary War, these authors sought to prove that black men were good soldiers and by extension good citizens. As black veterans laying claim to the citizen-soldier ideal, Williams and Wilson continued to see themselves as part of the vanguard in their race's demands for inclusion and equal rights. By the 1890s, however, the reality was that military service represented something of a dead end; the image of the middle-class professional would ultimately win out over that of the soldier in the ongoing African American struggle for civic equality.

Military Service and the Quest for Citizenship Rights

A full understanding of how the significance of military service evolved in the postwar African American community requires an examination of the primary argument made in favor of black enlistment during the Civil War. Regardless of whether they were slave or free, black males first wanted to prove their manhood to white members of society, and military service seemed a sure path to that goal. On the firing line, black men believed they could prove they were of the same mettle as white men. However, it was far more important, particularly among free blacks, to prove they were worthy of being recognized not simply as men but also as citizens. When African American men sought to enlist in the ranks of the Union army, they were making an overt claim on the white citizen-soldier ideal. In doing so, they sought to undermine the legal precedent set by the *Dred Scott* decision (1857), which held that no black man, whether slave or free, could be considered a citizen of the United States.[6] If African American men fulfilled one of the key duties of citizenship—namely, the defense of the nation—black men reasoned that society could not justly deny them the "fundamental privileges and immunities" guaranteed to a citizen.[7]

This belief is reflected in a speech given by Frederick Douglass to a Philadelphia audience on July 6, 1863, in which he stated, "The opportunity is given us to be men. With one courageous resolution we may blot out the hand-writing of the ages against us. Once let the black man get upon his person the brass letters U.S.; let him get an eagle on his button, and a musket on his shoulder, and bullets in his pocket, and there is no power on the earth or under the earth which can deny that he has *earned* the right of citizenship in the United States."[8] The timing of Douglass's speech is nearly as significant as its content. Similar arguments for black enlistment had been made since the beginning of the war but had largely been ignored by the Union government. Manpower shortages and growing northern discontent with the conscription law of March 1863 were the catalysts that finally made the use of black men as soldiers more appealing to white northerners.[9] The *Chicago Tribune* reasoned that "a thousand blacks will save a thousand white men from being drafted."[10] To this they might also have added that black enlistment would keep those same white men from being killed. In addition, the Emancipation Proclamation, which went into effect on January 1, 1863, offered black men a greater impetus to join the Union ranks. As the northern war aims shifted to include the abolition of slavery, it became both possible as well as desirable for black men to enlist.[11]

The ideals espoused in Douglass's speech were not limited to leading figures in the African American community. James Henry Hall, who at the age of thirty-eight left his job as a barber in Philadelphia to enlist in the Fifty-Fourth Massachusetts, fully understood the symbolic value of his military service. He noted in a letter published in the August 27, 1864, issue of the African American newspaper the *Christian Recorder*, "If we fight to maintain a Republican Government, we want Republican privileges. The rights of citizenship, and a free title and acknowledged share in our own noble birthplace."[12] Hall associated his willingness to sacrifice with what he saw as a reasonable request for inclusion in the national order as a citizen ("our own noble birthplace") and the right to rise and fall economically ("acknowledged share") on his own merit. Elijah Marrs, a fugitive slave from Kentucky, expressed a comparable sentiment in his 1885 memoirs. Recollecting his flight from slavery, Marrs described his first full day of freedom after putting on his new army uniform: "I felt freedom in my bones, and when I saw the American eagle, with outspread wings, upon the American flag, with the motto, 'E Pluribus Unum,' the thought came to me, 'Give me liberty or give me death.'"[13] By placing his decision to enlist within the context of the American Revolution, Marrs, even more explicitly than Hall, associates his military service with a desire for the rights and privileges that come with full legal inclusion in the nation.

Fulfilling one's military obligation to protect the state was a concrete way of proving allegiance and thereby affirming one's status as a citizen. Nonetheless, the concept of citizenship was poorly defined in the Civil War era. Determined primarily by one's state of residence, it was not until the Fourteenth Amendment was ratified in 1868 that the concept of citizenship was finally codified into American law.[14] The legal confusion that surrounded American citizenship, even

Figure 14. *24th Regiment U.S. Colored Troops. Let Soldiers in War, Be Citizens in Peace.* Carte de visite. Ca. 1865. Library of Congress. Washington, D.C.

more so than the *Dred Scott* decision, complicated any attempt on the part of black men to lay claim to social inclusion through the citizen-soldier ideal. One first had to prove he was a citizen to be a citizen-soldier, and yet military service, to a large degree, proved one's citizenship. A further complication in the African American project of attaining citizenship through enlistment in the Union ranks was the complex nature of black masculinity. In assuming the mantle of the soldier, black men reopened the problem of violence in relation to the black male. They had to prove simultaneously that they were virile enough to bear arms and yet restrained enough to be good citizens at war's end.[15]

Once the resistance to raising black regiments was broken, 178,975 African American men were mustered into federal service.[16] They were members of a separate department within the army known as the United States Colored Troops (USCT).[17] Since federal authority had allowed black men to enlist and many state governments were reluctant to recruit African American troops, the national government would take primary responsibility for mustering them. With the notable exception of Massachusetts, colored regiments were seen as separate from the traditional state militia system. They were perceived from the very beginning by most northern states as federal units. This would lead to a different demobilization experience for USCT veterans, but it also foreshadowed the difficulties they would face in attempting to take on the mantle of citizen-soldier. To the national imagination, black soldiers had more in common with "regular" soldiers than militia "volunteers."

Another visible difference between black military service and that of their white comrades appeared in the camps. Many black soldiers in USCT units saw their time in the military as an opportunity to learn skills that would be useful off the battlefield. They expressed a specific fervor for the ability to read and write.[18] The army camp became a school for many black soldiers, as either sympathetic white officers or educated black sergeants taught basic literacy as foundational skills needed for postwar citizenship. Elijah Marrs, a fugitive slave who had already learned to read and write on the plantation by professing a desire to read the Bible, shared his skills with fellow black soldiers. Marrs felt a great sense of pride and self-confidence in his "reputation as a writer." Not only was his ability to read and write valuable to his black comrades, but he also benefited from these skills in his relationship with the white officers. Due to his literacy Marrs was quickly promoted to the rank of duty sergeant in his regiment, a clerical position. Throughout the ranks of black regiments in the Union army, education in basic literacy was viewed as so important that a chaplain in a Louisiana black regiment argued that "the cartridge box and spelling book are attached to the same belt."[19]

If black men in the Union army were eager to procure skills that would prepare them for postwar citizenship rather than combat, the white population was more captivated by the question of whether black men could fight and, if so, how well. Illustrations appearing in the pages of prominent northern periodicals such as *Harper's Weekly* capture the contradictions inherent in the white population's understanding of black manhood. African American men were alternately viewed as too childlike to make good soldiers or as too animallike to be trusted with the weapons of war.

The black men portrayed in the scene "Teaching the Negro Recruits the Use of the Minie Rifle" in the March 14, 1863, issue of *Harper's Weekly* are decidedly nonthreatening and even, one might argue, nonchalant. At the center of the image stands a black soldier in a conventionally martial pose with a rifle in his hand. To his left is a white officer pointing off into the distance, toward what are presumably the enemy's positions. On the ground behind that officer are a pick and shovel lying inside a trench, which look as if they have only recently been discarded. Behind the black soldier at the center of this image stands what we might assume are the rest of his unit, who seem impatient to start moving. Far off in the distance behind them, we see a parapet filled with white soldiers staring down on the black troops as they prepare for action.

The relaxed attitude of the men in this scene suggests we are viewing a drill rather than the prelude to an assault. Nonetheless, the pressure associated with the outcome of this exercise is intense. Although the significance of the flag in the background is uncertain, the tools lying on the ground are filled with great meaning for the black men in this scene. Up to this point, they have more than likely been army laborers rather than combat soldiers. Their weapons have been the pick and shovel rather than a rifle. How well will they handle this more-complex machinery? Will they be able to operate as a disciplined unit? Once the enemy begins firing at them, will they be able to maintain their assault or will they retreat to the safety of their entrenchments? All these questions remain unanswered by the image even as it heightens the viewer's desire to know what the outcome will be. Just as the white unit on the hill behind them awaits an answer regarding the martial prowess of the black soldier, so, too, does the nation.

It would not be until May 27, 1863, at Port Hudson, Louisiana, and July 18, 1863, at Fort Wagner near Charleston, South Carolina, that black soldiers would have a chance to prove their mettle in combat. Again, however, the value of these actions would have a different resonance for African American men and the black community as a whole than it did for whites in the North and South. Elijah Marrs felt a greater sense of his authority as a sergeant while serving in noncombat

Figure 15. "Teaching the Negro Recruits the Use of the Minie Rifle." Engraving. March 14, 1863. *Harper's Weekly*.

roles, such as when he was assigned command of a contraband camp, first in Bowling Green and then at Camp Nelson in Kentucky. In this position, Marrs felt he had more power than he could ever wield with a gun in his hand. He tells the reader that hundreds of former slaves, hungry, destitute, and almost naked, "looked to me as if I were their Saviour."[20]

Admittedly, as a member of the Twelfth United States Heavy Artillery, Colored, Marrs's opportunities for frontline combat were limited. Typically these units were called on either for garrison duty or for siege warfare operations, neither of which were in great demand in the region of Kentucky where his unit was deployed. However, even in combat infantry units such as the First and Third Louisiana Native Guards and the Fifty-Fourth Massachusetts, which fought at Port Hudson and Fort Wagner, respectively, the overall sense of self-confidence that came with participation in combat was more important that its military value. Such activity encouraged black men, many of whom were unaccustomed to making public demands, to assert their rights as men.

One issue on which black soldiers were particularly vocal during the war was inequality in pay. Under the Militia Act of 1862, Congress had authorized the payment of ten dollars a month to black men employed by the U.S. government regardless of their mode of service. Not only was this three dollars less than their white comrades earned, but the amount of their pay was further reduced by the additional three dollars removed for clothing allowance.[21] Even though this discrepancy in pay must have created hardships for black soldiers, the fact remains that either amount was probably more than most of these men had earned before the war. Protests involving unequal pay were consequently a matter of principle for many members of the USCT, an attempt to gain government recognition that black soldiers deserved the same treatment as white men who served in the Union ranks.

This is the substance of Sergeant George E. Stephens's argument in a letter printed in the *Weekly Anglo-African* on September 19, 1863. Here he says, "$10 per month [is] the pay allowed to contrabands by statute when employed in the Commissary or Quartermaster's Department. There *may* be some reason for making a distinction between armed and unarmed men in the service of the government, but when the *nationality* of a man takes away his title to pay it becomes another thing."[22] Any differences in pay, Stephens suggests, should ultimately be based on the nature of one's job rather than social status.

Sergeant Stephens's complaint was one of many raised in protest against the inequality of pay experienced by USCT regiments. As a member of the Fifty-Fourth Massachusetts, Stephens would have been part of a boycott initiated in the summer of 1863, not long after their assault on Fort Wagner, by the Fifty-Fourth regiment and its sister unit, the Fifty-Fifth. Black soldiers in both units declined to receive any pay at all until Congress agreed to provide them the same compensation as combat troops in white regiments. An act of Congress passed in March 1864 eventually resolved the issue. Furthermore, it authorized the War Department to pay black men who had been free on April 19, 1861, the back pay allowed them by the passage of this act.[23]

The Ambivalent Legacy of the USCT

Issues such as pay inequality in the army taught black men how to operate openly within the official legal and political system both on their own behalf and for the interests of others. This was a new experience for a race used to oppression and the clandestine structures of politics and law that had developed in their local communities to help them resist and endure subjugation.[24] Black soldiers and veterans often served as early role models and guides for African American communities as they attempted to transform their grassroots conceptions of political organization and action into something the state and federal government would recognize. Sergeant A. R. Bryant, not long after the war's end, wrote a letter addressing the concerns of freed blacks living in Mount Pleasant, South Carolina. In this letter to the South Carolina Freedmen's Bureau, Sergeant Bryant reported that "the Rable [i.e., the rebels] is driving the pople of[f] they Plantation that is all that will cauld them masters can stay on the place But all that will not call them master they must Leve Rite away."[25] Concerned that former Confederates might try to treat freed blacks as if they were slaves, he requested that the Freedmen's Bureau representatives for that region investigate these complaints and provide legal assistance.

Eager to take part in the official legal and political processes of the nation, African Americans were nonetheless aware of the limits to full citizenship they faced without the right to vote. Corporal John H. B. Payne, a free man of color from Ohio, noted bitterly in a letter to the *Christian Recorder* on June 11, 1864, "The foreigner, when he enters this country, enters into life in an age full of a progressive spirit in the elective franchise." Payne lamented that even the Irish, whom he saw as responsible for the draft riots in New York City, had more political rights than he possessed as a defender of the Union. Nothing less, he argued, than "the rights that this Government owes me, the same rights that the white man has," would be sufficient payment for his service.[26] Although most black soldiers were not as vocal during the war as Payne in their demands for the franchise, his comments confirm the growing realization among black men that military service alone would not suffice to achieve the full rights of citizenship.

There was in fact a long tradition of black men defending the nation as soldiers only to see the hope for social equality associated with that service denied them. African American historian and native Bostonian William Cooper Nell explored the troubled history of black military service in his 1855 book *The Colored Patriots of the American Revolution*. Nearly a decade before the Civil War's conclusion, Nell sought to remind his white readers of the role black men, such as Crispus Attucks, played in creating the nation that still excluded them from citizenship. He laments that "the Revolution of 1776, and the subsequent struggles in our nation's history, aided, in honorable proportion, by colored Americans, have (sad, but true, confession) yet left the necessity for a second revolution, no less sublime than that of regenerating public sentiment in favor of Universal Brotherhood." As USCT units began to demobilize, the same dilemma explored by Nell in his antebellum research began to unfold for the African American heroes of the Civil War. In his farewell address to the men of the Sixty-Second USCT, their white commander, Colonel Barrett, tells them, "It is not the color which is hereafter to make the difference between men." However, he then goes on to say, "You wish to be citizens? Show to the country then that you are capable of citizenship."[27] Unlike the demobilization speeches given to white regiments, Barrett's speech separates the issue of manhood from that of citizenship. Black men have proven themselves on the battlefield to be men, but, in his opinion, they have yet to prove their worthiness of the title of citizen.

Barrett's comments illustrate, among other things, that the end of the Civil War did not represent the completion of the second revolution envisioned by African Americans like Nell. A new phase of the war had begun for black men, but before they could engage in this second struggle they first needed to return home. This in itself was an arduous task. Among the last units to be mustered in to federal service, many regiments of the USCT were not demobilized until well after the end of the war.[28] Also, due to the effects of slavery on the African American community, the concept of "home" and "homecoming" had a very different resonance for black veterans than it did for white. The denial of legal status to black slave families had led to the sale of mothers, wives, and children as individuals, scattering them all across the slave states. This made it much harder for black males in the army who had once been slaves to feel they "belonged" in any one part of the nation after the war. Furthermore, the continued reluctance of many state governments to raise black volunteer regiments, which was one of the factors that led to the creation of the USCT, ensured that African American men in these units would represent a wide cross-section of regions in the United States.²⁹

Demobilization policy in the USCT reflected all these realities, as black regiments were mustered out completely in the field rather than return to the states where they were enlisted. After mustering out, black veterans received paid transit to the location of their choice. Some former units like the Fifth USCT, whose members had been mustered in the same region of Ohio, chose to travel "home" together (as was the case with most white regiments). Also, in a few instances, black soldiers decided to stay at the site of their mustering out, as they had created new homes in these locations during their army service. Richard Reid notes that "pension records show a cluster of men from the 35th USCT living around Summerville, South Carolina, in a region where the regiment had served during the first year of Reconstruction. Several of them, while still in the army, had married local women."³⁰ However, a significant proportion of those who served in the USCT chose to travel alone in search of family members who had been scattered by slavery and war. Many black veterans felt that their families needed to be reunited before the construction of a home could safely be assured.

Whatever their individual circumstances, black veterans as group, even more than other African American males, exhibited a tendency to band together after the war. Using their strength in numbers, these former soldiers applied the symbolic power of military service to their advantage. In Nashville, black veterans sent an open letter to the local newspaper demanding voting rights in January 1865, nearly a full year before slavery was officially abolished throughout the United States. Emboldened by the experience of serving in the Union army, the authors argued, "If we are called on to do military duty against rebel armies in the field, why should we be denied the privilege of voting against rebel citizens at the ballot box?" Black veterans in Kentucky complained to the U.S. Congress in July 1867 that "many crimes have been committed upon [us] during the last year, for which [we] have failed to obtain redress." Since these petitioners "were *Soldiers*," they could not understand why the right to defend themselves through the vote was denied them. They claimed that only "enfranchisement will arrest the cruel spirit of robbery, arson, and murder in Kentucky, as it most evidently has done in more Southern States."³¹

Ironically, southern states subject to the Congressional Reconstruction Acts of 1867 offered a greater degree of authority to black men in the early postwar era. Granted the right to vote in these former rebel states three years before the rest of the nation, many black veterans chose to live in the South following their discharge from the army. For some, this migration meant a return to communities they had fled long before the war. This was the case with Andrew Jackson Chesnutt, father of the well-known late-nineteenth-century African American author Charles Chesnutt. Following his service as a teamster in the Union army, Andrew Chesnutt chose to return to his boyhood home of Fayetteville, North Carolina, rather than his prewar residence in Cleveland, Ohio. As was the case with many of the white "carpetbaggers and scalawags" living in the postwar South, black veterans who either moved to the South for the first time or were returning home did so out of both idealism and a desire for wealth and fame. They saw an opportunity in the Reconstruction-era South to rapidly improve their social status while at the same time reshaping race relations.

The short biographies collected in Eric Foner's *Freedom's Lawmakers* show that a significant number of USCT veterans, many of them non-commissioned officers during the war, held positions in state and local government as legislators and bureaucrats. One can only speculate on the social impact in the postwar nation of allowing more black men to be commissioned officers in the USCT. However, it is telling that the only black veteran (or black man for that matter) to serve as governor during Reconstruction was a former captain in the Seventy-Fourth USCT, P. B. S. Pinchback, who was governor of Louisiana from December 9, 1872, to January 13, 1873.[32] Despite the limitations for black men to rise within the ranks of the army and the related limit this placed on their postwar political potential, black veterans helped move forward the national discourse on black citizenship at a much faster pace than might otherwise have occurred. Sympathetic white politicians from the North were aware of the sacrifice of black soldiers in the war and its pressing need for some concrete form of social recognition.

In a speech delivered on the Senate floor in January 1866, Lyman Trumbull of Illinois recognized the heroism of black men in arms. At the same time, however, he noted that "there is very little importance in the general declaration of abstract truths and principles unless they can be carried into effect."[33] Realizing that the Thirteenth Amendment merely offered black men recognition as human beings, Trumbull argued that all blacks, whether former slaves or freemen before the war, must be allowed legal recognition as American citizens, including the right to vote. Both rights were finally granted with the passage of the Fourteenth and Fifteenth Amendments (1868, 1870), landmark pieces of legislation that would have been considerably more difficult to pass without the powerful image of the black veteran consistently kept in the nation's view.

This great official power and prestige were short-lived for black veterans, in most cases lasting only as long as southern Reconstruction. After his brief tenure as governor, Pinchback served in a variety of minor government posts in

Figure 16. *Distinguished Colored Men*. Chromolithograph. Ca. 1883. Library of Congress. Washington, D.C.

Louisiana until 1893, when he decided to permanently leave the South and move to Washington, D.C. There he conducted a small but lucrative private legal practice until his death in 1921. Similar highs and lows accompanied the experience of Josiah T. Walls, a former sergeant in the Third U.S. Colored Infantry. Walls was originally from Winchester, Virginia, but had decided to settle in Florida after the war, near the region where he had been mustered out of the army. In the early 1870s, Walls was living in Gainesville and served as its mayor for a number of years. He also purchased a plantation, which he turned into a lucrative produce farm, served as a congressman, ran a successful law practice, and operated the local newspaper, the *Gainesville New Era*. For Walls, 1883 was the pinnacle of his postwar public career. After this, he was gradually shut out of state politics, running unsuccessfully for legislative office in both 1884 and 1890. He also struggled economically after a severe freeze wiped out his farm in 1895. By the turn of the century, he was a fairly obscure figure, working in a secure but unremarkable job as the manager of Florida A&M's research farm in Tallahassee.

Charles Nash's decline was even more precipitous than that of P. B. S. Pinchback or Josiah Walls. A sergeant in the Eighty-Second U.S. Colored Infantry, Nash was elected to Congress, representing the state of Louisiana for the years 1875–77. Following the end of Reconstruction, he also served as postmaster for the town of Washington, Louisiana. At the time of his death in 1913, however, Nash had returned to his prewar career as a cigar roller, living in relative poverty in New Orleans.[34]

Enlisted men did not experience such a dramatic decline in the post-Reconstruction era in part because they did not experience so great a rise in social stature. Most of these rank-and-file soldiers "remained enmeshed in rural poverty" after the war. Pension records along with census data taken from the period confirm this generalization. James H. Mabin, a former private in the Sixtieth U.S. Colored Infantry, remarked in his pension application testimony, "I have worked for so many people at odd jobs I can hardly name them all." An unskilled laborer before the war, Mabin continued in that social position. The same was true of Henry Bates, a private in the Fourth U.S. Colored Heavy Artillery, who in 1900 at the age of sixty still considered himself "a day laborer, but had been unemployed for six months in the last year."[35]

Dudley Bostick and his brother Stephen had enjoyed modest success as farmers. Both served as coal heavers on the USS *General Bragg*, a Union steamship that had presumably been captured from the Confederates and not had its name changed. After the war, they established a small community of ex-slaves in Jackson County, Illinois, that became known as the Bostick settlement. Although the census records do not indicate how much money the brothers earned on the property or how much debt they incurred, the census of 1900 indicates that by that time Dudley Bostick no longer owned his land; rather, he was renting a small farm in Murphysboro, Illinois. Moreover, his brother Stephen, who still owned his own land, was heavily mortgaged.[36] Life in the city was not much better, as the fate of T. F. M. Kay, a resident of Quincy, Illinois, illustrates. A former musician in the Twenty-Ninth U.S. Colored Infantry, Kay studied law in the office of County Judge Thomas J. Mitchell. Politically active throughout the 1870s, presumably with the intent of achieving elected office, by 1892 he was working in the more modest jobs of pension agent for black veterans and notary public.[37]

Despite the passage of federal laws designed to ensure civil and political rights, equal treatment under the law for black men in the United States following Reconstruction still seemed out of reach. African American veterans such as Henry M. Turner became disgusted by the glacial pace at which racial prejudice was being eroded in American society, and therefore sought a solution outside the United States. In 1876, he gave up trying to reform his native state of Georgia and championed emigration to Africa.[38] Other black veterans like Alfred Fairfax suggested the less-drastic option of moving to the vast lands of the West. He led a group of settlers from Louisiana to Kansas who were part of a movement that began in 1879 known as the "Exodusters."[39] Even more former black soldiers, however, simply led lives of quiet destitution, struggling to get by as they pondered what had happened to their great dreams of social prominence.

Racial Uplift and the Search for New Role Models in the Jim Crow Era

Historians have attempted to mitigate this otherwise-depressing narrative of the black soldier's legacy by arguing that the support of black civilians in their local communities helped assuage these growing assaults by the white populace on veteran manhood.[40] Nevertheless, there was a divergence between how black veterans understood the legacy of their military service and how it was comprehended by civilians in the African American community in the post-Reconstruction era. Even though black veterans such as George Washington Williams, with the encouragement of white members of the Grand Army of the Republic, continued to insist that "looking back over the centuries, there would be little else to record of the poor, patient Negro save his suffering and degradation were it not for the luminous flashes of his martial glory," the view of many black civilians was much more jaundiced.[41]

The *Chicago Daily Inter-Ocean* noted in its September 26, 1896, issue that on Emancipation Day, when one might well expect public praise of black soldiers in the Civil War, African American community members in Chicago celebrated instead by hearing an "address on the principles of finance, illustrated by statistics."[42] In a similar vein, the *Southwestern Christian Advocate* in its January 7, 1897, issue recorded an Emancipation Day speech given by a Colonel Wicker in New Orleans that celebrated the incredible progress of the black race since the war in professional fields such as medicine, the religious ministry, and the law, but it makes no mention of the active role of black soldiers in helping to achieve freedom for the African American community.[43] One of the few newspapers to refer specifically to black military service on Emancipation Day during the years 1896–97 is the Emporia, Kansas, *Daily Gazette*. In the issue published for September 23, 1897, the paper notes that the Emancipation Day speaker for that year in Emporia "told how the negro had been the first to fight for the Union and the last to quit."[44]

Black civilians in the 1890s seemed reluctant to discuss the black military experience in the Civil War. This was true not only in public speeches but also in book publishing. Aside from the writings of African American veterans like George Washington Williams and Joseph Wilson, both of whom received support and encouragement for their histories from Union veterans' groups, the black middle-class professional held a greater degree of prominence in written representations during the late nineteenth century than did the black soldier. The former embodied the future hoped for by the African American community, while the latter appeared to recall an embarrassing past, a once-promising experiment in racial equality that had ultimately failed.

Paul Laurence Dunbar's poems "The Colored Soldiers" and "Robert Gould Shaw" along with his lesser-known novel *The Fanatics* are particularly strong examples of the shift in perspective within the African American community toward the significance of black military service in the Civil War. Dunbar openly questions in these works the relevance of what black soldiers had achieved, while at the same time attempting to honor their courage and the values for which they sacrificed their lives. Frances Ellen Watkins Harper, a well-known figure among antebellum abolitionist writers and speakers, shared Dunbar's ambivalence toward black military service in the Civil War. Her novel *Iola Leroy* has two black veterans as its male protagonists, but manages to largely obscure their military service. Instead, she highlights the postwar service of these men to their communities in the cause of creating civilian middle-class black professionals.

Harper's motivation for obscuring the war service of her protagonists is different from Dunbar's more open critique. She was primarily concerned by the association of black masculinity with "primitivism" and violence. Too openly celebrating black military success, she feared, might help support racist attacks on the African American community and lead to greater violence. Although Dunbar was interested in separating black manhood from the image of the instinct-driven savage, his response to the legacy of black soldiers in the Civil War had more to do with his sense of embarrassment at how far the race, and particularly free blacks, had declined in social stature since the close of the Civil War. Like his contemporary, the African American short story writer and novelist Charles Chesnutt, Dunbar struggled to come to terms with the class divisions inside the African American community at a time when racial solidarity was crucial for survival. The image of black soldiers in blue represented for Dunbar not just a lost hope for social advancement but a fissure in the black community that raised questions about whether all African Americans were capable of social uplift.

"Incongruous to the Point of Ghastly Humor"

Paul Laurence Dunbar is perhaps best known to contemporary readers for his poetry, and particularly his short piece "We Wear the Mask." In that poem he anticipates what W. E. B. Du Bois would refer to as the "double-consciousness" experienced by African Americans living in the age of Jim Crow. Dunbar remarks that "We smile, but, O great Christ, our cries / To thee from tortured souls arise / . . . But let the world dream otherwise, / We wear the mask!" The association of Dunbar's writing with the psychological repression and dissimulation necessary for blacks in the United States to survive at such a low point in race relations makes it seem natural that the dominant metaphor for understanding his literary works would come from his best-known poem—the mask. Through this metaphor, Dunbar is understood as a man of his times forced to compromise with his prejudiced readership, composed primarily of white northerners, in order to succeed.[45] Other critics looking at Dunbar's masking techniques have come to different conclusions, both positive and negative.[46] But the fact remains that he was a cunning author who rarely spoke directly to his readers when a more indirect approach would do.

This preference for indirection is what makes Dunbar's open remarks in the pages of the *Chicago Record* newspaper in December 1898 worthy of note. In an article titled "Recession Never," Dunbar accused northerners of hypocrisy for their criticism of southern race relations. He contended that "the race spirit in the United States is not local but general." Dunbar went on to state, "To the outsider, unacquainted with the vagaries of our national prejudice, the recent and sudden change of attitude of the American toward the Negro would appear inconsistent." Looking back to the once-promising era of the Civil War and Reconstruction, he observed that "the new attitude may be interpreted as saying: 'Negroes, you may fight for us, but you may not vote for us. You may prove a strong bulwark when the bullets are flying, but you must stand from the line when the ballots are in the air. You may be heroes in war, but you must be cravens in peace.'" This sudden shift from the great promise of the Reconstruction era to the horrific disappointments of the age of Jim Crow led Dunbar to remark bitterly that "the drama of this sudden change of heart is incongruous to the point of ghastly humor."[47]

Such "ghastly humor" and the incongruities that caused it are central to Dunbar's understanding of the Civil War and the black men like his father who fought in the Union ranks. Joshua Dunbar had been a slave in Kentucky until he escaped to Canada before the Civil War through the Underground Railroad. In 1863 he decided to return to the United States and enlist at the age of forty-seven in Company F of the Fifty-Fifth Massachusetts. After the war, Joshua settled in Dayton, Ohio, where he worked as a plasterer. It was there he met his wife, the much-younger widow Matilda J. Murphy. Paul Laurence Dunbar was their first child together. Born in June 1872, Paul was separated from his father at an early age. Matilda petitioned for and was granted a divorce from Joshua in 1876. Nonetheless, his father's idealism and the scant rewards he attained from it, dying nearly penniless in the Dayton soldiers' home in 1882, could not help but influence his understanding of black military service in the Civil War.[48]

A deep ambivalence colors all of Dunbar's attempts to narrate this great event in the life of an earlier generation of African Americans. In his poetry it is most evident in "The Colored Soldiers" and "Robert Gould Shaw." The first of these poems initially appeared in the 1895 collection *Majors and Minors* but was later included in the 1896 collection *Lyrics of Lowly Life*, which received praise from William Dean Howells for its ability "to feel the negro life aesthetically and express it lyrically." "The Colored Soldiers" begins with two conditional clauses: "If the muse were mine to tempt it" and "If my tongue were trained to measures."[49] Critics analyzing the poem have tended to move quickly from the hesitant opening of the first stanza to the more confident body of the poem.[50] Here Dunbar narrates the process whereby black men were finally allowed to fight and die in the Civil War. The poet tells us that "in the early days you scorned them" but "then distress fell on the nation" and "you called the colored soldiers, / and they answered your call." He also addresses in these seemingly more confident stanzas the relationship of what they accomplished then as soldiers (i.e., in the 1860s) with the plight of African Americans now (i.e., in the 1890s): "the traits that made them worthy,— / Ah! Those virtues are not dead."[51]

To a certain extent the decision by critics to move beyond the tentative syntax of the opening can be justified as a comment on the poem's overall form. Heroic odes often begin with a statement from the poet that protests their inability to do justice to the lofty subject of their verse.[52] This technique seems logical in a poem dedicated to the black heroes of the Civil War, written by a young poet born after the war's end. It would serve to excuse his presumption at addressing a theme that was perhaps too prestigious for his talent or social standing. Yet to view the opening stanza of the poem exclusively in that light gives the poetic voice in the body of the ode a greater sense of assurance than it actually possesses.

In the portion of the poem quoted most often, Stanza 8, critics have traditionally seen Dunbar as reaffirming the relevance of the Civil War past to the Jim Crow present that African American and white readers of his poem inhabit. Here he states:

> They were comrades then and brothers,
> Are they more or less to-day?
> They were good to stop a bullet
> And to front the fearful fray.
> They were citizens and soldiers,
> When rebellion raised its head;
> And the traits that made them worthy,—
> Ah! Those virtues are not dead.

This stanza makes both a request of its readers as well as a statement of fact. The request is for the reader, especially the white readers of the poem, to not forget the service of black men in the Union ranks. The statement of fact is that "the traits that made them [i.e., colored soldiers] worthy . . . those virtues are not dead."[53] However, the irony remains that the words "comrade," "brothers," and "citizen" do not describe race relations in the 1890s United States. This irony, rather than simply the demands of poetic form, dictates the conditional opening. It suggests that while Dunbar is not against his readers having a greater appreciation for the sacrifices of black men in the Civil War, he is skeptical that such appreciation will lead to improved race relations. The virtues of black soldiers, he implies, are still very much alive, but their cultural capital as a group has greatly diminished.

Dunbar's skepticism about the value of black military service as a metaphor for racial uplift appears again in a later poem, "Robert Gould Shaw." Published in 1903 in the collection *Lyrics of Love and Laughter*, Dunbar starts this sonnet with a question—why would a member of Boston's elite chose to leave "the classic groves" of his university studies and risk his life "to lead th' unlettered and despised droves / to manhood's home"? Unable to answer this question, the poet is still quick to honor Shaw's sacrifice and idealistic devotion to the cause of racial equality, which led him to consent "to lead th' unlettered and de- / spised droves." These men along with Shaw "died for right." Yet the poet cannot help but question what the actions of Shaw and his black soldiers had achieved. Looking back upon the Battle of Fort Wagner as a "hopeless fight," Dunbar connects the suicidal valor of Shaw and his men to their unrealized dreams of racial equality. He says that "since thou and those who with / thee died for right / Have, died, the Present teaches, / but in vain!"[54] The poet suggests that despite these soldiers' deaths long ago for a just cause, inequality as bad as if not worse than the prewar era continued to dominate the lives of African Americans in Dunbar's time.

Both poems fail to provide the tribute to black military service that critics have commonly ascribed to them. Instead, they are filled with discomforting questions about race, manhood, and the significance of the Civil War. Does black military service or, as the poem "Robert Gould Shaw" refers to it, "manhood's home," lead to a literal death like that experienced by Shaw and his men at Fort Wagner, or to a metaphorical death of social significance decades after the war's end? These questions persist in *The Fanatics*, which is the only one among Dunbar's four novels to address the Civil War as its main theme. Here we see developed at length the author's perspective on the legacy of the war that freed the slaves and created the mythic figure of the "colored soldier." We also see class-based tensions exposed within the black community. These distinctions manifest themselves in the novel based on four status markers—free blacks versus former slaves, and northern blacks versus southern blacks. Ultimately, *The Fanatics* suggests that the Civil War was a moment of temporary insanity that gripped northern communities; while the war may have helped southern blacks enmeshed in slavery, this interlude actually worsened the lives of many northern free blacks. This hideous irony heaped on the countless other ironies of deteriorating race relations in the early twentieth century leads Dunbar to conclude that memories of the past, including black military service in the Civil War, have little to offer African Americans but another opportunity for resentment and shame.

The plot and character types of the novel initially mark *The Fanatics* as an exemplar of the popular late-nineteenth-century American genre of reconciliation romance.⁵⁵ In Dunbar's narrative, however, the reunion is not between a white northern man and a white southern woman after the war. Political differences separate the white Van Doren and Waters families who both live in the Ohio town of Dorbury. The reader is told that before the war Stephen Van Doren and Bradford Waters "had loud and long discussions on the question of slavery and kindred subjects," but that "they had but one mind as to the welfare of their children." That welfare includes the engagement of Stephen's son Robert to marry Bradford's daughter Mary. With the onset of the war, the amity between these families is shattered. Bradford tells his daughter, "Let this be the last time I catch you talking with one of the Van Dorens. We are two families, on opposite sides of a great question. We can have no dealings, one with the other."⁵⁶ Bradford, a staunch Republican, is incensed that "rebels" have fired on government property at Fort Sumter, and he will no longer associate with Democrats like Stephen Van Doren who support their actions. The romantic union of two lovers, Mary and Robert, is shattered by the political disunion that now looms over the nation.

Dunbar adds an interesting twist to his already-intriguing reinterpretation of the reconciliation romance genre by adding two more pairs of lovers. The first is Tom Waters, Mary's brother, who is engaged to marry Nannie Woods; and the second is Walter Stewart, who will eventually meet and fall in love with the southern belle Dolly Etheridge. Tom and Nannie both agree politically and romantically. Were there no war, their marriage would be assured. The war, however, intervenes in their domestic bliss and eventually takes Tom away from Nannie, as he is killed while fighting in Tennessee. Although the chapter recording the return of Tom's body to Dorbury is highly stylized and filled with pathos, it nonetheless adds an element of realism to the narrative that breaks the tone needed for a reconciliation romance to work.⁵⁷ Here love does not conquer all; instead, death and mourning hold sway.

For Walter Stewart, the son of a Virginian who served in the Mexican War, political ambivalence blended with family loyalty leads him to find his mate. Walter's father shares the Democratic politics of Stephen Van Doren, but he chooses not to remain in the North as a perceived "Copperhead"; instead, he returns to his native Virginia and purchases a plantation. Walter initially serves in the Union army, but upon completion of his term of service he travels to Virginia to be with his dying father. There he becomes a prisoner on parole to Confederate authorities and watches by his father's side as the elderly Stewart dies. When the war ends, Stewart marries the daughter of his neighbor—Dolly Etheridge—and manages his father's plantation.

These plotlines suggest that Dunbar's novel is interested primarily in how the Civil War affected whites, an exploration of the "divided houses" theme so commonly applied to interpretations of the conflict. War divides the Van Doren and Waters houses, which are only brought together again by the death of Tom Waters and the permanent widowhood of his fiancée, Nannie Woods. It also divides the Stewart family, which again is brought together only by death, this time the death of an elderly father. This interpretation is challenged, however, by the presence in the novel of a figure straight out of the postwar plantation fiction branch of local color—"Nigger Ed"—and the inclusion of a chapter that explores the flight of former slaves or "contrabands" to the North during the war.

"Nigger Ed" is a free black who serves as both the town crier and the town drunk in Dorbury prior to the war. He joins the Dorbury regiment in its march to the battlefield as the servant to one of its officers, and returns home after the volunteer regiment's term of service expires.[58] Ed provides both comic relief in many sections of the novel and a troubling symbol of race relations in Dorbury. In an early section of the narrative, we see Ed running through the town telling its citizens of the "hanging of Mr. Vallandigham." Since Vallandigham is known as a Confederate sympathizer, Ed's assertion seems plausible to Mary and Nannie.[59] He tells them, "Yes'm, dey's hangin' him up by de co'thouse, a whole crowd o'men's a-hangin' him. Yo' fathah's 'mongst 'em, missy, he said turning to Mary." Mary is ready to accept the worst in her fanatically Republican father, until another townsperson named "Mr. Smith" tells her that the crowd is only hanging Vallandigham "in effigy." To this Ed replies, "Effigy, effigy, dat's whut dey said, but hit don't mek no diffunce how a man's hung, des so he's hung." Nannie and Mary then attempt to explain to Ed the meaning of the word "effigy." They tell him, "It's a stuffed Vallandigham they're hanging." Ed then exclaims, "Stuffed! I t'ought effigy meant his clothes. Lawd bell yo' soul, missy, an' me brekin' my naik runnin' f'om a stuffed co'pse. I reckon I' larmed half de town." Ed walks off in silence after this scene and Mary retorts, "And it's for those people our brothers and fathers are going to war?"[60]

Critics of the novel have typically used such passages to illustrate the limits of Dunbar's ability to portray non-stereotypical black characters.[61] However, the presence of "Nigger Ed" is meant to represent "Dunbar's bleak vision of the outcome of black military participation" in the Civil War. This vision is particularly pronounced in *The Fanatics* since "Nigger Ed" is "the sole representative of black military service" and enlists not as a soldier but follows a northern unit as an "officer's servant."[62] Ed's status as "servant" rather than soldier is further solidified later in the novel. Upon the disbanding of the original Dorbury unit, Ed stays in

Ohio; he only returns to the battlefield later in the narrative to retrieve the body of Tom Waters.

There is an ironic distance between the way Dunbar characterizes, or more properly fails to characterize, Ed and the beliefs about race held by the author. Readers interested in the cause of racial justice are supposed to be angered by the hideous irony that service in the war led to a lateral shift for Ed rather than any meaningful change. He has gone from being the town fool and spreader of rumor to the role of servant to and storyteller of the white community's memory of the war. But Dunbar's bleak portrayal of Ed's military service is not simply proof of the author's despair; the novel may well be "bitter," but Dunbar's bitterness has a goal. To fully understand that goal, we must examine "Nigger Ed" in relation to the only other portion of the narrative that examines race relations—the chapter titled "The Contrabands."

In this chapter Dunbar examines the influx of former slaves that began traveling north as the Union army captured large sections of Confederate territory, encouraged by changing northern legal codes that gave them some modicum of freedom. The narrator tells us that "the decree of General Butler making all slaves who came into camp contraband of war, affected the Negroes not only in his immediate vicinity, but wherever there was a Union camp." Drawn by the promise of freedom "women, children, young, able-bodied men and the feeble and infirm, all hastened towards the Union lines," and from there "work[ed] their way North to the free states." Gradually these groups of "contraband" begin to appear in the fictional Ohio town of Dorbury, whose white residents start to fear that their community will be overrun. We are told that "the cry rose for the enforcement of the law for the restriction of emancipated Negroes, while others went to the extreme of crying for the expulsion of all blacks, from the state." Free blacks in Dorbury, whose small community was not "founded upon mixed blood, but upon free birth or manumission before the war," join in on this cry for restricting the influx of "contrabands" into their quiet enclave. They attempt to restrict former slaves from entering into and participating in the services of their church. One free black member of the church says, "W'y, befo' I'd see dis chu'ch, dis chu'ch dat we free people built give up to dese conterbands, I'd see hit to'down, brick by brick."[63]

Dunbar presents a complex portrait of race relations in this wartime Ohio town that goes beyond a simple hatred of whites toward blacks. The presence of "Nigger Ed" suggests that the people of Dorbury were racist before the war, and that even if they were interested in ending slavery they were not interested in championing racial equality. However, the existence of a "Negro Aristocracy" and a well-developed albeit segregated free black community in Dorbury, also suggests a degree of racial tolerance. As long as the black community remained small, quiet, and known to the whites, Dorbury's white residents seemed content. As the volume of blacks grows and their individual identities remain mysterious, white opposition to African Americans as a group in their small town grows. The free blacks already living in Dorbury are alarmed by the change in mood. They are justifiably afraid of losing what little they possess, in terms of both material possessions and also social status. Thus, when one of the freed slaves says, "We's all colo'ed togetha," the free blacks hear this not as a comforting statement of racial solidarity but as a threat.[64] They are afraid of being misclassified by their neighbors as "contrabands" and expelled from the homes and lives they had quietly constructed next door to the whites.

The narrative demonstrates that those fears are indeed warranted. After a mob decides to rout the African American population out of Dorbury, they make "no distinction as to bond or free, manumitted or contraband." Warned by the southern sympathizer Stephen Van Doren of this plot, the blacks of Dorbury are brought together out of necessity. The mob, led by the drunken brother of the local prosecutor, Raymond Stothard, arrives at "old McLean Street, where stood the house of one of Dorbury's free black citizens." Here the entire African American community of Dorbury, former slave and free black, are gathered to defend themselves. Around midnight Stothard and his followers bang on the door. When no one answers, they break it down. Inside the house the white mob sees "instead of a cowering crowd of helpless men . . . a solid black wall of desperate men who stood their ground and fought like soldiers." The white mob fights with the determined group of free blacks and former slaves using the "fist, stave, club, and the swift knife."[65]

It's only when the fight appears to be turning in favor of the blacks that a solitary shot rings out. This leads to a general retreat, but the battle for Dorbury is not over yet. A young African American boy whose mother had earlier been insulted by Stothard emerges from the crowd. While Stothard rallies his men for the final assault, this young boy pulls out a knife and stabs the man in the heart. Stothard falls dead instantly. The death of their leader slows the mob's progress, but the damage has already been done. Stothard's killer, referred to by the narrator as a "wild-eyed boy," flees Dorbury "into the night to be lost forever." Not far behind him is the entire black population of Dorbury. We are told that "the rout of the Negroes was now complete, and they fled in all directions. Some ran away; only to return when the storm had passed; others, terrified by the horror of the night, went, never to return, and their homes are occupied in Dorbury today by the men who drove them from them."[66]

No less bitter than Dunbar's portrayal of the problematic character "Nigger Ed," this chapter nonetheless suggests a reason for the author's emotions. Dunbar published *The Fanatics* in 1901, just three years after the infamous race riots of 1898 in Wilmington, North Carolina, and the same year Charles Chesnutt published his novel *The Marrow of Tradition* that constructed a fictionalized portrait of those riots.[67] In *The Fanatics*, Dunbar responds obliquely to what for him were contemporary events. These events, viewed through the lens of the Civil War, suggest that the past is of limited utility to the African American community. For those who survive the war(s) in Dorbury, waged both at home and in the South, memory is the only real reward. The war veteran "Nigger Ed" may very well have "a place for life" in Dorbury, but it is only as a mirror for white recollections.[68] Moreover, white remembrance of the past does little to aid the postwar African American residents of the town who remain after its disastrous wartime racial confrontation.[69] Dunbar thus implies that for the black community to truly uplift itself in a new century that was increasingly removed from the context of the Civil War, a new model of manhood and with it a new tradition must be forged.

Even though Dunbar does not explore that model in *The Fanatics*, he does suggest the direction that African Americans must take in order to uncover a new model of manhood and establish a new black tradition. That direction would involve a greater articulation of class differences as they relate to the project of racial uplift and the creation of a black middle class.[70] The delicate task that Dunbar bequeaths to his racially conscious readers is to define more clearly what exactly it means for African Americans to rise, and to decide if all members of the race will be able to rise to the same level to which blacks like Dunbar aspire.

War by Other Means

Observing the failures of the Civil War generation at racial integration, Dunbar hoped to surmount this troubled legacy of black manhood and citizenship in the post-Reconstruction era by letting go of the past. Dunbar's attitude toward the memories of the Civil War and Reconstruction was due in large part to his age. Born in 1872, he was one year younger than Stephen Crane and shared many of the white author's frustrations about the older generation's stranglehold on the rules and roles for manhood. The influence of this generation gap on Dunbar's attitude becomes even more apparent after examining the works of the much-older abolitionist writer and poet Frances Ellen Watkins Harper. In the only novel published in book form during her lifetime, *Iola Leroy*, Harper attempts to recover rather than relinquish the best pieces of her race's anguished Civil War–era past.[71]

Published in 1893, at the height of lynch-mob violence against black men, Harper's *Iola Leroy* reveals the author to be more concerned about the role her novel might play in inciting further white aggression.[72] As a result, one of the few postwar works of African American fiction to portray black soldiers never shows them engaged in battle. Additionally, in the war's aftermath, Harper minimizes the value of her protagonists' military service, placing it within the larger context of the ongoing struggle for racial improvement that began decades before the Civil War and, she believed, would continue well into the twentieth century. The Civil War and black military service thus become, in Harper's novel, a brief episode in an ongoing insurgency against race prejudice, which is carried on in stealth by black women and children as well as men.

The author's unique perspective helps explain why *Iola Leroy* was interpreted for decades after its rediscovery in the 1970s not as a Civil War novel but as a late example of the antebellum "tragic mulatta tale."[73] Her narrative, however, is not solely focused on the lives of its female characters. Harper is indeed interested in rewriting "the war story [in order to make] black women central actors in the war," but she believed that by redefining the war she would also be able to alter the existing conception of black manhood.[74] In order to find a new model of black masculinity that is more appropriate to the Jim Crow age, Harper reintroduces an archetype with roots in the antebellum period—the figure of the "wily slave."

Starting her Civil War novel not with Fort Sumter, but with a coded conversation between two slaves in a North Carolina marketplace, the author tells us that "during the dark days of the Rebellion . . . some of the shrewder slaves, coming in contact with their masters and overhearing their conversations invented a phraseology to convey in the most unsuspected manner news to each other from the battle-field." Because she provides the reader with the key, we are aware of the true significance of Bob and Tom's conversation in this opening scene. Seemingly innocuous phrases such as "the butter [is] fresh, or that the fish and eggs [are] in good condition" convey important military information involving Union victories and defeats as well as troop movements.[75] Were it discovered, their exchange of this information, even more than their possession of it, could easily have led to Bob and Tom's punishment as spies. For their actions represent not only sympathy with the enemies of the South, but also, at least in the view of their masters, a desire to revolt against white authority.

Harper thus suggests that, although Bob and Tom lack military rank and uniform, they are already soldiers engaged in an undercover war against slavery and racial prejudice. Consequently, even though Bob and Tom are eventually associated with the Union forces, army life does not serve as a major catalyst for change in their sense of identity. When Bob Johnson joins the Union army, his shift in name to Private Robert Johnson merely signals a change in official status.[76] Given a rank and a uniform, Robert is now part of a formally declared war, but the substance of his actions remains the same; it is only the means that have changed, becoming far more conventional and direct than before his enlistment. The invaluable service of Robert's friend, Tom, who is not allowed to enlist because of unspecified "physical defects," further underscores the thin line that demarcates the fighting in which these slaves have already been engaged from what they are currently doing. Even though the army leadership recognizes him only as a "laborer" rather than as a "soldier," Tom saves the lives of an entire combat unit by rowing them across a river to safety.

Harper's redefinition of war and, with it, the black military experience paves the way for a new understanding of the role that army service will play in the lives of black men following the conflict. Just as combat is marginalized in the novel, because of Harper's belief that an unrecognized conflict had already been going on for a long time before the conflict began, the value of being a veteran in the postwar nation is also diminished. Both officially recognized black soldiers in the novel, who are also its main male protagonists, Robert and his nephew Harry, are already prepared for freedom and full citizenship *before* the war. Robert is literate and a leading figure in his North Carolina slave community before enlistment. The only thing holding him back is his legal status as a slave. The same is true of the other veteran in the novel, Iola's brother Harry. Having gone to school in the North before he found out he was a slave, Harry does not need the education the army could theoretically provide any more than his Uncle Robert does.

The only immediate benefit that seems to accrue from their enlistment is the opportunity it afforded to travel in search of family members scattered by slavery. Harry, in fact, claims this as his main reason for joining the army, saying, "I made up my mind to enter it [i.e., black army regiment], actuated by a desire to find my mother and sister."[77] In the war's aftermath, Harry and Robert put their record of military service to use for economic as well as political purposes. Robert moves to the North and uses his reputation as a Union officer to advance his economic status and take care of his newly extended family, which includes his mother and sister. Harry, in contrast, decides to live in the South and employs his military service as a shield that allows him to engage in bold political actions on behalf of his race. Although the narrative lauds the actions of Robert, it expresses some concern regarding those of Harry. Harry's mother, Marie, says to him, "I am afraid that you will get into trouble and be murdered, as many others have been."[78] Harry disregards her warning as the anxiety of an overprotective parent, but it echoes the author's fears about the boldness of some black veterans in the post-Reconstruction era.

Frances Harper was searching for the vigor and sacrifice of war without its violence, a position that William James would much later call "the moral equivalent of war." She felt that finding this position would aid the black community in its continuing struggle against race prejudice, while at the same time protecting it from unnecessary reprisals. Harper first indicated her desire for a moral equivalent of war in a speech delivered at the Centennial Anniversary of the Pennsylvania Society for Promoting the Abolition of Slavery in 1875. She told her audience, "Before young men is another battle—not a battle of flashing swords and clashing steel—but a moral warfare, a battle against ignorance, poverty, and low social condition."[79] Nearly twenty years later, her perspective had not materially changed. If anything it had intensified, as her call to arms in *Iola Leroy* no longer summoned just the action of young men. The army, she argues in the novel, has not been disbanded but, in fact, expanded to include all members of the African American community. Its goal, however, has altered—no longer focused on killing, this new black army has as its goal the education and social advancement of the entire black race in the United States.

At the end of *Iola Leroy*, each of the main characters moves to the South in order to further this objective. Harry, already living in North Carolina, marries a fellow teacher, Miss Delany, and works toward the education of former slaves. His sister Iola, the title character of the novel, marries Dr. Latimer, who moves to North Carolina in order to practice medicine. Harry's Uncle Robert, who had built a life for himself in a northern city, moves to North Carolina as well, buying a plantation that he rents out to less-fortunate members of his race. He also devotes his waning years to caring for his mother and his sister, Marie, the mother of Harry and Iola. Now that the entire family has been reunited, a true home has been created and anything seems possible. Yet this vision of home seems more appropriate to the early years of Reconstruction than it does to the Jim Crow South of the 1890s. Perhaps that is why some critics have interpreted *Iola Leroy* as essentially a rewriting of her earlier novella, *Minnie's Sacrifice*, which appeared in serial form in the *Christian Recorder* in 1869.[80]

Nevertheless, whether we interpret *Iola Leroy* as a new composition or the revision of an earlier one, the novel's ironic attitude toward Uncle Robert is palpable. He is portrayed near the end of the novel as "a relic of the past"; "his voice increasingly fades as the text marches past the Civil War and into Reconstruction."[81] Moreover, this process of silencing occurs despite the fact that his financial investments make possible the reunion of the family and its life in North Carolina. In her anxiety to make the black veteran characters in her novel less threatening to white readers, Harper inadvertently empties black military service of its meaning. As in Dunbar's writing, military service becomes an interlude that is best forgotten while preparing for the better day that is about to dawn for the black race.

A Rearguard Defense of Martial Manhood

The works of African American authors Paul Laurence Dunbar and Frances Ellen Watkins Harper reveal the conflicting opinions that existed within the black community about the meaning and value of black military service. During the Civil War and the height of Reconstruction, martial manhood—the African American equivalent of the citizen-soldier—seemed to open the door to black male participation in the full rights of American citizenship. Over time, however, it became clear that army service alone would not suffice to aid the black community in transcending race prejudice. The early postwar thunder of voices that had celebrated black soldiers and black military service began to fade to a whisper. The efforts of black soldiers and to a certain extent the Civil War itself had begun to lose their relevance to the black community. This was especially true for the black men of the rising generation such as Paul Laurence Dunbar who served as spokesmen for a new era.

Dunbar's attitude was shared by the authors of inspirational works such as the *Progress of a Race; or, The Remarkable Advancement of the Afro-American Negro*, in which black soldiers were included in the historical section of the narrative but were conspicuously absent from the volume's hundreds of biographies of eminent black men.[82] Those African Americans who had lived through the war, like Frances Ellen Watkins Harper, understood the need for new, non-warlike models of manhood in the black community. But they were more cautious about jettisoning the entire legacy of the war. Where this older generation agreed with the younger, however, was in their view that the black soldier was no longer useful in the project of racial uplift. It was time for the civilian black professional to take the stage.

In essence, black veterans found themselves assaulted on two fronts in the late 1880s and 1890s: first by the culture of sectional reconciliation and the virulent white racism of the Jim Crow era, and second by the lack of interest within the African American community in the specifically warlike aspects of their Civil War–era achievements. This unpleasant reality adds a new dimension to our understanding of the defensive tone in Joseph Wilson's history of black troops, *The Black Phalanx*. Wilson desperately wanted to prove to both the white and black members of his reading audience that martial manhood was still relevant to discussions on the black race and specifically the future of the black male. By reaching back into the past, he hoped to demonstrate that the military service of black men during the Civil War and the wars that preceded it had proved an ongoing commitment to defend the life of the nation. He also felt that their service provided a visible sign of the manliness of the black male, who showed himself worthy of freedom by fighting to earn it.

To a certain extent, the beliefs of veterans like Wilson were encouraged by the Union veterans' groups to which some of them belonged. Wilson was a longtime member of the Grand Army of the Republic and served at one point as aide-de-camp to the organization's commander in chief. Recent research has shown that "black and white veterans [of the Union army] were able to create and sustain an interracial organization in a society rigidly divided on the color line" because they shared the memory of "service in a war against slavery."[83] Joseph Wilson recalls this bond between comrades in the preface to *The Black Phalanx*. Here he recounts a conversation with other members of the Farragut post of the Grand Army of the Republic as they sit around a campfire. He tells us, "It was proposed that the history of the American negro soldier should be written. The task of preparing the history fell to my lot."[84] Despite the patronizing tone inherent in the proposal of his comrades that he write a book about black soldiers, as if he were incapable of writing about anything else, Wilson's assigned task nonetheless represented a qualified acceptance by his peers of the value of African American military service during the Civil War.[85] Such acceptance would have been denied to Wilson in nearly all other venues outside the Grand Army in late-nineteenth-century America.

Consequently, Wilson was disposed to accept his duty to record the deeds of African Americans in arms. He allowed himself to be typecast in the role of "black" historian for his post because he felt no one else (including black civilians) would take up the torch of remembrance when men like him were gone. Wilson hoped to remind both his black and white readership that "the story of an oppressed race" included martial manhood, and that through military service African American men had contributed to the "improvement" of the race as well as guarded the "liberties and boundaries of the land."[86] Among the many difficulties black veterans like Wilson faced was that of convincing an African

American readership of the validity of his point of view. This was particularly challenging given the massive gap between the wartime arguments for martial manhood he still espoused and the realities of life for black veterans in the post-Reconstruction era.

By the time Wilson was writing, black veterans were more likely to be targets of racial violence than symbols of the potential for "improvement" in race relations in the United States. They were in many instances the vulnerable rear guard of the racial uplift movement rather than its front line. An article in the November 21, 1888, *New York Times* captures the truth of this perspective, recording the brutal assault on a black veteran, James McIntyre, by three younger white men.[87] McIntyre owned a home as well as a small store in the town of Oceanville, New Jersey. Although the author of the article does not go into details, he notes that the three men convicted in McIntyre's assault had been harassing him for months. Their hope was to force him to close his store and leave town. Because he refused to leave, the youths increased their violence toward him, savagely beating McIntyre and the housekeeper who lived with him. The writer of the article asserts the great indignation of the paper as well as that of the "better element" of the community of Oceanville at McIntyre's assault. However, the title of the piece, "Protecting a Colored Veteran," commits its own form of violence (in this case symbolic) on this old soldier. It suggests that the indignation of the white community at his assault comes less from McIntyre having been a Union soldier than his current status as an old man and amputee. He is a defenseless person in need of protection by the white community rather than a self-reliant and heroic veteran of the Civil War.

Well before the decline of the African American veterans' legacy in the heart of the Jim Crow era, numerous factors insured that black military service in the Civil War would be different from the experience of white soldiers. The institution of slavery paired with racial discrimination toward free blacks initially made it seem that African American men would not be allowed to enlist at all in the ranks of the Union army. When wartime manpower shortages along with changing northern political goals finally led to black enlistment in the northern army, recruits still faced great challenges, such as unequal pay, demeaning assignments, a lack of black officers, and segregation from white army units. Despite these challenges, however, the African American community viewed the birth of the USCT as a chance for black males to prove not only their manhood but also their worthiness as citizens. Serving alongside other volunteers, these men understood themselves as citizen-soldiers who deserved the rights of citizenship after having fulfilled one its highest duties—national defense.

After the war, veterans of black regiments used their wartime service to full advantage. They were vocal supporters of the Fourteenth and Fifteenth Amendments and active participants in the political movements associated with Reconstruction. The decision to align so closely their fortunes to that of Reconstruction would have dire consequences as the northern desire to reshape social relations began to fade. Black veterans saw their stars gradually tarnished as their cultural capital vanished along with their financial success. Soon "freedom's soldiers" were visible only to the African American community, and even there the legacy of these wartime heroes became increasingly mixed. A new generation of black males such as Paul Laurence Dunbar saw little use in emulating the mythic figure of the black soldier. Instead, they sought middle-class professional role models such as doctors, teachers, and lawyers, who exemplified the peaceful approach of racial uplift and eventual entry into the American mainstream. Even those African Americans who had lived through the war, such as Frances Ellen Watkins Harper, saw limited utility in the mythic figure of the black soldier. War had ended slavery, but military service proved incapable of providing the lasting civic equality the black community desired.

Black veterans recognized this shift in civilian perception toward what they had achieved during the Civil War. They were convinced like their white comrades that the war was highly significant to their identity and to the future of the nation as a whole. However, they lacked access to the avenues of publication and the high degree of literacy possessed by white veterans. It was only through association with veterans' groups such as the Grand Army of the Republic that black veterans like Joseph Wilson were able to distribute their defense of "martial manhood" to white and African American readers. Regrettably, the claims of these veterans fell on deaf ears as whites were willing to concede that a handful of black men had proven their manliness in battle but not that this manliness held greater portents for the entire race. Moreover, African Americans, viewing the precipitous decline of a large number of veterans in the post-Reconstruction period, couldn't help but be skeptical of claims that black military service had advanced the race's prospects. Heroism in the past would be recognized and remembered, at least as long as the war remained in living memory, but as the black military experience in the Civil War demonstrated, remembrance did not necessarily lead to influence. The quest for racial equality continued, and new non-martial role models were sought to lead the way.

Epilogue

In a true war story, if there's a moral at all, it's like the thread that makes the cloth. You can't tease it out. You can't extract the meaning without unraveling the deeper meaning.

—Tim O'Brien, *The Things They Carried*

Contemporary readers of war narratives and audiences of war films are generally in agreement with veteran authors like Tim O'Brien that the experience of combat is a solid "cloth" that is damaged or cheapened by a conventional search for "meaning." The "deeper meaning" is only fully available to those who have lived through the mysterious phenomenon of war and been forever changed by that experience.[1] Veterans understand their wars intuitively in a way that standard forms of communication cannot explain. Consequently, any attempt to represent war is of necessity incomplete.

This perspective toward war seems universal, but it has not always been the standard response. *New Men* shows that the United States Civil War was a watershed moment for these beliefs in American culture. Whereas civilians and former soldiers alike had once seen military service as an episode in a man's life, after the war it was understood to be a transformative experience. This new conception was crystalized in the term "veteran," which came to represent a new identity rather than simply a set of skills. From their sufferings had come a wisdom that Civil War veterans could not and would not casually throw away. Thus, even though many former soldiers longed for a return to the way of life they enjoyed before the war, most came to realize that such longings were utopian in nature, unlikely to ever see fruition. They had crossed a threshold of experience on the battlefield that they believed had made them enlightened in comparison to the civilian populace.

Many reasons exist for why scholars have not typically viewed the Civil War as a defining moment in America's cultural understanding of what it meant to be a veteran. Foremost among them is the perception that war has *always* been a transformative experience. This critical blindness obscures the connection between the largely philosophical view of warfare as "experience" rather than "event," and the historical emergence of "modern" war. Military historian Yuval Noah Harari notes that the perceived "connection between war and the revelation of truth" is a hallmark of the modern combat experience.[2] Peace is consistently described as a realm of illusions whereas war, "the ultimate experience," provides insights to its participants that were once reserved solely for philosophers, saints, and mystics. These insights in turn lead to a changed sense of consciousness and new perception of the world.

For scholars of the Civil War era, a tacit acceptance of the transformative power of war on self-conception serves two functions. The first is that it sidesteps ongoing arguments over whether the war was in fact a "modern" conflict. These typically involve exhaustive examination of the types of weapons used along with the strategies and tactics adopted by commanders. The second is that it avoids the question of "bad" wars versus "good" ones and the nature of their legacies. Because the legacy of the Civil War remains divisive, there is strong resistance to any research that might heighten that division, unless it focuses on the positive outcome of slavery's abolition. A paradox that follows from this series of omissions is the claim that Civil War veterans were shaped by their participation in the war but did not experience any lasting changes to identity.[3]

The focus in *New Men* on the war's lasting impact on Civil War veterans' self-conception demonstrates a belief that the conflict began as a premodern struggle but developed into an early version of modern war. To a large extent this shift was due to the changed rhythm of war more than to the preexisting beliefs on the part of soldiers of what a war should be like. Nearly continuous fighting in the last two years of the war replaced the set-piece battles of earlier campaigns. Soldiers received little or no time to conceptualize what they had lived through or to physically and mentally recuperate. This great fatigue to both mind and body changed them in ways they never completely understood. All that was certain was they could not fully return to their antebellum sense of identity. Civil War soldiers, raised in a strongly Christian nation, turned to religion as the closest analogy capable of expressing the change they felt. They had been baptized by war and born again as new men.

Veterans on both sides of the struggle felt this change to their self-conception, which contradicts the assumption that only "bad wars" lead to reintegration problems for soldiers returning home. Were this perspective true, it would follow that Confederate veterans, fighting to preserve the discredited institution of slavery, should exhibit the greatest symptoms of social alienation.[4] Defeat in the pursuit of a "bad" cause, however, was not necessary for the decay of a soldier's faith in the values he held prior to enlistment. In fact, many northern veterans, like Albion Tourgée and Oliver Wendell Holmes, whose hopes for the nation were limitless at the war's end, became far more disillusioned than their southern opponents. They watched as the nation descended from the promise of being a workingman's democracy, premised on "free labor," into the economic morass of the Gilded Age. They also carried within them disturbing reminders of their violation of supposedly sacred social beliefs, most notably the prohibition against killing.

The troubled lives of significant numbers of veterans reveal that their process of reentry into civilian life was distinct from the political and racial struggles of the era in which they lived. This insight does not detract from the excellent research on sectional reconciliation and the fight for African American civil rights in the nineteenth- and early-twentieth-century United States. Rather, it highlights the fact that even necessary wars have a human cost difficult to quantify. That cost goes beyond the number of dead on the battlefield, and requires us to contemplate the living who walk away from combat with scars that sometimes are not so visible. For a large portion of Civil War veterans, the mere fact of survival in a struggle where life and death seemed impersonal and random made them view themselves and their purpose in a radically different way. These beliefs trickled down to American society as a whole and created a new way of thinking and writing about war and its survivors.

Exposing the origins of this new way of writing about war and its veterans shows that the "Lost Generation" of Ernest Hemingway and John Dos Passos was preceded in its observations on the transformative influence of war by nearly forty years. Ironically, a generation of men who were far more obsessed with the accurate representation and preservation of the past than the men of the post–World War I era left behind a largely metaphysical rather than historical legacy. Severed from its roots in the Civil War–era nation, the belief that war was an experience that made "new men" became the true inheritance that the Civil War veteran provided subsequent generations of American males—to alternately strive for, ponder, or contest. We are left with that legacy today.

Even though the details have changed over time to fit the specific needs of each generation, the theme of war as a threshold that transforms the self-conception and worldview of soldiers remains the starting point when we attempt as a society to understand the men and women who return home from war. In narratives as diverse as Tim O'Brien's *The Things They Carried* and Colby Buzzell's *My War: Killing Time in Iraq*, former soldiers continue to struggle in their attempts to explain the transformative experience of war. Tim O'Brien states in his well-known sketch "How to Tell a True War Story" that "War is hell, but that's not the half of it, because war is also mystery and terror and adventure and courage and discovery and holiness and pity and despair and longing and love. War is nasty; war is fun. War is thrilling; war is drudgery. War makes you a man; war makes you dead."[5] This series of contradictions highlights the elusive quality of war that Civil War veterans attempted to describe through the lens of religious belief, and which we attempt today to explain primarily through scientific metaphors.

Among the current attempts to explain the combat experience through a scientific perspective is Kathryn Bigelow's film *The Hurt Locker*. In this work about the Second Iraq War (2003–11), addiction is initially used as a metaphor to explain the soldier's relationship to combat. Explosives technician Sergeant William James enjoys the adrenaline rush he receives from cheating death with each bomb he defuses and detonates.[6] When he returns home unharmed at the end of his tour of duty, Sergeant James seems out of place in civilian life. He is more lost and afraid in the aisles of the suburban supermarket that he ever was in the war-torn streets of Iraq. We are thus led to believe that James returns to the battlefield not simply to retrieve his adrenaline high but to reclaim his "true self" as well. War has changed James's biochemistry and with it his sense of identity. The army and the battlefield are his true home.

The constant search for the right metaphor to explain the long-term effects of war on its participants suggests that much research remains to be done on the subject. *New Men* provides a valuable context for scholars engaged in this research. My hope is that this study will encourage not only a new approach to academic inquiry on the Civil War and the culture it spawned, but also the growth of a new "veterans studies" movement that systematically explores the elements of the combat experience that are truly universal and those that are context-specific. Without such specificity, civilians and former soldiers will continue to misunderstand each other, and full social reintegration for soldiers returning home will remain a frustrated dream.

Notes

Introduction

1. For Whitman's comment on later representations of the war, see "The Real War Will Never Get in the Books" in *Specimen Days*. Michael Moon reproduces this section of Whitman's prose reminiscence of the war on pp. 778–79 of the Norton Critical Edition of *Leaves of Grass*. Edmund Wilson in *Patriotic Gore* and Daniel Aaron in *The Unwritten War* use Whitman's comments as a point of departure and source of inspiration for their studies of Civil War literature and the supposed lack of great literary representations of the war.

2. See the introductions by Alice Fahs to *The Imagined Civil War*, and Elizabeth Young, *Disarming the Nation*. Here they formulate their argument against the theme of the "unwritten war."

3. Cynthia Wachtell's *War No More* examines the phenomenon of the "unwritten war" as a by-product of the Civil War's status as the first modern war in the United States. Authors were uncomfortable writing about a conflict that challenged their conceptions of heroic war. See Chapter 8 of Wachtell.

4. Craig Warren argues that veteran claims to representational authority intimidated would-be writers of Civil War literature. However, he leaves the origins of their claims largely unexamined. See in particular Chapter 1 of Warren, *Scars to Prove It*.

5. This narrative, initiated by Paul H. Buck's *Road to Reunion*, was popularized by David Blight in *Race and Reunion*. It has since become the dominant paradigm for understanding the post–Civil War era in the United States. See *Race and Reunion*, particularly Chapters 4 and 5, for his interpretation of the road to reunion.

6. Among the recent scholarship examining friction between Union and Confederate veterans are *Remembering the Civil War* by Caroline Janney and *Across the Bloody Chasm* by Keith Harris. Janney contends that political "reunion" rather than emotional "reconciliation" was what veterans and civilians were able to achieve in the postwar nation. All sides remembered the causes of the war as they understood them but nonetheless chose to work together for the cause of postwar national advancement. Harris takes a similar approach to that of Janney but chooses to focus primarily on veterans, examining the ways in which they sought to work within the climate of reconciliation while remaining true to their memories of the war. See Janney, pp. 5–7, and Chapters 5 and 6. See also Harris's introduction to *Across the Bloody Chasm*. Chief among the recent scholarship on manhood and disability relating to Civil War veterans is James Marten's *Sing Not War*. Marten shows that for many former soldiers, especially those veterans who received pensions or lived in soldiers' homes, it was important to prove to the civilian populace that the war had not made them unfit for life in the peacetime nation. See Marten, Chapters 4 and 5. Additional scholarship on the subject of Civil War veterans,

manhood, and disability includes Brian Matthew Jordan, "Living Monuments"; Susan Mary-Grant, "The Lost Boys"; and Chapter 4 of Megan Kate Nelson, *Ruin Nation*.

7. An excellent example of a regional history of Civil War veterans is Jeffrey McClurken's *Take Care of the Living*, which examines the postwar lives of families of Confederate veterans in Pittsylvania and Danville counties, Virginia.

8. To a certain extent, divisions between regulars and volunteers persisted during the Civil War and in its immediate aftermath. Union volunteer John William De Forest makes this division a key aspect of the plot in his novel *Miss Ravenel's Conversion*, which I examine at length in Chapter 1. General and politician John Logan, one of the founders of the Grand Army of the Republic, also remained vocal in his disregard for regular army troops after the war. By the end of Reconstruction, however, this distinction was mostly ignored. Former soldiers saw one another as comrades regardless of how they had served. The diaries and letters of Union and Confederate soldiers suggest that they felt a greater affinity for their officers than veterans of prior U.S. wars had. Speeches and letters written by officers indicate that the feeling was mutual. This stands in contrast to the outright hostility and disgust that many officers felt toward their men in the Mexican War. For more information on relations between officers and enlisted men in the Mexican War, see Paul Foos, *A Short Offhand Killing Affair*, particularly Chapter 5. Richard Bruce Windars provides an extensive description of the differences between volunteers and regular soldiers in the Mexican War in Chapters 4 and 5 of his *Mr. Polk's Army*. Social norms during the Revolutionary War era held that officers were by nature "gentlemen" and therefore of higher status than the men they commanded. The consequences of this belief are explored by Caroline Cox in *A Proper Sense of Honor*; see in particular Cox, Chapter 1. Gregory T. Knouff examines the relationship between the militia and the regular soldiers of the Continental Army in Chapter 3 of his book *The Soldiers' Revolution*.

9. In addition to his research on differences between Regulars and Volunteers in the Mexican War, Richard Bruce Windars also explores the role of politics in what many Americans saw as the Democrats' war. He argues that volunteers were often selected who shared the views of President James K. Polk's Democratic Party while the Regulars who bore the brunt of the fighting tended to be Whigs. This intensified the divisions within the army and ensured that any legacy of the war would be fractured rather than creative of solidarity among all the soldiers who fought. See Windars, Chapter 3. This was not the first time, however, that a president sought to create an army of voters rather than simply an army in the field. Theodore J. Crackel in *Mr. Jefferson's Army* examines the efforts of President Thomas Jefferson to shape the Regular Army into an institution more friendly toward his Democratic-Republican Party. See Crackel, Chapter 2.

10. See Charles Royster, *A Revolutionary People at War*, 356–60.

11. See John Resch, *Suffering Soldiers*, 90–92, 148–51. Sarah J. Purcell also describes the new generation's reaction to Revolutionary War veterans in *Sealed with Blood*; see Purcell, 187–94.

12. John Limon's *Writing After War* begins with a brief analysis of the pre–Civil War novel *Rip Van Winkle*, then quickly shifts to the post–Civil War writing of Henry James, William Dean Howells, and Stephen Crane; James Dawes's *The Language of War* starts

directly with Crane's *The Red Badge of Courage*; and Cynthia Wachtell's *War No More* opens with popular fiction written during the Civil War.

13. Although the origins of the phrase are uncertain, soldiers in the Civil War era commonly described their first experience of combat as "going to the see the elephant."

14. An expansive literature debating the status of the U.S. Civil War as the nation's first "modern" or "total" war has developed in the past twenty years. For an overview of the issues involved in this debate, see Stig Förster and Jörg Nagler (eds.), *On the Road to Total War*. Of particular interest are the essays by Mark E. Neely Jr., "Was the Civil War a Total War?" Edward Hagerman, "Union Generalship, Political Leadership, and Total War Strategy," and James M. McPherson, "From Limited War to Total War in America."

15. Recent scholarship on Sherman's march through Georgia and the Carolinas questions the destructiveness or "totality" of the campaign. Jacqueline Glass Campbell and Wesley Moody both argue that the psychological impact of Sherman's march on the southern population was greater than its physical destruction. See Campbell, *When Sherman Marched North from the Sea*, Chapter 5; and Moody, *Demon of the Lost Cause*, Chapter 7.

16. Earl J. Hess provides an extensive examination of the impact of the rifled musket and trench warfare on combat tactics and strategy in the Civil War. See *The Rifle Musket in Civil War Combat* and *Trench Warfare Under Grant and Lee*.

17. The Napoleonic origins of early Civil War tactics are a recurring theme in much of the scholarship on the war. However, the degree to which Civil War commanders consciously studied and applied these precepts is a subject of debate. See James McPherson, *The Battle Cry of Freedom*, 331–38, and Carol Reardon, *With a Sword in One Hand and Jomini in Another*, particularly Chapter 2.

18. Civil War casualty statistics remain inexact. Scholars must remain cautious, therefore, about using casualty statistics alone as markers of the unique character of the war. Nicholas Marshall provides a critique of the use of casualty statistics to prove the war's unprecedented destructiveness in his article "The Great Exaggeration."

19. Grant stated in an official report that "the armies in the East and West [have] acted independently like a balky team." Hereafter Grant claimed that he intended to "use the greatest number of troops practicable against the armed force of the enemy, preventing him from using the same force at different seasons against first one and then another of our armies." See the United States War Department, *The War of the Rebellion*, Series 1, Volume 36 (Part 1), p. 12.

20. For more on the Overland Campaign and Grant's ascendance to the position of general in chief of the Union army, see Mark Grimsley, *And Keep Moving On*, Chapter 8, and Ernest B. Furguson, *Not War But Murder*, 12–16.

21. For casualty statistics on the Battle of Cold Harbor, see Edward H. Bonekemper III, *Ulysses S. Grant*, 306–7. Statistics on casualties from the Battle of Gettysburg can be found in John W. Busey and David G. Martin, *Regimental Strengths and Losses at Gettysburg* (4th ed.), 125. These statistics are similar to those listed by William F. Fox in his *Regimental Losses in the American Civil War* (1889), which at one time served as the standard text on combat casualties during the conflict; see Fox, 541. The ongoing debate over the significance of Civil War casualty statistics is addressed above, in note 18.

22. Daniel Bond, *Unpublished Memoir and War Diary*, June 21, 1864.

23. See Barbara Gannon, *The Won Cause*, particularly Chapters 1 and 11.

24. For Samito's discussion of the black soldier's successful role in passing the Fourteenth and Fifteenth amendments, see Chapter 6 of *Becoming American Under Fire*.

1. Demobilization, Disability, and the Competing Imagery of the Wounded Warrior and the Citizen-Soldier

1. See "Military Politicians," *The Nation*, 291; "Re-organization of Parties," *New York Herald*, 4; and "Crime in Chicago," *Washington Daily Intelligencer*.

2. For an overview of the ideology of sentiment and examples of its deployment in antebellum culture, see the essays in Shirley Samuels (ed.), *The Culture of Sentiment*. Of particular interest are Samuels's critical introduction to the collection and Dana Nelson's essay "Sympathy as Strategy in *Hope Leslie*."

3. Resch, *Suffering Soldiers*, 66.

4. See the introduction to this volume, notes 18 and 21.

5. A vast body of literature exists on the topic of the citizen-soldier. For an excellent overview of the citizen-soldier tradition in the United States, see John K. Mahon's *History of the Militia and the National Guard* and Jerry Cooper's *The Rise of the National Guard*. R. Claire Synder's book *Citizen-Soldiers and Manly Warriors* provides an excellent examination of the theoretical concept of the citizen-soldier. See in particular her introduction, where she examines the connection between military service and citizenship within the republican tradition in the United States.

6. Historian Marcus Cunliffe notes that "the experiences of seventeenth and eighteenth century England were, to a somewhat surprising degree, recapitulated in the New World; and the cautionary tales they embodied made a profound impression upon the colonies." See *Soldiers and Civilians*, 31.

7. Army demobilization is discussed in passing by a wide variety of Civil War scholars. Most focus either on the mythology of homecoming—such as James Marten in *Sing Not War*—or on the parades that welcomed some Union veterans home—such as Stuart McConnell in *Glorious Contentment*. Relatively few studies, however, have focused specifically on the logistics necessary to dismantle the northern and southern armies at the end of the war. The description of the process of army disbandment in this section relies on the secondary analysis of William Holberton, *Homeward Bound*, and Newell and Shrader, "The U.S. Army's Transition to Peace."

8. George Henry Mills, *History of the Sixteenth North Carolina Regiment in the Civil War*, 70.

9. C. I. Walker (ed.), *Rolls and Historical Sketch of the Tenth Regiment, SO. CA. Volunteers in the Army of the Confederate States*, 130–31.

10. Elbert Decatur Willett (ed.), *History of Company B, 40th Alabama Regiment, Confederate States Army*, 89.

11. For a list of the various field rendezvous sites see Holberton, *Homeward Bound*, Appendix A. The same information can also be found in United States War Department, *The War of the Rebellion*, Series 3, Volume 5, 20–23.

12. Marvin (ed.), *The Fifth Regiment Connecticut Volunteers*, 391. The idiom "French leave" in this quote refers to soldiers departing from their unit without permission.
13. Blakeslee (ed.), *History of the Sixteenth Connecticut Volunteers*, 106.
14. Field, *Letter to Kittie Field*.
15. De Forest, *Miss Ravenel's Conversion*, 434, 430.
16. Ibid., 434–35.
17. Qtd. in Holberton, *Homeward Bound*, 69. The "eagle" referred to by Turner is presumably the hard currency he was paid in rather than the paper money circulated during the war.
18. Committee of the Regiment, *The Story of the 55th Volunteer Illinois Infantry*, 438.
19. Marshall, *Letter to Hattie Marshall*.
20. Barber, *Letter to His Aunt*.
21. De Forest, *Miss Ravenel's Conversion*, 429.
22. Finch, *Letter to Thirza Finch*.
23. Mitchell, *Civil War Soldiers*, 59.
24. Qtd. in ibid., 60.
25. Charles A. Partridge, *History of the Ninety-Sixth Regiment Illinois Volunteer Infantry*, 501.
26. Gary Gallagher examines this sentiment at length in Chapter 4 of his book *The Union War*.
27. Charles Royster's seminal research on the Revolutionary War era indicates that "while Americans considered hierarchical regimentation necessary for an army, they disliked its existence, even though they were not personally subject to it . . . freedom and a standing army [they believed] could not both survive in the United States." See *A Revolutionary People at War*, 358.
28. "Military Politicians," *The Nation*, 291.
29. Andy Slap offers his own interpretation of the term "Caesarism" and the political beliefs associated with it in Chapter 9 of his book *The Doom of Reconstruction*. See in particular pp. 211–12.
30. "Have We Come to Caesarism?" *The Nation*, 352–53. There are many studies available on the political upheaval in France during the period 1848–52, but one of the best works to examine the influence of this period on American culture is Timothy Roberts's *Distant Revolutions*. See in particular Chapter 2.
31. The classic text examining this wartime crisis is David Long *The Jewel of Liberty*. Recent studies have questioned Long's assertion that Union soldiers voted overwhelmingly or voluntarily for Lincoln. These include White "Canvassing the Troops," and Timothy Orr, "A Viler Enemy in Our Rear."
32. "Ought Soldiers to Vote?" *The Nation*, 331.
33. For information on the stigma associated with a military career, see Chapter 4 of Edward M. Coffman, *The Old Army*. Here he discusses how the enlisted soldier in particular was viewed as the antithesis of the energetic entrepreneurialism favored in Jacksonian America.
34. See in particular "Immorality in Richmond," *Daily Mississippian*; "Temperance in Our Armies," *Daily Palladium*; "Profanity Among Soldiers," *Vermont Chronicle*; "Soldiers

Riot in Washington," *Newark Advocate*; and "Crime in Chicago," *Washington Daily Intelligencer*.

35. See above, notes 2 and 3.

36. Megan Kate Nelson provides a brief but similar analysis of this image and the story accompanying it in her recent book *Ruin Nation*, 193–95.

37. The separate spheres concept was influential in interpreting gender relations in the nineteenth-century United States well into the twentieth century. It argued that men took part in the activities of the public sphere (i.e., the world of work and commerce) whereas women were active in the private sphere (i.e., the home). For a critical examination of the separate spheres concept of nineteenth-century culture see Cathy N. Davidson and Jessamyn Hatcher (eds.), *No More Separate Spheres!*

38. "The Empty Sleeve at Newport; or, Why Edna Ackland Learned to Drive," *Harper's Weekly*, 534.

39. There are two biographies of John William De Forest. The first is part of the Twayne United States Authors Series: James F. Light's *John William De Forest*. A more recent critical biography of the author and his works is James Hijiya's *J. W. De Forest and the Rise of American Gentility*.

40. For more on Sidney Lanier's biography see Edwin Mims, *Sidney Lanier*, and Aubrey H. Starke, *Sidney Lanier*.

41. See Karen Keely, "Marriage Plots and National Reunion," and Chapter 2 of Nina Silber's *The Romance of Reunion* for more on the genre of the reconciliation romance. Refer to Martin Buinicki's article "John W. De Forest's *Miss Ravenel's Conversion* and the Limits of Sentimental Citizenship" for an argument that the novel critiques rather than represents the genre.

42. See Chapter 5 of Cynthia Wachtell, *War No More*, and Michael Schaefer, *Just What War Is*, for an examination of the novel's "realistic" portrayal of war.

43. Although he is eventually promoted to the brevet rank of brigadier general near the novel's end, for the sake of consistency I will continue to refer to him as Colonel Carter throughout the chapter.

44. De Forest, *Miss Ravenel's Conversion*, 20.

45. Ibid., 29.

46. See Fick, "Genre Wars and the Rhetoric of Manhood in *Miss Ravenel's Conversion from Secession to Loyalty*."

47. Kemble, *The Image of the Army Officer in America*. See in particular Chapters 3 and 4.

48. Ball, *Army Regulars on the Western Frontier*, 85.

49. De Forest, *Miss Ravenel's Conversion*, 424.

50. Ibid., 386.

51. Ibid., 467–68.

52. Ibid., 427.

53. Ibid., 429.

54. Ibid., 427–28.

55. Ibid., 437.

56. Sidney Lanier, *Tiger-Lilies*, 185.

57. For more on this special connection between southern soldiers and civilians see Chapter 4 of Gary Gallagher, *The Confederate War*.

58. Garland Greever, "Introduction," in Lanier, *Tiger-Lilies*, xx.

59. See William J. Kimball's essay "Realism in Sidney Lanier's *Tiger-Lilies*," and Garland Greever, "Introduction," in Lanier, *Tiger-Lilies*.

60. Lanier's war flower was more than likely inspired by the *blaue blume* (blue flower) of Novalis in his novel *Heinrich von Ofterdingen*, which became a symbol of the German romantic movement. The blue flower represents a desired but unattainable ideal. See Greever, "Introduction," in Lanier, *Tiger-Lilies*.

61. Edmund Wilson in his book *Patriotic Gore* picks up on this prelapsarian imagery, but interprets it as yet another example of the Lost Cause mythology that develops in the postwar South. Wilson's disdain for Lanier's flowery narration leads him not only to pass over the specifics of Lanier's contribution to the Lost Cause mythology but also to miss the novel's message relating to former Confederate soldiers. See Wilson, 450–56.

62. Lanier, *Tiger-Lilies*, 102.

63. Ibid., 108.

64. Emory M. Thomas in his book *The Confederacy as a Revolutionary Experience*, and Michael Barton in his essay "Did the Confederacy Change Southern Soldiers?" both examine Confederate identity. They do so, however, solely within the context of political identity (i.e., did these soldiers see themselves as part of a Confederate nation?). I am more interested here in the question, posed by Lanier, of how these men saw themselves after having killed other men and taken part in the experience of combat—not totally divorced from issues of nationalism, but nevertheless distinct.

65. For an in-depth examination of the psychology behind killing in combat see *On Killing* by Lt. Col. David Grossman. See in particular Chapter 1 on the stages of the "killing response."

66. For further information on Lanier's portrayal of "poor white trash" characters in the novel see Nathalia Wright's essay "The East Tennessee Background of Sidney Lanier's *Tiger-Lilies*."

67. Lanier, *Tiger-Lilies*, 184.

68. Ibid., 190.

69. Ibid., 142.

70. Ibid., 154–55.

71. Ibid., 160.

72. When he finds out that his brother Gorm has deserted from the Confederate army, he tells him, "Gorm Smallin, you has cheated me, an' ole father an' mother an' all, out of our name which it was all we had; you has swore to a lie . . . you has stole our honest name, which is more than ye can ever make to give to your wife's baby." Ibid., 121.

73. Ibid., 191.

2. Veterans, Artisanal Manhood, and the Quest for Postwar Employment

1. For more information on the cycles of boom and bust in the Gilded Age, see Elmus Wicker, *Banking Panics of the Gilded Age*, and Robert Sobel, *Panic on Wall Street*.

M. John Lubetkin provides useful insights into the role of railroad speculation in these panics in *Jay Cooke's Gamble*. See particularly Chapters 17 and 18.

2. The authoritative overview of the 1877 railway strikes remains Philip Foner's *The Great Labor Uprising of 1877*. David Stowell's essay collection *The Great Strikes of 1877* provides a useful review of more recent scholarship on this historical event, which many labor historians see as the beginning of the modern labor movement.

3. For a recent interpretation of political corruption in the Grant administration see Chapter 6 of Andrew Slap's *The Doom of Reconstruction*.

4. See the epilogue to Gerald Linderman's *Embattled Courage*.

5. In Chapter 6 of James J. Broomall's unpublished dissertation "Personal Confederacies," he discusses the economic dimension of veteran silence in the late 1860s and 1870s among former soldiers in the South. He adds this factor to the already-existing hypothesis that the war was still too emotional a topic for veterans to discuss at that stage of their lives.

6. The authoritative source on northern free labor ideology remains that of Eric Foner, who examines it in *Free Soil, Free Labor, Free Men* as part of his study on the birth of the Republican Party. See in particular Chapter 1, which provides an overview of the concept of free labor in the antebellum North. Although the self-made man has received extensive attention over the years, Irvin Wyllie's classic *The Self-Made Man in America* remains the most reliable and accessible work on this still-influential belief.

7. For more information on the modernization of the army during the Civil War, see in particular Chapter 2 of Edward Hagerman's *The American Civil War and the Origins of Modern Warfare*. Here the author discusses the reorganization and growing professionalization of the Army of the Potomac under the leadership of General McClellan.

8. See Alan Trachtenberg, *The Incorporation of America*. Trachtenberg explains what he means by "incorporation of America" in the preface, with the following chapters serving as evidence of his theory.

9. The Roman historian Livy has provided us with the most widely known version of the Cincinnatus story. See *The History of Rome*, Book 3, Chapter 26. For the biblical quote about turning swords into ploughshares see Isaiah 2:4.

10. The caption that accompanies the digital image of this painting on the New York Metropolitan Museum of Art's website identifies the man's unit as part of the Second Corps, First Division, Sixty-First New York Volunteer Regiment.

11. On page 431 of John De Forest's novel *Miss Ravenel's Conversion from Secession to Loyalty* (examined in the previous chapter), the returned veteran Edward Colburne asserts, "I want some clothes. I can't go out in these filthy rags. I am loaded and disreputable with the sacred southern soil. I must be measured for a citizen's suit immediately."

12. Christopher Kent Wilson, "Winslow Homer's *The Veteran in a New Field*," 12.

13. Cyrus McCormick patented his horse-drawn reaper in 1854. Although it would not become a commonplace sight on American farms until the 1880s, company records show that in 1865 nearly four thousand of his "self-rakers" and "mowers" were produced. For an examination of the McCormick reaper works see Chapter 4 of David Hounshell's *From the American System to Mass Production*. A chart derived from data contained in the McCormick estate papers appears on page 161 of that chapter. Chapter 5 of Carroll

NOTES TO PAGES 52–60

Pursell's *The Machine in America* provides an excellent overview of the mechanization process of American agriculture.

14. Russell Sturgis, "The Sixth Annual Exhibition of the Artist's Fund Society of New York," 663.

15. "Review of *The Veteran in a New Field*," 268 (my emphasis).

16. Ibid., 268.

17. There is some uncertainty about the date of publication for Cummings's pamphlet, as no year is included on the title page and multiple editions seem to be in circulation. Two copies of Cumming's work are housed at the Newberry Library in Chicago, both of which were examined for inclusion in this chapter. The first is dated by the Newberry catalog as circa 1885 and the second as circa 1888. These dates have been determined from references in the pamphlet to Grand Army national encampments. An additional version of this work, dated circa 1892, was uncovered in the collection of the William L. Clements Library in Ann Arbor, Michigan. Unless otherwise noted, all quotations from *The Great War Relic* in this chapter come from the circa 1888 edition, which contains the most complete version of Charles Cummings's biography. For a brief record confirming Cummings's military service with the Twenty-Eighth Michigan, see *The Civil War Soldiers and Sailors Database*, operated by the United States National Park Service.

18. Charles Cummings, *The Great War Relic*, 7.

19. Ibid., 8.

20. Ibid., 8–9.

21. Ibid., 9.

22. Unlike Cummings's pamphlet, Robson's publication has the date printed on the title page of each edition. The Newberry Library owns two copies of the work, one dated 1876 and the other 1888. Both editions were examined for inclusion in this chapter. It is not clear how many other editions of the work were originally published.

23. John Robson, *How a One Legged Rebel Lives*, 47–48, 113.

24. Ibid., iii–v.

25. Ibid., 115–17.

26. William Jones, "Letter," 1.

27. *Soldiers' and Patriots' Biographical Album*, 52.

28. Trimble, *History of the Ninety-Third Regiment Illinois Volunteer Infantry*, 363.

29. The first Homestead Act of 1862 allowed the head of a family who was a U.S. citizen and at least twenty-one years of age to claim 160 acres of federal land for a nominal filing fee. If the person lived on that land for five years, they were eligible to receive a title for it. They could also purchase the land after six months for $1.25 per acre. The Homestead Act of 1864 revised the original act, making special provisions for Union veterans. In particular, it allowed veterans to claim land through a representative if unable to do so in person due to military service or disability. See HR Bill 242 and S Bill 60, 38th Congress, First Session. As in past wars, homesteads rather than pensions were originally envisioned as the primary means of government recompense for its veterans, with pensions going primarily to those permanently disabled in battle and unable to work. For more information on veterans and homesteads in the antebellum United States, see James W. Oberly, *Sixty Million Acres*.

30. Trimble, *History of the Ninety-Third Regiment Illinois Volunteer Infantry*, 363.
31. Ibid., 363.
32. *Soldiers' and Patriots' Biographical Album*, 100.
33. Levi Downs, *Letter to His Sister*.
34. Downs, *Letter to His Sister Louisa*.
35. Todd DePastino, *Citizen Hobo*, 17.
36. See Judy Hilkey, *Character Is Capital*, 58, 102–3.
37. For a nineteenth-century perspective on the growing power of the railroads and their corrosive effect on government see Adams, "The Government and the Railroad Corporations."
38. The literature on the "Lost Cause" mythology is extensive. Perhaps the best overview is that provided by Gaines Foster in *Ghosts of the Confederacy*. For more information on the "New South" movement, which provided an alternative to the Lost Cause, see Paul M. Gaston's, *The New South Creed*.
39. Literary critic Edmund Wilson referred to Cooke as "an amiable Virginian, who inhabited a world of chivalry that was partly perhaps real but was in any case very much colored by the fantasies of chivalric fiction." See *Patriotic Gore*, 192.
40. The basic distinction between a natural gentleman and his aristocratic counterpart (i.e., the gentry) is the factor of socialization. Gentry are trained to their social role as gentleman, whereas natural gentleman seem born to their social position and often belie their origins in how they comport themselves. An excellent example of the natural gentleman can be found in the antebellum fiction of James Fenimore Cooper, whose character Natty Bumppo is the quintessential natural gentleman. In southern fiction, the natural gentleman (especially after the war) had been conspicuously absent, which is what makes Cooke's attempt to utilize this figure in 1870 so interesting. For an in-depth examination of the natural gentleman concept, see Chapter 3 of Stow Persons's *The Decline of American Gentility*.
41. John Esten Cooke, *The Heir of Gaymount*, 12, 14, 16.
42. Ibid., 32, 33, 35.
43. Mary Jo Bratton argues in her essay "John Esten Cooke and His 'Confederate Lies'" that Cooke "was at best an ambivalent apostle of the traditional Southern way of life." According to Bratton, Cooke's prewar fiction already showed a preference for the "natural gentleman" of western Virginia as opposed to the tidewater gentry of eastern Virginia. See Bratton, n.p.
44. John Beaty, *John Esten Cooke, Virginian*, 124.
45. Although Tuggmuddle's antecedents are debatable, his progeny are numerous, ranging from Jonadab Leech in Thomas Nelson Page's novel *Red Rock* (1899) to Faulkner's famous Snopes family that appears in the narrative trilogy begun by *The Hamlet* (1940). What these poor white characters have in common is that they are objects for the projection of southern cultural anxieties: their negative portrayals absorb a wide variety of concerns connected with social changes in the South.
46. Critics have noted the prescient attitude toward southern agriculture in *The Heir of Gaymount*. Jack Wills observes in his biography of John Esten Cooke for the *Dictionary of Literary Biography* that *The Heir of Gaymount* "anticipates Ellen Glasgow's *Barren*

Ground (1925) by half a century." Wayne Mixon makes a similar observation regarding Cooke's forward-looking commentary on agricultural practices in the postwar South. See Wills, n.p.; and Mixon, *Southern Writers and the New South Movement*, 23–28.

47. Cooke, qtd. in Beaty, *John Esten Cooke, Virginian*, 161.

48. A review of Tourgée's body of work demonstrates that his interest in the shifting nature of northern political economy was not limited to *Figs and Thistles*. His later novels *Eighty-Nine; or, The Grand Master's Secret* (1888), an attack on the Standard Oil Company, and *Murvale Eastman, Christian Socialist* (1890) are both scathing critiques of corporate capitalism in the late-nineteenth-century United States.

49. The concept of the "jeremiad" as a distinct literary form and rhetorical technique is explored by Sacvan Bercovitch in *The American Jeremiad*. My understanding of Tourgée's narrative as a "corporate jeremiad" suggests a new theme for the jeremiad, rather than arguing for a new understanding of the concept as a whole.

50. Markham Churr's combat experiences in the novel echo those of the author, including Tourgée near-paralyzing accident during his first engagement. Tourgée was hit in the back by the wheel of a racing gun carriage, and it was uncertain after Bull Run whether he would be able to walk again. The main area where imagination takes over from biography is in Churr's promotion to brigadier general and his eventual election to Congress. Tourgée left the war at the rank of lieutenant, resigning from the army due to ongoing problems with his back. Moreover, his highest-ranking government post was that of American consul at Bordeaux, France, held in the last years of his life.

51. Tourgée, *Figs and Thistles*, 338.

52. Ibid., 353.

53. Given the novel's date of publication and the way the T.C.R. company scandal is described, it seems likely that Tourgée had in mind the Crédit Mobilier scandal (1872–73). In order to cover its potential losses, the board of directors of the Union Pacific Railroad created a shell construction corporation known as Crédit Mobilier of America. Charging inflated prices for construction contracts, the excess money went straight into the pockets of these Union Pacific Railroad executives. They then used a considerable portion of this money to influence congressmen to vote for more government subsidies and land grants for the transcontinental railroad. The scandal was uncovered by the *New York Sun* in September 1872 in the middle of Grant's campaign for a second term in office, and implicated his vice president, Schuyler Colfax. Many other politicians (including James Garfield) were caught up in this scandal, but the only ones to be officially censured were congressmen Oakes Ames of Massachusetts and James Brooks of New York. Ames had been responsible for distributing Crédit Mobilier stock to other legislators in return for their votes. Brooks, as government director of the Union Pacific Railroad, was prohibited from owning its stock. For more information on the scandal and its investigation see Logan Douglas Trent, *The Credit Mobilier*, as well as Chapter 16 of Mark Wahlgren Summers's *The Era of Good Stealings*.

54. Tourgée's claim that Union veterans were a bulwark against Gilded Age corruption seems odd given the scandal-plagued political reputation of Union general turned president Ulysses S. Grant. On this particular Union veteran's postwar record, Tourgée remains strangely silent in the novel.

55. For more information on the surprise presidential nomination of James Garfield at the 1880 Republican National Convention in Chicago, see Chapter 5 of Kenneth Ackerman's *Dark Horse*.

56. Although numerous passing references to Garfield's assassination can be found in a number of works on politics during the period, the most extensive examination of the assassination and its aftermath is James Clark's *The Murder of James A. Garfield*.

57. "Review of *Figs and Thistles*," *Chicago Daily Inter-Ocean*, 4.

58. Hilkey, *Character Is Capital*, 127.

3. Narrating Traumatic Experience in Civil War Memoir

1. For more on this supposed period of veteran silence see the epilogue to Gerald Linderman's *Embattled Courage*, and also the opening chapters to Mary Dearing's history of the Grand Army of the Republic, *Veterans in Politics*. Gaines Foster addresses the issue of silence among Confederate veterans in Chapters 1 and 2 of *Ghosts of the Confederacy*.

2. The list of research studies on combat trauma written since the end of the Vietnam War is too large to cite in its entirety. Among the more influential studies on the topic are Jonathan Shay, *Achilles in Vietnam*, and Bessel Van der Kolk, Alexander McFarlane, and Lars Weisaeth (eds.), *Traumatic Stress*. For an overview of attitudes toward trauma within the academic community during the twentieth and twenty-first century see Nigel Hunt, *Memory, War, and Trauma*, and Ruth Leys *Trauma: A Genealogy*.

3. Dean, *Shook over Hell*, 100.

4. Research by David Blight and Drew Gilpin Faust are two examples of this intriguing trend. In *Race and Reunion*, Blight notes that "Civil War soldiers saw innocence collide with evil, beauty with hideous destruction, heroism with venality, absurdity with idealism, and with time they were to write . . . about those ironies" (140). He insinuates in this statement that Civil War veterans experienced combat trauma, and yet, rather than further develop that assertion, Blight shifts the focus from matters of personal reconciliation of those traumas to the role that veterans exerted (or in some cases failed to exert) in matters of national political reconciliation. Drew Gilpin Faust's *This Republic of Suffering* engages in a rhetorical strategy similar to Blight's. She acknowledges the role that killing on a mass scale played in creating trauma among veterans, but sees veteran trauma as a sign of the paradigm shift in national understanding of death that resulted from the Civil War. See in particular Chapters 5 and 6, which address the civilian need to assign meaning to the vast numbers of Civil War dead and the changed rites of mourning. Blight's and Faust's casual way of invoking the concept of veteran trauma suggests it is an established fact in the study of Civil War veterans that does not need further discussion. Paradoxically, the rest of their work serves to undermine the suggestion that veterans of the Civil War experienced the phenomenon. Trauma thus develops into simply another way of understanding the generalized experience of suffering by soldiers as well as civilians in the war.

5. Posttraumatic stress disorder was not officially recognized until 1980, when it first appeared in the DSM-III, the standard handbook for treatment and classification

of psychiatric disorders. See Chapter 1 of Dean, *Shook over Hell*, for an overview of the emergence of PTSD as a medical condition.

6. One of the best-known proponents of the Civil War as the "good war" is James McPherson. See in particular *For Cause and Comrades*.

7. J. M. Da Costa, "On Irritable Heart," 38.

8. The terms "melancholy" and "nostalgia" were used interchangeably by nineteenth-century American doctors as they sought to understand mental illnesses among Civil War veterans. Consequently, these terms are used as synonyms throughout this chapter even though contemporary research tends to examine them separately from each other. Although currently out of print, the best history of the medical understanding of melancholy remains Stanley W. Jackson's *Melancholia and Depression*. For an overview of the now-superseded medical concept of nostalgia see George Rosen's essay "Nostalgia."

9. Janet discovered an area in the psyche that housed what he called "subconscious fixed ideas." These "idées fixe" included what we would know refer to as traumatic memories. He argued that such memories were "apt to be very dangerous . . . because they are no longer under the control of the personality." Furthermore, the obsessive quality of these memories ensured the sufferer would be indelibly attached to them, despite their destructiveness to the patient's health and well-being. See *Psychological Healing*, 596.

10. The first soldier's homes were created before the Civil War as asylums or long-term hospital facilities for severely physically disabled veterans from the Regular Army and the United States Navy, but a vast influx during the war of wounded Union soldiers strained this system to the breaking point. Furthermore, the societal distinction between the citizen-soldier volunteer and members of the Regular Army seemed to necessitate the creation of a separate system of soldiers' homes for volunteers. Judith Cetina's unpublished dissertation "A History of Veterans' Homes in the United States, 1811–1930" offers a comprehensive history of the system of soldiers' homes; in fact, it is one of the few studies to examine the first home for veterans created in the United States, the sailors' home in Philadelphia that opened in 1811. Patrick Kelly's *Creating a National Home* examines the movement to create homes for Union volunteer soldiers after the Civil War. For information on the much-later movement to create soldiers' homes for Confederate veterans, see R. B. Rosenburg's *Living Monuments*, particularly Chapter 4, which examines the creation of a Confederate soldiers' home in Georgia.

11. See "Advertisement for the Missouri Soldiers' Home," *Confederate Veteran*, 302.

12. Dean, *Shook over Hell*, 141–42.

13. Cathy Caruth, *Unclaimed Experience*, 4.

14. Bessel van der Kolk, "The Body Keeps the Score," 229; "Trauma and Memory," 287.

15. Ruth Leys, *Trauma*, 305. Leys offers a lengthy critique of Cathy Caruth's theory of trauma in Chapter 8.

16. James Pennebaker and Janel Seagal, "Forming a Story," 1243, 1250–51.

17. Ambrose Bierce, "What I Saw of Shiloh," 110.

18. "Review of *In the Midst of Life*," 15

19. Kalí Tal, *Worlds of Hurt*, 16.

20. The most commonly cited example is that of the German *Freikorps* that arose following the First World War. In his book *The Culture of Defeat*, Wolfgang Schivelbusch

compares the Ku Klux Klan movement in the South to the later German *Freikorps*. My contention in this chapter, and to a certain extent throughout the project as a whole, is that defeat was not a necessarily correlative for such a sense of alienation. In fact, many northern veterans whose hopes for the nation were unbounded at the war's end, became far more disillusioned than their southern opponents as they watched the nation descend into economic turmoil in the 1880s and '90s and turn away from what they believed to be its core "American" values.

21. Oliver Wendell Holmes, Jr., "Memorial Day," 15.
22. Gerald Linderman, *Embattled Courage*, 280.
23. Robert Johnson, *Remembered Yesterdays*, 213–15.
24. See Chapter 19 of John Marszalek, *Sherman*, for more information on Sherman's struggles with politicians as commanding general of the Army.
25. See Marszalek, *Sherman*, 465, and Stanley Hirshson, *The White Tecumseh*, 357.
26. See Marszalek, *Sherman*, 164–65.
27. "General Sherman's Book," *St. Louis Globe-Democrat*, 4; "New Publications," *San Francisco Daily Evening Bulletin*, 1.
28. See Hirshson, *The White Tecumseh*, 356.
29. See "Sherman–Boynton," *Arkansas Gazette*, 5.
30. Michael Fellman, introduction to Sherman, *Memoirs*, xix.
31. William Tecumseh Sherman, *Memoirs*, 613.
32. Ibid., 479.
33. Ibid., 486, 487, 488, 489, 492.
34. Ibid., 496, 497.
35. Ibid., 544–47.
36. Marszalek, *Sherman*, 249.
37. Sherman, *Memoirs*, 595, 597.
38. Much ink has been spilled on whether the Civil War was the first "total war" in the history of the United States. In an effort to avoid getting mired in this controversy, I have taken the view throughout this project that the Civil War was a "transitional war" that blended elements of "modern" war with older models of combat. As such, it seems reasonable to assume that Sherman and his army would engage in a limited war of destruction against the civilian population rather than the type of "total war" later practiced by the Germans in Europe or the Japanese in the Pacific during the Second World War. For more information on the distinction between "hard war" and "total war," see Chapter 8 of Mark Grimsley, *The Hard Hand of War*.
39. Sherman, *Memoirs*, 583, 643.
40. Ulysses S. Grant, *Personal Memoirs*, xxix.
41. See above, note 39.
42. Sherman, *Memoirs*, 304.
43. Ibid., 724.
44. For more information on the military memoir genre see Harari, "Military Memoirs."
45. For more information on life writing among the upper classes in nineteenth-century America see Scott Casper's *Constructing American Lives*. Ann Fabian's *The Un-*

varnished Truth provides one of the few book-length studies of personal narrative that doesn't focus exclusively on one type, such as slave narrative or conversion narrative.

46. For more information on the publication history of Watkins's narrative see M. Thomas Inge's introduction to *Company Aytch*, vii–viii.

47. In his essay "Reconstructing Rebellion," Andrew Higgins suggests a connection to the writings of the southern humorist Bill Arp. Arp was the pen name of Charles Henry Smith, a popular southern journalist who wrote for the *Atlanta Constitution* during the height of the period of reconciliation.

48. Sam Watkins, *Company Aytch*, 178–80.

49. Ibid., 108–9.

50. Ibid., 110.

51. Ronnie Janoff-Bulman, *Shattered Assumptions*, 51.

52. Watkins, *Company Aytch*, 74.

53. Ibid., 181.

54. It also must be noted that both the deaf–mute child and Peyton Farquhar are southerners living in close proximity to a war zone. Even though Bierce does not refrain from satirizing these two characters, he actually reserves his strongest scorn for northern civilians far removed from the sites of war. See in particular his short story "Killed at Resaca," in which a dead officer's sweetheart drops a letter from him to the ground because she notices a spot of blood on the edge of the paper.

55. C. Hartly Grattan was among the first scholars to see the author's "bitter" personality as a defining factor in his works, titling his 1929 biography *Bitter Bierce*. Subsequent critics like Edmund Wilson, Paul Fatout, and Daniel Aaron have further suggested that this bitterness developed from Bierce's war experiences. Although these critics do make the connection between the author's service in the war and the morbid nature of his tales, they do not examine at any length the narrative technique favored by the author in his war stories or consider its full significance.

56. Lawrence Berkove notes that "What I Saw of Shiloh" first appeared in the April 1874 issue of the *London Sketch-Book*. See page 17 and note 33 on page 194 of *A Prescription for Adversity*.

57. Besides its appearance in the *London Sketch-Book*, "What I Saw of Shiloh" also appeared in the San Francisco newspapers *The Wasp* in 1881 and the *Examiner* in 1898 before being printed as part of the "Bits of Autobiography" section of Bierce's collected works in 1909.

58. Ambrose Bierce, "What I Saw of Shiloh," 98, 104–5, 110.

59. Bierce, "Devil's Dictionary," 379.

60. G. Thomas Couser notes in his reading of "Jupiter-Doke, Brigadier General," "Dense and subtle in its historical allusions, it incorporates a sly but trenchant burlesque of some identifiable Civil War luminaries, most notably Ulysses S. Grant." He uses as evidence for this claim the name Jupiter-Doke, which he claims has a similar sound to that of Ulysses S. Grant, as well as Bierce's documented disdain for Grant's leadership at Shiloh. See "Writing the Civil War," 87.

61. Bierce, "Jupiter Doke, Brigadier-General," 80.

62. Ibid., 82.

63. Michael Schaefer, *Just What War Is*, 84.

64. Bierce, "One of the Missing," 246; "The Affair at Coulter's Notch," 160.

65. Because the story was later placed in the *Can Such Things Be?* group of stories in Bierce's *Collected Works* (1909), there is some confusion regarding its publication history. In their collection of Bierce's war fiction *Phantoms of a Blood-Stained Period*, Duncan and Klooster mistakenly note the date of the story's appearance as 1903. Bierce scholars S. T. Joshi and David Schultz, however, in their definitive work, *Ambrose Bierce*, list the story as first appearing in *Cosmopolitan* magazine in September 1908 under the title "The Man." I have decided to follow their dating for the genesis of this tale, based on the depth of their research, as the more authoritative.

66. Bierce, "A Resumed Identity," 303.

67. Ibid., 306–7.

68. As Stephen Kern notes in his book *The Culture of Time and Space*, the conceptualization and measurement of time was an obsession in the late nineteenth century. William James's essay "The Perception of Time" in the October 1886 issue of the *Journal of Speculative Philosophy* offers one example of horology in this period. For an extensive examination of the use of time in Bierce's fiction see Paul Juhasz's "No Matter What the Actual Hour May."

69. Bierce, "A Resumed Identity," 307–8.

70. Mary Grenander suggests as much in her analysis of the story. See Grenander, *Ambrose Bierce*, 99–102.

4. The Glorious Burden of the Aging Civil War Veteran

1. See in particular Chapter 1 of Kristin Hoganson's *Fighting for American Manhood*.

2. Gail Bederman addresses the perceived "crisis" in middle-class white manhood in the opening chapter of *Manliness and Civilization*, where she explores the impact of black male masculinity and the rising social status of middle-class white women on the dominant conception of manhood. For a thorough examination of the class issues involved in the late-nineteenth-century crisis in male identity, see Judy Hilkey's *Character Is Capital*, and Chapter 3 of Michael Kimmel's *Manhood in America*, which illustrate the corrosive effect of corporate life on the concept of the self-made man. See Mark Carnes, "Middle-Class Men and the Solace of Fraternal Ritual," for a discussion of how fraternal group formation combatted the perceived assaults against middle-class white manhood.

3. Hoganson, *Fighting for American Manhood*, 26.

4. For an overview of northern policies used to financially compensate Civil War veterans see Theda Skocpol, *Protecting Soldiers and Mothers*. James W. Oberly outlines pre–Civil War compensation policies for veterans in *Sixty Million Acres*. See Judith Cetina, "A History of Veterans' Homes in the United States, 1811–1930," for an overview of soldiers' homes. Patrick J. Kelly's *Creating a National Home*, and R. B. Rosenburg's *Living Monuments*, provide an outline of soldiers' home policies and construction in the post–Civil War nation.

5. The exact language of the act is quoted in the address of GAR commander in chief Russell Alger at the Twenty-Fourth National Encampment in 1890: "All persons who

served ninety days or more in the military or naval service of the United States during the late war of the rebellion, and who have been honorably discharged therefrom, and who are now or who may hereafter be suffering from a mental or physical disability, of a permanent character, not the result of their own vicious habits, which incapacitates them from the performance of manual labor in such a degree as to render them unable to earn a support, shall, upon making due proof of the fact, according to such rules and regulations as the Secretary of the Interior may provide, be placed upon the list of invalid pensioners of the United States, and be entitled to receive a pension not exceeding twelve dollars per month, and not less than six dollars per month, proportioned to the degree of inability to earn support." See Grand Army of the Republic, *Journal of the Twenty-Fourth Annual Session of the National Encampment*, 9. The key passages of the Dependent Pension Act were also published on the front page of the *New York Tribune*'s June 29, 1890, edition along with information on how to apply for a pension under the new act.

6. "Robbing the Soldiers," *Philadelphia Times*, 1.

7. "Veterans in the Census," *New York Times*, 5.

8. The actual cost of Civil War pensions is rarely discussed by the popular press during the period of great debate over pension expansion in the late 1880s and 1890s. In the annual report of the commissioner of pensions for 1891, one year after the passage of the Dependent Pension Act, $118,548,960 is recorded for total pension disbursements to veterans of the United States Army and Navy as well as their widows and dependents. For 1889, $89,131,968 was disbursed. This represents a 33 percent increase in government expenditures on veterans and their dependents. Although this number includes veterans of the army and navy from earlier wars as well as their dependents, it seems reasonable to assume that the majority of those persons receiving government pensions in both 1889 and 1891 would have been veterans of the Union army. These numbers suggest that public concern over pension expenditures was warranted, but a full study of the national economy during this period would be necessary to substantiate that concern in quantitative terms. See Bureau of Statistics, *Statistical Abstract of the United States*, 320–23.

9. "Time to Halt," *New York Daily Tribune*, 6; "Untitled Editorial," *Daily News*, 4. The phrase "read out of the party" is a political idiom meant to remind readers of the important role newspaper editors played in nominating candidates for office. It suggests that the paper's political influence within the Republican Party might be negated through their poor choice of editorial.

10. Pierre Nora, "Between Memory and History," 8.

11. See Chapter 6 of Kirk Savage, *Standing Soldiers, Kneeling Slaves*.

12. "More Than Half Are Dead," *Galveston News*, 19.

13. Department of the Interior, *Report on the Population of the United States at the Eleventh Census*, 803; Grand Army of the Republic, *Journal of the Thirty-First Annual Session of the National Encampment*, 91–92.

14. John Palmer, in Grand Army of the Republic, *Journal of the Twenty-Sixth Annual Session of the National Encampment*, 46.

15. An interesting study of the tortured mechanics of this relationship might be done through examining the institutional interplay between Sons of Veterans organizations

and the Civil War veteran organizations themselves. Founded much later than the Grand Army of the Republic, the United Confederate Veterans allowed their sons (and in some cases daughters) a far greater level of participation in reunions and day-to-day activities than did the Grand Army.

16. George Merrill, in Grand Army of the Republic, *Journal of the Sixteenth Annual Session of the National Encampment*, 869.

17. Duke Goodman, "Report of the Inspector General," 435.

18. Both interpretations are present in Perry Lentz's *Private Fleming at Chancellorsville*. Lentz says in his introduction, "*The Red Badge of Courage* is set firmly within the American Civil War. Its men are dressed, organized, arrayed, commanded, maneuvered, and above all armed as soldiers in the American Civil War were dressed, organized, arrayed, commanded, maneuvered, and armed." Then, paradoxically, after proving in eight chapters that Crane conducted extensive historical research to complete his novel and show us what Civil War combat was really like, Lentz concludes that Crane's final message to the reader is that "in a malevolent universe 'ideals' are ridiculous. There may be things worth cherishing . . . but the term 'ideals' implies that there is some system of nonmaterialistic value that the cosmos will validate; a ludicrous notion in a world where in fact 'they will get you in the end.'" See Lentz, 2, 257. Craig Warren also confronts this difficulty in *Scars to Prove It*, where the novel is read simultaneously as setting in motion twentieth-century writing on the Civil War while engaging in an accurate and affectionate reconstruction of the Civil War soldier's experience; see Chapter 1. To date, Matthew Bolton is the only critic to specifically identify the 1890s as the novel's proper context, but he understands that context as one of industrialization rather than tension between Civil War veterans and a new generation of middle-class white males. See "*The Red Badge of Courage* in the Context of the 1890s."

19. See Linda Davis, *Badge of Courage*, 64. Here she speculates on some of the novel's possible sources, including hypothetical conversations with Civil War veterans, something she extrapolates from the much-later recollections of Crane's friend Frederic Lawrence: "For years he had never failed to draw out from Civil War veterans their memories, their experiences in the everyday life of an army, and he knew more of war as it appears to the private in the ranks than most of the historians." Lawrence, "The Real Stephen Crane," 120.

20. Department of the Interior, *Report on the Population of the United States at the Eleventh Census*, 803–4; Grand Army of the Republic, *Journal of the Twenty-Sixth Annual Session of the National Encampment*, 128, 130.

21. Christopher Benfey, *The Double Life of Stephen Crane*, 47.

22. Lew Wallace, in Grand Army of the Republic, *Journal of the Thirty-First Annual Session of the National Encampment*, 230.

23. Bill Brown offers an alternate reading of Crane's relationship to college sports in *The Material Unconscious*, 125–42. Here he suggests a connection between football and war in *The Red Badge of Courage* that ties both activities to the emerging late-nineteenth-century culture of spectatorship. For an overview of the history of American football and its role on college campuses in the nineteenth century, see Chapter 7 of

Ronald Smith's *Sports and Freedom*. Kim Townsend provides a more intimate portrait of college athletics at Harvard University in the 1890s and early 1900s in *Manhood at Harvard*, 97–120.

24. Miles Orvell states that in *The Red Badge of Courage* "the author seems to identify effortlessly with the point of view of his main character, a youth enamored of war." Although I agree that Crane, like his main character, is "enamored of war," "effortless" is precisely the wrong word for describing Crane's connection to Henry Fleming. The author may indeed be enamored of the veteran's social position represented by his main character, but that does not mean he fully sympathizes with his protagonist. See Orvell, *The Real Thing*, 130.

25. Stephen Crane, *The Red Badge of Courage*, Appleton edition, 21. Citations of the Appleton Text refer to the standard edition of the text published in 1895 that is still commonly used. I will also be referring in this chapter to the manuscript edition as published by Henry Binder, see note 34, below, and the newspaper edition of the narrative that was syndicated in 1894 by Irving Bacheller.

26. One of the few critics to resist this trend is John Clendenning, who uses the Oedipus complex to interpret Henry's relationship to the man-making power of war. He says of the protagonist that "when the father is dead, absent, or otherwise unavailable, sons tend to develop a sense of manhood based on fantasy." Even though this may prove true of Henry Fleming, who is a fatherless boy trying to live up to the ideals of the "Greek-like struggles" he had read about as a child, it does not adequately address the more intriguing struggle that goes on between Crane and the Civil War generation his main character represents. See Clendenning, "Visions of War and Versions of Manhood," 27.

27. Crane, *Correspondence*, 69.

28. Of these two pieces, the first sounds much closer in language to the Crane we have come to know. Thus, even though "The Gratitude of a Nation" can easily be traced back to Crane through handwriting analysis, the preeminent Crane scholar Stanley Wertheim states in his *Stephen Crane Encyclopedia*, "'Veterans' Ranks Thinner by a Year' seems closer than the report unpublished in his lifetime to Crane's description of the piece he submitted to the New York *Press*" (351).

29. Crane, "Veterans' Ranks Thinner by a Year," reprinted in Gullason, 158.

30. Ibid., 159.

31. This previously unpublished manuscript was found by Daniel Hoffman in 1957 on a scrap of paper that also contained the short poem "A soldier, young in years, young in ambitions." It is included in the Harper edition of *The Red Badge of Courage*, edited by Hoffman, and also can be found in *The New York City Sketches*, a collection of Crane's journalism edited by R. W. Stallman and E. R. Hagemann.

32. Crane, "The Gratitude of a Nation," 57.

33. Ibid., 58–59.

34. It is impossible to discuss Henry Binder and the manuscript version of *The Red Badge of Courage* without addressing the controversy associated with it. Binder, supported by his mentor Hershel Parker, claimed that Stephen Crane's editor at Appleton,

Ripley Hitchcock, prevented Crane from publishing the novel he originally intended. He argued that Hitchcock compelled the author to remove offensive passages from the novel, thereby "maiming" the text. Binder edited and published the handwritten manuscript, which he believed to be the authoritative text of the novel. Although I will be referring to the manuscript edition of the novel as well as the syndicated newspaper version of the story, I do not believe that either of these texts holds a privileged position over the standard Appleton text. They are cited as evidence of the linguistic compromises Crane needed to make in order to meet and (hopefully) shape the "horizon of expectations" of his audience. For the most recent examination of this textual controversy see Michael Guemple's "A Case for the Appleton *Red Badge of Courage*."

35. Crane, *The Red Badge of Courage*, Appleton edition, 54.
36. Crane, *The Red Badge of Courage*, manuscript edition, 55.
37. Crane, *The Red Badge of Courage*, Appleton edition, 26.
38. Crane, *Correspondence*, 161.
39. Alexander McClurg, "The Red Badge of Hysteria," 179.
40. In late 1894, Bacheller sold this version to a number of newspapers in the United States, including the *Philadelphia Press*, the *New York Press*, the *San Francisco Examiner*, and the *Nebraska State-Journal*, where a young Willa Cather helped set the type for the press.
41. Corwin Knapp Linson, *My Stephen Crane*, 37. Crane scholars have typically turned to these comments for clues about the novel's origins.
42. Crane, *The Red Badge of Courage*, newspaper edition, 117.
43. Crane, *Correspondence*, 81.
44. Crane, *The Red Badge of Courage*, Appleton edition, 69.
45. Randall Allred, "The Gilded Images of Memory," 100.
46. Crane, "The Veteran," 230–31. Little Jimmie's loss of idealism should not come as a surprise. It seems natural given the circumstances and fits a general theme about the youthful loss of innocence found in Crane's works as a whole. Maggie's attempt to re-create in her Bowery apartment the scenery of the conventional domestic novel and her vision of the womanizing Pete as the "beau ideal" of a man are just two of the more poignant examples in Crane's fiction of this process of disillusionment at work.
47. Ibid., 231.
48. The concept of "storm and stress," or Sturm und Drang, first became associated with the maturation period known as adolescence in the work of the nineteenth-century psychologist G. Stanley Hall. See Chapter 8 in the first volume of Hall's major work, *Adolescence*.
49. General Dan Sickles was in fact present at the Battle of Chancellorsville, where the fictional Private Henry Fleming claims to have run away. Sickles was also a resident of New York after the war, the state to which Henry, a member of the fictional 304th New York Volunteers, would have presumably returned.
50. Crane, "The Veteran," 233.
51. Ibid., 231.
52. Bill Brown, *The Material Unconscious*, 160, 164.
53. Crane, "Marines Signaling Under Fire at Guantanamo," 150–51.

54. "The Union's New Decoration Day," *New Orleans Daily Picayune*, 9
55. "Veterans Unfit for War," *New York Times*, 2.

5. Racial Uplift and the Figure of the Black Soldier

1. The Second Confiscation Act of July 17, 1862, was the first legislation to use the phrase "forever free" in relation to fugitive slaves. Although the act did not require that a slave enlist in the Union army to be considered free, enlistment made it less likely that a master would sue to prove his allegiance to the northern government and thereby reclaim his slave. Legislation passed in March 1865 freed the families of fugitive slaves serving in the northern army nine months before the ratification of the Thirteenth Amendment (abolishing slavery in the United States) in December 1865. However, in practice, many black men serving in the U.S. Army used military authority to their advantage (regardless of legal precedent) in helping their families escape slavery. For the text of the Second Confiscation Act, see United States, *Statutes at Large*, Volume 12, pp. 589–92. Mary Berry examines the government's policy toward the families of fugitive slaves serving in Union regiments in Chapter 6 of her book *Military Necessity and Civil Rights Policy*. See especially pages 80–82.

2. An extensive body of research exists on the experience of black men in the Union army. The classic study of the United States Colored Troops is Dudley Taylor Cornish's *The Sable Arm*. Other works examining black enlistment and service in the Civil War include Noah Andre Trudeau, *Like Men of War*; Richard M. Reid, *Freedom for Themselves*; Christian Samito, *Becoming American Under Fire*; and John David Smith (ed.), *Black Soldiers in Blue*.

3. For more on the relationship between black soldiers and their white officers see Joseph T. Glatthaar, *Forged in Battle*.

4. Black men were already serving in combat roles in the U.S. Navy prior to the outbreak of the Civil War, although a quota initiated in 1839 limited black enlistment to 5 percent of the navy's annual recruiting goals. I have chosen to examine African American soldiers rather than sailors in this chapter primarily because of the greater rhetorical power wielded by the image of the black soldier. Courting the image of the citizen-soldier, black troops had a greater cultural cachet than did black sailors, who were associated with an outcast profession. For more information on black enlistment in the navy prior to the Civil War, see Chapter 1 of Steven Ramold's *Slaves, Sailors, Citizens*. His study also offers an excellent overview of black service in the navy from the Revolutionary War up to the Civil War. Barbara Tomblin's *Bluejackets and Contrabands* focuses primarily on the U.S. Navy's policy toward fugitive slave enlistment but offers some excellent insights into the role played by that branch of the military in the ongoing process of emancipation.

5. Historian Christian Samito has boldly claimed that without the extensive letter writing and speeches of these outspoken veterans, the passage of the Fourteenth and Fifteenth Amendments would not have been possible. See Chapter 6 of *Becoming American Under Fire*.

6. For a thorough examination of the court's opinion on black citizenship in the *Dred Scott* decision, see Chapter 15 of Don Fehrenbacher's *The Dred Scott Case*.

7. James Kettner, *The Development of American Citizenship*, 287.

8. Frederick Douglass, "Address for the Promotion of Colored Enlistments," 365 (my emphasis).

9. It is interesting to note that the infamous New York City draft riots broke out only a week after Douglass gave his speech. For information on the northern military draft see James W. Geary's *We Need Men*, particularly Chapters 6 and 9. See Chapter 4 of Paul D. Escott's *Military Necessity* for manpower mobilization in the southern states.

10. Ira Berlin, Joseph Reidy, and Leslie Rowland (eds.), *Freedom's Soldiers*, 95.

11. The First Confiscation Act of August 6, 1861, created the legal category of "contraband," and allowed the Union government to employ as laborers fugitive slaves that had been used to aid the Confederacy. However, it was not until the passage of the Militia Act of July 17, 1862, enacted on the same day as the Second Confiscation Act, that black men were legally allowed to serve in the United States armed services. Before that date they were prohibited from serving in state militias by the Militia Act of 1792 and in the Regular Army by recruiting policies dating from the 1820s. Following the passage of the 1862 Militia Act, black men were fighting as part of the Union army in Kansas, Louisiana, and South Carolina. Of these units, only those created by General Benjamin Butler, the 1st and 2nd Louisiana Native Guards, were recognized by the federal government prior to January 1, 1863. However, they were still considered primarily a state militia and not part of the U.S. Army. This would remain the case until the creation of the United States Colored Troops as a department within the army bureaucracy on May 22, 1863. For an overview of the evolution in Union enlistment policy in regard to black males see Dudley Taylor Cornish, *The Sable Arm*, particularly Chapters 2, 4, and 7. The text of both Confiscation Acts and the Militia Act of 1862 can be found in Volume 12 of United States, *Statutes at Large*, 319, 589–92, 597–600, respectively. The Regular Army policy toward black enlistment can be found in United States, *Revised United States Army Regulations*, Article 60, Section 929.

12. Edwin Redkey (ed.), *A Grand Army of Black Men*, 205.

13. Elijah Marrs, *Life and History of the Rev. Elijah P. Marrs*, 22.

14. Samito examines the numerous ambiguities associated with the concept of citizenship in the antebellum era in Chapter 1 of *Becoming American Under Fire*. Chapter 10 of James Kettner's *The Development of American Citizenship* examines the same phenomenon but from a perspective more legal than cultural.

15. For more on the paradoxical view of black manhood in the Civil War era and its implications for military service see Jennifer James, *A Freedom Bought with Blood*, 19; Richard Yarborough, "Race, Violence, and Manhood," 174; and Carole Emberton, "Only Murder Makes Men."

16. This number is taken from George Washington Williams, *The Negro Troops in the War of the Rebellion*, 139–40. Noah Trudeau's research on the enlistment of black soldiers in *Like Men of War* further supports this enlistment figure. See Trudeau, xviii.

17. It is interesting to note that no such policy of segregation existed in the U.S. Navy. Black sailors served alongside white midshipmen. As in the army, however, African Americans were denied promotion to positions that would have placed them in charge

of whites. For more information on conditions of service for black sailors during the Civil War, see Chapter 4 of Steven J. Ramold's *Slaves, Sailors, Citizens*.

18. Heather Andrea Williams notes in her essay "Commenced to Think Like a Man" that "African American soldiers, even more so than black civilians, expressed a special fervor for literacy." See Williams, 212.

19. Marrs, *Life and History of the Rev. Elijah P. Marrs*, 22; Berlin, Reidy, and Rowland (eds.), *Freedom's Soldiers*, 618.

20. Marrs, *Life and History of the Rev. Elijah P. Marrs*, 61. Black soldiers were not the only ones to feel a greater sense of authority from their work on behalf of former slaves in contraband camps. Chandra Manning examines how black women, children, and noncombatants re-created their sense of self in these camps, and in the process came to redefine what it meant to be a U.S. citizen. See "Working for Citizenship in Civil War Contraband Camps."

21. The historian Ira Berlin notes, "The general poverty of the black community made the pay question an especially sensitive issue . . . black soldiers needed regular wages to support themselves and their families and a few extra dollars a month could mean the difference between subsistence and destitution." See Berlin, Reidy, and Rowland (eds.), *Freedom's Soldiers*, 363.

22. Redkey (ed.), *A Grand Army of Black Men*, 233 (my emphasis).

23. The congressional appropriations act to equalize the pay of black soldiers can be found in United States War Department, *The War of the Rebellion*, Series 3, Volume 4, p. 448. Ira Berlin, Joseph P. Reidy, and Leslie S. Rowland (eds.) offers an overview of the pay equalization issue in *Freedom, Series 2: The Black Military Experience*, pp. 362–68, as does Joseph Glatthaar in Chapter 9 of *Forged in Battle*.

24. Steven Hahn's *A Nation Under Our Feet* is an important reminder that African American communities already possessed a form of political and legal organization prior to the end of the Civil War. These systems were of necessity localized and hidden from the white population to avoid reprisals, but they served as the foundation for blacks to learn official legal and political procedures in the era of Reconstruction. They were thus not starting their lessons in citizenship rights with a blank slate. See Hahn, especially Chapters 2 and 4.

25. Steven Hahn et al. (eds.), *Freedom, Series 3, Volume 1: Land and Labor*, 970.

26. Redkey (ed.), *A Grand Army of Black Men*, 209.

27. William Cooper Nell, *The Colored Patriots of the American Revolution*, 380; Berlin, Reidy, and Rowland (eds.), *Freedom's Soldiers*, 784.

28. The all black Twenty-Fifth Corps, consisting of over forty regiments, was sent to the Texas border in June 1865 to prevent the Mexican Civil War from spreading onto U.S. territory. Other black units were scattered all over the former Confederacy, providing a much-needed police force to its war-torn cities and towns. According to Trudeau, the last black regiment to be mustered out was the 124th USCT, which left the service on December 20, 1867. See *Like Men of War*, 461. For more information on the service of black soldiers on the Texas border and in southern states during Reconstruction see Trudeau, Chapter 18. Chapter 7 of Richard Reid's *Freedom for Themselves* offers a more in-depth

examination of the USCT's role in garrisoning southern towns, but focuses exclusively on North Carolina African American regiments that served in their "home" state.

29. Because officers were chosen by examination boards appointed by the USCT rather than state officials, it was rare that the officers of a black regiment came from one predominant state or locality. The ranks of the enlisted men were even more diverse than were those of the officer corps. A chart in the back of Edward A. Miller Jr's *The Black Civil War Soldiers of Illinois* show that in Company A only two of the men came from Illinois. The majority were from the border states of Missouri and Kentucky, where slavery had yet to be abolished.

30. Richard Reid, *Freedom for Themselves*, 304.

31. Berlin, Reidy, and Rowland (eds.), *Freedom's Soldiers*, 811–12, 822.

32. The rationale behind denying black men the right to serve as officers was partially based on the white belief in black racial inferiority. Few believed that black men possessed enough discipline and self-control to be a soldier let alone command troops in battle. Additionally, army officials feared that allowing black soldiers to obtain commissions, even if they were earned for bravery on the battlefield, would lead to dissension within the ranks. Colonel C. W. Foster, assistant adjutant general in charge of the Bureau of Colored Troops, put it succinctly, saying, "The real question presented then is—are white officers and men prepared to acknowledge and obey the colored man, or officer as a military superior?" See Berlin, Reidy, and Rowland (eds.), *Freedom, Series 2: The Black Military Experience*, 304. The answer to Foster's question clearly was no. Thus literate black men were frequently promoted only to the rank of sergeant unless they found promotion outside the ordinary chain of command in the positions of chaplain or surgeon. For a list of black officers in the Union army see Appendix 3 of Joseph T. Glatthaar's *Forged in Battle*. The highest volume of black officers in the Union army was in the regiments that once comprised the Louisiana Native Guard, in which Pinchback had served as a captain. These were state militia regiments authorized by General Butler in the fall of 1862, and were largely composed of free men of color from the upper-class mulattos of New Orleans.

33. Qtd. in Samito, *Becoming American Under Fire*, 160.

34. Foner, *Freedom's Lawmakers*, 158, 222–23.

35. Donald Shaffer, *After the Glory*, 53; Elizabeth Regosin and Donald Shaffer (eds.), *Voices of Emancipation*, 88; P. M. Jones (ed.), *Forgotten Soldiers*, 25.

36. Jones, *Forgotten Soldiers*, 28–29, 31.

37. For T. F. M. Kay's full biography see *Soldiers' and Patriots' Biographical Album*, 741–42.

38. Foner, *Freedom's Lawmakers*, 216.

39. Biographical information on Alfred Fairfax comes from ibid., 73. For more information on the Exodusters see Nell Irvin Painter's *Exodusters*.

40. Donald Shaffer argues that "the idolization they received each Memorial Day and at many other times must have been a balm for the poverty that many still faced and for the fact that their numbers diminished [from death] more quickly than those of their Union and Confederate counterparts." Fitzhugh Brundage makes a similar claim that "public celebrations . . . provided blacks with highly visible platforms for both the

expression of black collective memory in general and the commemoration of black veterans in particular." See Shaffer, *After the Glory*, 65; Brundage, "Race, Memory, and Masculinity," 143.

41. George Washington Williams, *The Negro Troops in the War of the Rebellion*, 332.

42. "Friends of Illinois Club Celebrate Emancipation Day," *Chicago Daily Inter-Ocean*, 3.

43. "Emancipation Day in New Orleans," *Southwestern Christian Advocate*. Throughout the nineteenth century, there were three days on which the black community celebrated emancipation. The first was September 22, the date on which Abraham Lincoln initially signed the Emancipation Proclamation, and the second was January 1, the date that the proclamation officially became active in the rebel states. A third date used for the celebration of emancipation was in August, the month that Great Britain's law abolishing slavery in the West Indies went into effect. African American communities seem to have chosen their own dates to celebrate this event depending on local priorities, including such mundane but important factors as the weather.

44. "Emancipation Day," *Daily Gazette*, 2.

45. Paul Laurence Dunbar, "We Wear the Mask," 71. Literary critic Kenny J. Williams states that Dunbar "must have been fully aware of the demands which the times made upon the novelist who desired popularity and who sought the approval of the American reading public." To meet those demands, Williams claims, Dunbar engaged in "veiling his views of life and masking his ideas of society." These attempts at misdirection, he argues, centered in his prose around the author's choice of characters and storylines, and in his poetry the heavy reliance on dialect. See Williams, "The Masking of the Novelist," 201.

46. By and large, critics have responded favorably to Dunbar's literary aesthetic. See Williams, "The Masking of the Novelist," and Lena Ampadu, "The Poetry of Paul Laurence Dunbar and the Influence of African Aesthetics." For a negative assessment read Addison Gayle Jr., "Literature as Catharsis."

47. Dunbar, "Recession Never," 36–37.

48. Unless otherwise noted, all biographical material on Dunbar comes from Peter Revell, *Paul Laurence Dunbar*.

49. William Dean Howells, "Introduction to 'Lyrics of Lowly Life,'" viii; Dunbar, "The Colored Soldiers," 50.

50. Jennifer Terry and Sharon D. Raynor bypass these conditional clauses in their otherwise-perceptive analyses of the poem. See Terry, "When Dey 'Listed Colored Soldiers,'" and Raynor, "Sing a Song Heroic."

51. Dunbar, "The Colored Soldiers," 51.

52. Critic Nassim Balestrini refers to this hesitant opening of the poem as a *captatio benevolentiae*. See, "National Memory and the Arts in Dunbar's War Poetry," 21.

53. Dunbar, "The Colored Soldiers," 51.

54. Dunbar, "Robert Gould Shaw," 221.

55. See James, *A Freedom Bought with Blood*, 84–97.

56. Dunbar, *The Fanatics*, 177, 181.

57. To the best of my knowledge, no critic has yet commented on the uncanny resemblance of the chapter title that precedes the narrative of the dead Captain Tom Waters's

return to Dorbury for burial—"The Homecoming of the Captain"—to the narrative written by Oliver Wendell Holmes Sr. for *The Atlantic*—"My Hunt After the Captain"—published in December 1862. Other similarities in phrasing suggest the need for further research on the connection between this section of Dunbar's novel and Holmes Sr.'s earlier narrative.

58. Many northern volunteer regiments raised in the early years of the Civil War were enlisted to serve for periods less than the duration. These varied between ninety days, nine months, and three years. As the war dragged on, these regiments were encouraged to reenlist for the duration as "veteran" units. Those units that chose not to reenlist, or which too small in numbers to retain their regimental status, returned home to muster out. For more on northern army enlistment policies see Eugene Murdock, *One Million Men*, and James Geary, *We Need Men*.

59. Clement L. Vallandigham served in the U.S. House of Representatives from May 1858 to March 1863, representing Ohio's 3rd Congressional District. Known for his outspoken defense of slavery and states' rights, Vallandigham was arrested by Union officials on May 5, 1863, and tried by a military court for expressing his desire for peace with the Confederacy on any terms. He was deported to Confederate territory during the war, but returned to Ohio a short time later via Canada. For more on Vallandigham, see Frank L. Klement, *The Limits of Dissent*.

60. Dunbar, *The Fanatics*, 186.

61. Addison Gayle claims that Ed is "analogous to Nelse of *The Leopard's Spots* and Thomas Dixon's description of his black character is apropos Dunbar's description of Nigger Ed." Most critics do not go as far as Gayle, comparing Dunbar's fictional creation to that of an avowedly white racist author such as Dixon. Instead, they take the approach suggested by Kenny J. Williams, who sees Dunbar's writing style as masking his true opinions to shape the beliefs of his white audience. See Gayle, "Literature as Catharsis," 186. For Williams's argument see note 46, above.

62. James, *A Freedom Bought with Blood*, 92, 102.

63. Dunbar, *The Fanatics*, 240–44.

64. Ibid., 244.

65. Ibid., 246–49.

66. Ibid., 249.

67. For more information on the 1898 race riots in Wilmington, see David S. Cecelski and Timothy B. Tyson (eds.), *Democracy Betrayed*.

68. Dunbar, *The Fanatics*, 304.

69. The question of how valuable shared memories of the war were to black veterans is paramount in Barbara Gannon's *The Won Cause*. There she convincingly argues that Union veterans were able to recognize the heroism of black comrades while at the same time overlooking the social injustice carried out against African Americans as a whole in the postwar nation. Their white comrades treated black veterans with respect and a certain degree of equality, but they were not viewed as representative men of their race.

70. Andreá Williams asserts, "African-American literature as a medium does not simply reflect class relations but rather works to reproduce them." Dunbar, as Williams notes, enacts his vision of race and class articulation using "spatial boundaries" through

which "he attempts to make room for upwardly mobile black Americans on the written page and in his readers' imaginations." These boundaries exist in *The Fanatics*, but only as traces of a small-town Ohio way of life for antebellum free blacks that was destroyed by the emotional excess of war, which led the white citizens of Dorbury to mistake their free black neighbors for "contraband." See Williams, *Dividing Lines*, 6, 79.

71. Known primarily for her poetry, Frances Harper published only one novel prior to *Iola Leroy*, *Minnie's Sacrifice* (1867), which was serialized in the African American newspaper the *Christian Recorder*.

72. According to Stewart Tolnay and E. M. Beck, the number of black men lynched in the southern United States reached its peak in the last decade of the nineteenth century. For their analysis of black male lynchings in this decade see Chapter 2 of their study *A Festival of Violence*.

73. For an example of the traditional interpretation of Harper's novel see Lori Robison, "An 'Imperceptible Infusion' of Blood."

74. Elizabeth Young, *Disarming the Nation*, 211.

75. Frances Ellen Watkins Harper, *Iola Leroy*, 9.

76. This perspective counters the view of most veteran authors publishing in the 1880s and '90s. It is also contrary to the view of contemporary literary critics such as Don Dingledine. Examining a passage from Thomas Wentworth Higginson's memoir *Army Life in a Black Regiment*, in which a former slave who is now a soldier confronts his onetime mistress, Dingledine argues that military enlistment for this former slave represented a great "physical transformation from slave—'Bob'—to a federal soldier—Corporal Robert Sutton." See "The Whole Drama of the War," 1113.

77. Harper, *Iola Leroy*, 202.

78. Ibid.

79. Harper, "The Great Problem to Be Solved," 219.

80. P. Gabrielle Foreman makes this argument in her essay "Reading Aright."

81. Michael Borgstrom, "Face Value," 786.

82. See Kletzing and Crogman, *Progress of a Race*.

83. Barbara Gannon, *The Won Cause*, 5.

84. Joseph Wilson, *The Black Phalanx*, "Preface," n.p.

85. Historian Andrew Fleche notes that "joint war service provided white and black Union soldiers with shared experiences that set them apart from non-combatants regardless of their race or regional affiliation." See "Shoulder to Shoulder as Comrades Tried," 201.

86. Joseph Wilson, *The Black Phalanx*, 462.

87. "Protecting a Colored Veteran," *New York Times*, 1.

Epilogue

1. Tim O'Brien, "How To Tell a True War Story," 77.

2. Harari, *The Ultimate Experience*, 1, 6.

3. We see this paradox at work in the scholarship of Gerald Linderman. He describes a shift in the worldview of Civil War soldiers, from that of the premodern concept of

courage to the modern conception of war as an impersonal struggle between small pieces trapped in a vast engine of war. Yet he seems uncomfortable accepting that this shift has a lasting impact on veterans' identity. By their twilight years, in his view, somehow a faith in courage has been restored. See *Embattled Courage*, 296–97.

4. See note 20 in Chapter 3.

5. O'Brien, "How To Tell a True War Story," 80.

6. There is something uncanny about the fact that the protagonist of this film shares the same name as the Civil War–era philosopher and psychologist William James, who created the concept of a "moral equivalent of war." It is unclear whether this was an intentional decision on the part of the screenwriter, Mark Boal, or the director, Kathryn Bigelow. This intriguing choice of name, however, does encourage an in-depth analysis of the main character that might not otherwise be warranted.

Bibliography

Primary Sources

"1863–1878: Freedom, Emancipation, Equal Rights, Emancipation Day!" *The Register* [Raleigh, N.C.]. December 27, 1878.

"Abuse of Widow Pensions." *Chicago Daily Tribune*. November 30, 1897.

Adams, Charles F. "The Government and the Railroad Corporations." *North American Review* 112.230 (1871): 31–62.

Addeman, J. M. *Reminiscences of Two Years with the Colored Troops*. Providence: Soldiers and Sailors Historical Society of Rhode Island, 1880.

"Advertisement for 'Battles and Leaders of the Civil War.'" *News and Observer* [Raleigh, N.C.]. September 10, 1884.

"Advertisement for the Missouri Soldiers' Home." *Confederate Veteran* 1 (1893): 302.

Ambler, I. W. *"Truth Is Stranger Than Fiction": The Life of Sergeant I. W. Ambler*. New York: Lee and Dillingham, 1883.

"American Railways." *Philadelphia North American and United States Gazette*. May 23, 1871.

Anthony, George. *George Tobey Anthony Papers*. William L. Clements Library. Ann Arbor, Mich.

"Anything to Get Gifts: An Incident of the Grand Army Pension Program." *New York Times*. August 21, 1890.

Applin, George. *George Applin Papers*. William L. Clements Library. Ann Arbor, Mich.

"Arrested for Pension Frauds." *New York Tribune*. May 30, 1890.

Barber, William Harrison. *Letter to His Aunt*. May 29, 1865. William Harrison Barber Papers. William L. Clements Library. Ann Arbor, Mich.

"Battles and Leaders of the Civil War." *News and Observer* [Raleigh, N.C.]. September 10, 1884.

Bergson, Henri. *Matter and Memory*. Boston: Macmillan, 1919.

Berlin, Ira, Barbara J. Fields, Steven F. Miller, Joseph P. Reidy, and Leslie S. Rowland (eds.). *Free at Last: A Documentary History of Slavery, Freedom, and the Civil War*. New York: New Press, 1992.

Berlin, Ira, Joseph P. Reidy, and Leslie S. Rowland (eds.). *Freedom: A Documentary History of Emancipation. Series 2: The Black Military Experience*. New York: Cambridge U P, 1982.

———. *Freedom's Soldiers: The Black Military Experience in the Civil War*. New York: Cambridge U P, 1998.

Berlin, Ira, and Leslie S. Rowland (eds.). *Families and Freedom: A Documentary History of African-American Kinship in the Civil War Era*. New York: New Press, 1997.

Bernard, George (ed.). *War Talks of Confederate Veterans*. Petersburg, Va.: Fenn and Owen, 1892.
Bierce, Ambrose. "The Affair at Coulter's Notch." *Phantoms of a Blood-Stained Period: The Complete Civil War Writings of Ambrose Bierce*. Eds. Russell Duncan and David Klooster. Amherst: U of Massachusetts P, 2002.
———. "The Devil's Dictionary." *The Collected Writings of Ambrose Bierce*. Eds. Clifton Fadiman. New York: Citadel Press, 1946.
———. "Jupiter-Doke, Brigadier General." *Phantoms of a Blood-Stained Period: The Complete Civil War Writings of Ambrose Bierce*. Eds. Russell Duncan and David Klooster. Amherst: U of Massachusetts P, 2002.
———. "One of the Missing." *Phantoms of a Blood-Stained Period: The Complete Civil War Writings of Ambrose Bierce*. Eds. Russell Duncan and David Klooster. Amherst: U of Massachusetts P, 2002.
———. "A Resumed Identity." *Phantoms of a Blood-Stained Period: The Complete Civil War Writings of Ambrose Bierce*. Eds. Russell Duncan and David Klooster. Amherst: U of Massachusetts P, 2002.
———. "A Sole Survivor." *Phantoms of a Blood-Stained Period: The Complete Civil War Writings of Ambrose Bierce*. Eds. Russell Duncan and David Klooster. Amherst: U of Massachusetts P, 2002.
———. "What I Saw of Shiloh." *Phantoms of a Blood-Stained Period: The Complete Civil War Writings of Ambrose Bierce*. Eds. Russell Duncan and David Klooster. Amherst: U of Massachusetts P, 2002.
The Bivouac: An Independent Military Monthly. Boston: Edward F. Rollins, 1883.
"Black Men as Soldiers: Facts That Have a Bearing on the War in Cuba." *New York Times*. May 3, 1896.
Blakeslee, B. F. (ed.). *History of the Sixteenth Connecticut Volunteers*. Hartford, Conn.: Case, Lockwood, and Brainard Co. Printers, 1875.
Bond, Daniel. *Unpublished Memoir and War Diary*. 1864–65. Special Collections. Newberry Library. Chicago.
Brown, William Wells. *The Negro in the American Rebellion: His Heroism and Fidelity*. Ed. John David Smith. Athens: Ohio U P, 2003.
Bureau of Statistics. *Statistical Abstract of the United States: 1891*. Washington, D.C.: GPO, 1892.
"The Business Era in Politics." *Rocky Mountain News* [Denver]. October 10, 1874.
Califf, Joseph Mark. *Record of the Services of the Seventh Regiment, U.S. Colored Troops, from September, 1863, to November, 1866, by an Officer of the Regiment*. Providence, R.I.: E. L. Freeman & Co., Printers to the State, 1878.
Canfield, William A. *A History of William A. Canfield*. Manchester, N.H.: Charles F. Livingston, Printers, 1869.
"Celebration at Jamaica: Emancipation Day on Long Island." *New York Age*. September 7, 1889.
"Celebration for Emancipation Day: Colored Citizens Will Carry Out a Novel Program." *Milwaukee Sentinel*. April 17, 1898.

Chenery, William H. *The Fourteenth Regiment Rhode Island Heavy Artillery (Colored), in the War to Preserve the Union, 1861–1865*. Providence, R.I.: Snow and Farnham, Printers and Publishers, 1898.
Cohen, Hennig (ed.). "The Autobiography of John Esten Cooke." *American Literature* 30.2 (1958): 234–37.
"Colored Soldiers Orphans." *North American and United States Gazette* [Philadelphia]. December 11, 1867.
"The Colored Soldiers: Serfdom in the United States Army." *New York Freeman*. January 1, 1887.
"The Colored Troops: Attacked by a Mob Yesterday." *North American and United States Gazette* [Philadelphia]. April 19, 1880.
"The Colored Troops (Unveiling the Shaw Memorial)." *Boston Daily Advertiser*. June 1, 1897.
"The Colored Veterans' Appeal." *New York Times*. May 18, 1876.
"Colored Veterans Are Victorious: The Leading White (G.A.R.) Post of New Orleans Votes to Retain Its Charter." *Chicago Daily Tribune*. June 12, 1892.
"Colored Voters in the Campaign." *New York Age*. July 7, 1888.
"Coming Home from the Wars: The Orderly Conduct of the Soldiers." *New York Herald*. June 14, 1865.
Committee on Public Lands. United States. Cong. House. *H.R. Bill 242*. 38th Cong., 1st sess. February 15, 1864.
———. United States. Cong. Senate. *S. Bill 60*. 38th Cong., 1st sess. January 15, 1864.
Committee of the Regiment. *The Story of the 55th Volunteer Illinois Infantry*. Clinton, Mass.: W. J. Colter, 1887.
"Confederate Archives: The Sherman–Johnston Convention." *Galveston News*. June 16, 1875.
Connecticut Adjutant General's Office. *Record of Service of Connecticut Men in the Army and Navy of the United States During the War of the Rebellion*. Hartford Conn.: Case, Lockwood, and Brainard Co. Printers, 1889.
Conwell, Russell H. *Magnolia Journey: A Union Veteran Revisits the Former Confederate States*. Tuscaloosa: U of Alabama P, 1974.
Cooke, John Esten. *The Heir of Gaymount*. New York: Van Evrie, Horton, 1870.
"Corporate Absolutism." *San Francisco Daily Evening Bulletin*. May 26, 1873.
Cowden, Colonel Robert. *A Brief Sketch of the Organization and Services of the Fifty-Ninth Regiment of United States Colored Infantry, and Biographical Sketches*. Dayton, Ohio: United Brethren Publishing House, 1883.
Crane, Stephen. *The Correspondence of Stephen Crane*. Eds. Stanley Wertheim and Paul Sorrentino. New York: Columbia U P, 1988.
———. "The Gratitude of a Nation." *The New York City Sketches*. Eds. R. W. Stallman and E. R. Hagemann. New York: NYU Press, 1966.
———. "Marines Signaling Under Fire at Guantanamo." *The War Dispatches*. Eds. R. W. Stallman and E. R. Hagemann. New York: NYU Press, 1964.

———. *The Red Badge of Courage*. 1895 Appleton text. 4th ed. Eds. Donald Pizer and Eric Carl Link. New York: W. W. Norton, 2008.

———. *The Red Badge of Courage*. Manuscript edition. Ed. Henry Binder. New York: W. W. Norton, 1982.

———. *The Red Badge of Courage*. Newspaper edition (*New York Press*, December 9, 1894). Ed. Joseph Katz. Gainesville, Fla.: Scholars' Facsimiles and Reprints, 1967.

———. "The Veteran." *The Red Badge of Courage*. 4th ed. Eds. Donald Pizer and Eric Carl Link. New York: W. W. Norton, 2008.

"Crime in Chicago." *Washington Daily Intelligencer* [Washington, D.C.]. October 27, 1865.

Cummings, Charles L. *All About It: The Great War Relic*. n.p., ca. 1885.

———. *The Great War Relic*. n.p., ca. 1888.

———. *The Great War Relic*. n.p., ca. 1892.

"Current Literature: Twenty-Two Years' Work at the Hampton Institute." *Chicago Daily Inter-Ocean*. April 1, 1893.

Da Costa, J. M. "On Irritable Heart: A Clinical Study of a Form of Functional Cardiac Disorder and Its Consequences." *American Journal of the Medical Sciences* 61.121 (1871): 18–52.

"Decoration Day." *Elizabeth Daily Journal* [Elizabeth, N.J.]. May 30, 1891.

"Decoration Day." *The Independent* [Bloomfield, N.J.]. May 30, 1891.

"Decoration Day in New York." *Whig and Courier* [Bangor, Maine]. May 31, 1873.

De Forest, John William. *Miss Ravenel's Conversion from Secession to Loyalty*. New York: Penguin, 2000.

———. *A Union Officer in the Reconstruction*. Eds. James Croushore and David Potter. Baton Rouge: Louisiana State U P, 1997.

———. *A Volunteer's Adventures: A Union Captain's Record of the Civil War*. Ed. James Croushore. Baton Rouge: Louisiana State U P, 1996.

De Menil, Alexander. "One Estimate of John Esten Cooke." *St. Louis Magazine*. Rpt. in *Detroit Free Press*. November 13, 1886.

Department of the Interior. *Report on the Population of the United States at the Eleventh Census, 1890: Part II*. Washington, D.C.: GPO, 1897.

"Department of the Interior Report: In 1894 the Maximum Expenditure for Pensions Will Be Reached." *Chicago Daily Tribune*. December 7, 1892.

"The Dependent Pension Act: A Circular for the Information of Those Coming Within Its Provisions." *New York Tribune*. June 29, 1890.

De Pew, Chauncey M. *Instructions for the Soldier's Voting Law*. Albany, N.Y.: Office of the Secretary of State, 1864.

Douglass, Frederick. "Address for the Promotion of Colored Enlistments, Delivered at a Mass Meeting in Philadelphia, July 6, 1863." *The Life and Writings of Frederick Douglass*. Vol. 3. Ed. Philip S. Foner. New York: International Publishers, 1952.

Downs, Levi. *Letter to His Sister*. June 20, 1866. Levi Downs Papers. William L. Clements Library. Ann Arbor, Mich.

———. *Letter to His Sister Louisa*. April 22, 1872. Levi Downs Papers. William L. Clements Library. Ann Arbor, Mich.

Du Bois, W. E. B. *Black Reconstruction in America: 1860–1880*. New York: Atheneum, 1973.
Dunbar, Paul Laurence. "The Colored Soldiers." *The Complete Poems of Paul Laurence Dunbar*. New York: Dodd, Mead, and Co., 1980.
———. *The Fanatics*. Rpt. in *The Collected Novels of Paul Laurence Dunbar*. Eds. Herbert Woodward Martin, Ronald Primeau, and Gene Andrew Jarrett. Athens: Ohio U P, 2009.
———. "Recession Never." *The Paul Laurence Dunbar Reader*. Eds. Jay Martin and Gossie H. Hudson. New York: Dodd, Mead, and Co., 1975.
———. "Robert Gould Shaw." *The Complete Poems of Paul Laurence Dunbar*. New York: Dodd, Mead, and Co., 1980.
———. "We Wear the Mask." *The Complete Poems of Paul Laurence Dunbar*. New York: Dodd, Mead, and Co., 1980.
Dupré, Louis J. *Fagots from the Campfire*. Washington, D.C.: Emily Thornton Charles and Co., 1881.
Durang, John. *John T. Durang Papers*. William L. Clements Library. Ann Arbor, Mich.
"The Empty Sleeve at Newport; or, Why Edna Ackland Learned to Drive." *Harper's Weekly*. August 26, 1865.
"The Effects of Railroads upon the Industrial and Farming Interests of a People." *Bangor Daily Whig and Courier* [Bangor, Maine]. May 2, 1871.
"Emancipation Celebration." *Freedom's Champion* [Atchison, Kans.]. August 8, 1867.
"Emancipation Day." *Atchison Daily Champion* [Atchison, Kans.]. September 23, 1890.
"Emancipation Day." *Daily Gazette* [Emporia, Kans.]. September 23, 1897.
"Emancipation Day." *The Observer* [Fayetteville, N.C.]. January 8, 1891.
"Emancipation Day Celebrated: A Brilliant Army of Oratorical Talent at Battle Creek." *Chicago Daily Inter-Ocean*. August 2, 1895.
"Emancipation Day: Celebrated by the Morris Brown Congregational Church." *New Orleans Daily Picayune*. January 3, 1898.
"Emancipation Day Celebrated Here on a More Elaborate Scale Than Formerly." *New Orleans Daily Picayune*. January 2, 1898.
"Emancipation Day Celebration: Colored People Preparing for a Big Time at Dickinson Saturday." *Galveston News*. June 13, 1897.
"Emancipation Day Here Will Be Fittingly Observed by Colored People Today." *News and Observer* [Raleigh, N.C.]. January 1, 1898.
"Emancipation Day: How It Was Celebrated Yesterday in Portland." *Morning Oregonian* [Portland, Ore.]. January 1, 1894.
"Emancipation Day: Muster of Colored Militia in Charleston South Carolina." *Frank Leslie's Illustrated Newspaper*. February 3, 1877.
"Emancipation Day in New Orleans." *Southwestern Christian Advocate* [New Orleans]. January 7, 1897.
"Emancipation Day Notice: To the Colored Veterans of Lyon County." *Daily Gazette* [Emporia, Kans.]. September 20, 1897.
"Emancipation Day at Pueblo." *Rocky Mountain News* [Denver]. August 5, 1897.

"Emancipation Day: The Celebration Last Night by the Chicago City Rifles." *New Orleans Daily Inter-Ocean*. January 2, 1878.
Emerson, Horace. *Emerson Family Papers*. William L. Clements Library. Ann Arbor, Mich.
Field, Joseph F. *Letter to Kittie Field*. September 15, 1865. Joseph F. Field Papers. William L. Clements Library. Ann Arbor, Mich.
"Fighting the Battles Over." *San Francisco Daily Evening Bulletin*. January 30, 1886.
Finch, Edwin. *Letter to Thirza Finch*. May 16, 1865. Thirza Finch Copybook and Diary. William L. Clements Library. Ann Arbor, Mich.
Fish Family Papers. William L. Clements Library. Ann Arbor, Mich.
Foner, Eric (ed.). *Freedom's Lawmakers: A Directory of Black Officeholders During Reconstruction*. New York: Oxford U P, 1993.
Fox, William F. *Regimental Losses in the American Civil War, 1861–1865*. Albany, N.Y.: Albany Publishing, 1889.
Freeman, Henry V. "A Colored Brigade in the Campaign and Battle of Nashville." *Military Essays and Recollections: Papers Read Before the Commandery of the State of Illinois, Military Order of the Loyal Legion*. Vol. 2. Chicago: A. C. McClurg and Co., 1894.
"Friends of Illinois Club Celebrate Emancipation Day." *Chicago Daily Inter-Ocean*. September 26, 1896.
Furness, William Eliot. "The Negro as a Soldier." *Military Essays and Recollections: Papers Read Before the Commandery of the State of Illinois, Military Order of the Loyal Legion*. Vol. 2. Chicago: A. C. McClurg and Co., 1894.
Garrison, E. Augustus. *Diary*. William L. Clements Library. Ann Arbor, Mich.
"General Sherman's Book." *St. Louis Daily Globe Democrat*. October 12, 1875.
"General Sherman's Memoirs." *Chicago Daily Inter-Ocean*. September 30, 1874.
Goodman, Duke. "Report of the Inspector General: United Confederate Veterans, Texas Division." *Confederate Veteran* 11 (1903): 435.
"The Governor's Messenger: A Sketch of Wm. Nesbitt Rose, Colored Soldier and Democrat." *Weekly News and Courier* [Charleston, S.C.]. June 3, 1896.
Grand Army of the Republic. *Journal of the Sixteenth Annual Session of the National Encampment*. Lawrence, Mass.: Daily American Job Printing Establishment, 1882.
———. *Journal of the Twenty-Fourth Annual Session of the National Encampment*. Detroit: Richmond and Backus Company, 1890.
———. *Journal of the Twenty-Sixth Annual Session of the National Encampment*. Albany, N.Y.: S. H. Wentworth, 1892.
———. *Journal of the Thirtieth Annual Session of the National Encampment*. Indianapolis: William B. Burford, 1896.
———. *Journal of the Thirty-First Annual Session of the National Encampment*. Lincoln, Neb.: State Journal Company, 1897.
Grant, Ulysses S. *Personal Memoirs*. New York: Barnes and Noble, 2003.
"A Green Private Under Fire: Review of *The Red Badge of Courage*." *New York Times*. October 19, 1895.
Grigsby, John. *John Warren Grigsby Papers*. Filson Historical Society. Louisville, Ky.

Grigsby, Melvin. *The Smoked Yank*. Rev. ed. n.p., 1888.
Gullason, Thomas. "Veterans' Ranks Thinner by a Year." Rpt. in "Additions to the Canon of Stephen Crane." *Nineteenth Century Fiction* 12.2 (1957): 157–60.
Hahn, Steven, Steven Miller, Susan E. O'Donovan, John C. Rodrigue, and Leslie S. Rowland (eds.). *Freedom: A Documentary History of Emancipation, 1861–1867. Series 3, Volume 1: Land and Labor, 1865*. Chapel Hill: U of North Carolina P, 2008.
Hall, G. Stanley. *Adolescence: Its Psychology and Its Relations to Physiology, Anthropology, Sociology, Sex, Crime, Religion and Education*. 2 vols. New York: D. Appleton, 1904.
Hanaford, P. A. *The Empty Sleeve: A Song with Chorus*. Boston: Oliver Ditson and Co., 1866.
Harper, Frances E. W. "The Great Problem to Be Solved." *A Brighter Coming Day: A Frances Ellen Watkins Harper Reader*. Ed. Frances Smith Foster. New York: Feminist Press at the City University of New York, 1990.
———. *Iola Leroy; or, Shadows Uplifted*. New York: AMS Press, 1971.
Hartzell, Calvin. *Ohio Volunteer: The Childhood and Civil War Memoirs of Captain John Calvin Hartzell, OVI*. Ed. Charles Switzer. Athens: Ohio U P. 2005.
"Have We Come to Caesarism?" *The Nation*. November 1, 1866.
"Heavy Cost of Pensions." *New York Times*. October 5, 1903.
"He's Taken to Drink." *Raleigh Register* [Raleigh, N.C.]. January 31, 1863.
The History of Jo-Daviess County. Chicago: H. F. Kett and Co., 1870.
The History of Union County Ohio. Chicago: W. H. Beers and Co., 1883.
"Hoke Smith on Pensions." *Newark Evening News*. September 23, 1893.
Holmes, Oliver Wendell. "Memorial Day: An Address Delivered May 30, 1884, at Keene, NH, Before John Sedgwick Post No. 4, Grand Army of the Republic." *The Occasional Speeches of Justice Oliver Wendell Holmes*. Cambridge, Mass.: Harvard U P, 1962.
Homer, Winslow. "The Veteran in a New Field." *Frank Leslie's Illustrated Newspaper* 24.615 (1867): 268.
"Honor Their Liberator: Colored People Generally Observe Emancipation Day at Springfield." *Chicago Daily Inter-Ocean*. September 23, 1896.
Houts, S. B. "The Battle of Shiloh." *St. Louis Globe-Democrat*. April 19, 1881.
Howells, William Dean. "Introduction to 'Lyrics of Lowly Life.'" *The Complete Poems of Paul Laurence Dunbar*. New York: Dodd, Mead, and Co., 1980.
"How the Western Soldiers Come Home." *Daily Cleveland Herald*. July 1, 1865.
"How Weissert Was Beaten (A Report on the G.A.R. Encampment)." *Milwaukee Daily Journal*. August 7, 1891.
Hubbell, Jay B. (ed.). "The War Diary of John Esten Cooke." *Journal of Southern History* 7.4 (1941): 526–40.
Hunter, R. M. T. *Post-bellum Mortality Among Confederates*. Confederate Survivor's Association. Augusta, Ga.: Chronicle Publishing, 1887.
Hussey, George. *Hussey-Wadsworth Papers*. William L. Clements Library. Ann Arbor, Mich.
"Immorality in Richmond." *Daily Mississippian* [Jackson]. April 7, 1863.
"The Increasing Pension List." *New York Times*. November 7, 1897.
"In Honor of Their Dead." *Newark Evening News*. May 30, 1893.

"Intemperance in Our Armies." *Daily Palladium* [New Haven, Conn.]. June 30, 1863.
"Intemperance in the Army." *Daily Whig and Courier* [Bangor, Maine]. May 13, 1864.
James, John G. *Cadet File*. Special Collections. Preston Library. Virginia Military Institute, Lexington.
———. *John G. James Papers*. Special Collections. Preston Library. Virginia Military Institute, Lexington.
James, William. "The Moral Equivalent of War." *McClure's Magazine* 35 (1910): 463–68.
———. "The Perception of Time." *Journal of Speculative Philosophy* 20.4 (1886): 374–407.
Janet, Pierre. *Psychological Healing: A Historical and Clinical Study*. Boston: Macmillan, 1925.
"Jeff Davis Scalps Tecumseh." *Daily Arkansas Gazette*. June 8, 1875.
"John Esten Cooke." *New Mississippian* [Jackson]. October 5, 1886.
Johnson, Robert Underwood. *Remembered Yesterdays*. Boston: Little, Brown, 1923.
Johnson, Robert Underwood, and Clarence Clough Buel (eds.). *Battles and Leaders of the Civil War*. New York: Century Publishing, 1887.
"Johnston Defends Himself Against Southern Historical Society Charges." *Chicago Daily Inter-Ocean*. August 25, 1874.
"The Johnston–Hood Controversy." *Galveston News*. May 24, 1874.
Jones, William. "Letter." *Grand Army Journal* 1.2 (1870): 1.
"Joy and Sorrow Mingled: Memorial Day Fittingly Observed by Thousands." *New York Tribune*. May 31, 1891.
"Juvenile Generals." *Newark Evening News*. July 22, 1893.
Kletzing, H. F., and W. H. Crogman. *Progress of a Race; or, The Remarkable Advancement of the Afro-American Negro*. Atlanta: J. L. Nichols and Co., 1898.
Lanier, Sidney. *Letters: 1857–1868*. Vol. 5 of *The Centennial Edition of the Works of Sidney Lanier*. Eds. Charles R. Anderson and Aubrey H. Starke. Baltimore: Johns Hopkins U P, 1945.
———. *Tiger-Lilies: A Novel*. Vol. 5 of *The Centennial Edition of the Works of Sidney Lanier*. Ed. Garland Greever. Baltimore: Johns Hopkins U P, 1945.
Lawrence, Frederic. "The Real Stephen Crane." *Stephen Crane Remembered*. Ed. Paul Sorrentino. Tuscaloosa: U of Alabama P, 2006.
"Life in the Army." *Daily Citizen and News* [Lowell, Mass.]. December 24, 1864.
Linson, Corwin Knapp. *My Stephen Crane*. Ed. Edwin H. Cady. Syracuse, N.Y.: Syracuse U P, 1958.
"Liquor in the Army." *Daily Cleveland Herald*. May 1, 1863.
"Literary Notes." *Milwaukee Sentinel*. April 24, 1881.
"Literary Notices: Review of *Tiger-Lilies*." *North American and United States Gazette* [Philadelphia]. January 4, 1868.
"Looking for Pensions." *Newark Evening News*. September 30, 1893.
"Mad for Pensions." *Chicago Tribune*. February 20, 1898.
"Make Young Patriots: The Schools and Citizenship." *Newark Evening News*. May 2, 1890.
Marrs, Elijah P. *Life and History of the Rev. Elijah P. Marrs*. Miami: Mnemosyne Publishing, 1969.

Marshall, Henry Grimes. *Letter to Hattie Marshall.* October 9, 1865. Henry Grimes Marshall Papers. William L. Clements Library. Ann Arbor, Mich.

Marvin, Edwin E. (ed.). *The Fifth Regiment Connecticut Volunteers: A History Compiled from Diaries and Official Reports.* Hartford, Conn.: Wiley, Waterman, and Eaton, 1889.

Maxim, Charles. *Charles M. Maxim Papers.* William L. Clements Library. Ann Arbor, Mich.

McClurg, Alexander. "The Red Badge of Hysteria." *The Crane Log: A Documentary Life of Stephen Crane.* Eds. Paul Sorrentino and Stanley Wertheim. New York: G. K. Hall and Co., 1994.

McDonald, Marshall. *Cadet File.* Special Collections. Preston Library. Virginia Military Institute, Lexington.

———. *Marshall McDonald Papers.* Special Collections. Preston Library. Virginia Military Institute, Lexington.

McGee, Charles M., Jr., and Ernest M. Lander Jr. (eds.). *A Rebel Came Home: The Diary of Floride Clemson.* Columbia: U of South Carolina P, 1961.

Meacham, Henry. *The Empty Sleeve; or, The Life and Hardships of Henry M. Meacham in the Union Army.* Springfield, Mass.: n.p., 1869.

Metcalf, Stephen. *Metcalf-White Papers.* William L. Clements Library. Ann Arbor, Mich.

"Military Politicians." *The Nation.* October 11, 1866.

Mills, George Henry. *History of the Sixteenth North Carolina Regiment in the Civil War.* Hamilton, N.Y.: Edmonston, 1992.

"More Pensions and Bounty." *Perth Amboy Republican.* August 31, 1888.

"More Pensioners Than Soldiers." *New York Times.* April 19, 1894.

"More Than Half Are Dead." *Galveston News.* May 30, 1897.

Morgan, Thomas J. *Reminiscences of Service with Colored Troops in the Army of the Cumberland, 1863–65.* Providence: Soldiers and Sailors Historical Society of Rhode Island, 1885.

Morris, David. *Letters: 1865–1867.* Special Collections. Chicago Public Library.

Morton, Joseph W., Jr. (ed.). *Sparks from the Campfire; or, Tales of the Old Veterans.* 3rd ed. Philadelphia: Keystone Publishing, 1892.

The National Tribune Scrapbook. Washington, D.C.: National Tribune, 1909. https://archive.org/details/nationaltribunes00wash.

"The Nation's Pensioners: A Great and Ever Growing Army of Treasury Raiders." *New York Times.* December 21, 1890.

Nell, William Cooper. *The Colored Patriots of the American Revolution.* Boston: R. F. Wallcut, 1855.

"A New Pension Scandal Brewing." *New York Tribune.* July 2, 1890.

"New Publications: *Memoirs* of General Sherman." *San Francisco Evening Bulletin.* June 5, 1875.

"New Publications: Review of *Tiger-Lilies.*" *News and Herald* [Savannah, Ga.]. December 10, 1867.

"New York Veterans Ready." *New York Times.* March 16, 1898.

"No Color Line Allowed: The Grand Army Settles Its Race Question." *New York Times.* August 7, 1891.
"No Negro Need Apply for Membership in the Grand Army in Connecticut." *New York Times.* October 22, 1889.
Northcott, Dennis, and Thomas Brooks (eds.). *Grand Army of the Republic: Transcription of the Death Rolls, 1879–1947.* Dennis Northcott, 2003.
"Obituary: Col. A. H. Belo." *New York Times.* April 20, 1901.
Ohio Adjutant General's Office. *87th–108th Regiments: Infantry.* Vol. 7 of *Official Roster of the Soldiers of the State of Ohio in the War of the Rebellion, 1861–1866.* Cincinnati: Ohio Valley Press, 1888.
Olcott, Henry. "The War's Carnival of Fraud." *The Annals of the War Written by Leading Participants in the North and South. Originally Published in the Philadelphia Weekly Times.* Philadelphia: Times Publishing Company, 1879.
"Once Foes Now Friends." *New Orleans Daily Picayune.* March 24, 1890.
"One Estimate of John Esten Cooke." *Detroit Free Press.* November 13, 1886.
"Opposed to the Negro: A Grand Army Post Orders Two Courts-Martial." *New York Times.* December 7, 1889.
"Ought Soldiers to Vote?" *The Nation.* October 25, 1866.
"Our Colored Soldiers." *Chicago Daily Inter-Ocean.* February 28, 1878.
"Our Colored Troops." *Chicago Daily Inter-Ocean.* April 21, 1876.
"Our Railroad Land-Grant Policy." *Boston Daily Advertiser.* June 1, 1870.
"Our War History." *St. Louis Daily Globe-Democrat.* September 19, 1878.
Owens, Ira S. (ed.). *Greene County in the War: Being a History of the Seventy-Fourth Regiment.* Xenia, Ohio: Torchlight Job Books, 1872.
Parker, Hilon. *Hilon A. Parker Papers.* William L. Clements Library. Ann Arbor, Mich.
Partridge, Charles A. *History of the Ninety-Sixth Regiment Illinois Volunteer Infantry.* Chicago: Brown, Pettibone, and Company Printers, 1887.
"Passing Away." *Elizabeth Daily Journal* [Elizabeth, N.J.]. February 16, 1891.
"Patriotism Recognized at Last." *New York Times.* December 24, 1893.
Peck, Hiram T. *Army Journal: Private Record of Life in the Federal Service During the Great Rebellion.* New Haven, Conn.: n.p., 1874.
"A Peculiar Situation: Southern Brigadiers and Black Veterans Meeting at the Festive Board." *New York Globe.* June 30, 1883.
"Pension Agents to Go." *Elizabeth Daily Journal* [Elizabeth, N.J.]. December 5, 1890.
"Pension Reform Begun." *Newark Evening News.* May 29, 1893.
"Profanity Among Soldiers." *Vermont Chronicle* [Brattleboro, Vt.]. March 24, 1863.
"Protecting a Colored Veteran." *New York Times.* November 21, 1888.
"Race Relations in the Grand Army of the Republic." *The Congregationalist* [Boston]. August 13, 1891.
"Railroad Progress." *Daily Republican* [Little Rock, Ark.]. January 18, 1870.
"Reception of the Colored Soldiers at Harrisburg." *The Liberator* [Boston]. November 24, 1865.
Redkey, Edwin S. (ed.). *A Grand Army of Black Men: Letters from African American Soldiers in the Union Army, 1861–1865.* New York: Cambridge U P, 1992.

Reece, J. N. *1861–1900*. Vol. 1 of *Report of the Adjutant General of the State of Illinois*. Springfield, Ill.: Phillips Brothers, 1900.

Regimental Reunion Association of the Seventy-Third Illinois. *A History of the Seventy-Third Regiment of Illinois Infantry Volunteers*. n.p.: Regimental Reunion Association of the Seventy-Third Illinois, 1890.

Regosin, Elizabeth A., and Donald R. Shaffer (eds.). *Voices of Emancipation: Understanding Slavery, the Civil War, and Reconstruction Through the U.S. Pension Bureau Files*. New York: NYU Press, 2008.

"Remarkable Incidents: Generals W. T. Sherman, Jos. E. Johnston, G. T. Beauregard, and Mr. Jefferson Davis in the St. Louis Railroad Convention." *Galveston News*. November 30, 1875.

"Re-organization of Parties: Proposed Formation of a National Citizen Soldier's Party." *New York Herald*. June 13, 1865.

Reunion Committee of the Ninety-Fourth Ohio. *Record of the Ninety-Fourth Regiment Ohio Volunteer Infantry, in the War of the Rebellion*. Cincinnati: Ohio Valley Press, n.d.

"Review of *Figs and Thistles*." *Chicago Daily Inter-Ocean*. July 21, 1881.

"Review of *Figs and Thistles*." *Denver Daily News*. November 30, 1879.

"Review of *In the Midst of Life*." *Critical Essays on Ambrose Bierce*. Ed. Cathy N. Davidson. Boston: G. K. Hall and Co., 1982.

"Review of *Tiger-Lilies*." *North American and United States Gazette* [Philadelphia]. January 4, 1868.

"Review of *The Veteran in a New Field*." *Frank Leslie's Illustrated Newspaper*. July 13, 1867.

"Reviews and Literary Notices: Review of *Tiger-Lilies*." *Atlantic Monthly* 21.125 (1868): 382–83.

"Robbing the Soldiers: How the Demagogues Plunder in the Name of the Veterans of the Civil War." *Philadelphia Times*. March 21, 1891. Rpt. in *Milwaukee Sentinel*. March 23, 1891.

Robson, John. *How a One Legged Rebel Lives; or, A History of the 52nd Virginia Regiment*. Richmond, Va.: W. H. Wade and Co., 1876.

Rollin, Frank A. *Life and Public Services of Martin R. Delany*. Boston: Lee and Shepard, 1883.

Shaw, William (ed.). *Illustrated Roster of the Grand Army of the Republic*. n.p., 1914.

Sherman, William Tecumseh. *Memoirs*. New York: Penguin, 2000.

"Sherman and Johnston: The Atlanta Campaign as Viewed by the Two Generals." *St. Louis Daily Globe-Democrat*. September 5, 1875.

"Sherman and Thomas." *St. Louis Daily Globe-Democrat*. October 12, 1875.

"Sherman's Book." *Georgia Weekly Telegraph and Journal & Messenger* [Macon]. May 25, 1875.

"Sherman-Boynton: A Farewell Shot from the Belligerents." *Arkansas Gazette*. February 28, 1880.

"Sherman's Historical Raid." *North American and United States Gazette* [Philadelphia]. October 29, 1875.

"Soldiers Above All Others." *New York Times*. November 1, 1885.

Soldiers' and Patriots' Biographical Album. Chicago: Union Veteran Publication Company, 1892.
"Soldiers Riot in Washington." *Newark Advocate* [Newark, Ohio]. March 11, 1864.
The Southern Bivouac. Louisville, Ky.: Southern Historical Association, 1882–1887.
"Southern Complaint of Union Pensions." *Morning Oregonian* [Portland, Ore.]. February 14, 1888.
Stone, Kate. *Brokenburn: The Journal of Kate Stone, 1861–1868*. Ed. John Q. Anderson. New introd. by Drew Gilpin Faust. Baton Rouge: Louisiana State U P, 1995.
Sturgis, Russell. "The Sixth Annual Exhibition of the Artist's Fund Society of New York." *The Nation* 1.21 (1865): 663.
"The Surprise at Pittsburg Landing." *Frank Leslie's Illustrated Newspaper* [suppl.]. May 17, 1862.
"Talks on Timely Topics: General Joseph E. Johnston." *Frank Leslie's Illustrated Newspaper*. December 27, 1879.
Taylor, Richard. *Destruction and Reconstruction*. Ed. Charles Roland. Waltham, Mass.: Blaisdale Publishing, 1968.
"Temperance in Our Armies." *Daily Palladium* [New Haven, Conn.]. June 30, 1863.
"Time to Halt." *New York Daily Tribune*. July 7, 1890.
"Topics of the Time: Battles and Leaders of the Civil War." *Century* 28.6 (1884): 943–44.
Tourgée, Albion. *Figs and Thistles*. New York: Fords, Howard, and Hulbert, 1879.
Trimble, Harvey M. *History of the Ninety-Third Regiment Illinois Volunteer Infantry*. Chicago: Blakely Press, 1898.
Tunnard, W. H. (ed.). *Southern Record: The History of the 3rd Regiment Louisiana Infantry*. Baton Rouge: Printed for the Author, 1866.
Turner, John R. "The Battle of the Wilderness." *War Talks by Confederate Veterans*. Ed. George Bernard. Petersburg, Va.: Fenn and Owen, 1892.
Twitchell, A. S. (ed.). *History of the Seventh Maine Light Battery*. Boston: E. B. Stillings and Co., 1892.
"Union Sentiment Among Confederate Veterans." *Century Magazine* 34.2 (1887): 309–10.
"The Union's New Decoration Day." *New Orleans Daily Picayune*. May 28, 1899.
United States. *Revised United States Army Regulations*. Washington, D.C.: GPO, 1861.
———. *Statutes at Large*. Washington, D.C.: GPO, 1859–63.
United States National Park Service. *The Civil War Soldiers and Sailors Database*. Washington, D.C.: National Park Service, 2013. http://www.nps.gov/civilwar/soldiers-and-sailors-database.htm.
United States War Department. *The War of the Rebellion: A Compilation of the Official Records of the Union and Confederate Armies*. Washington, D.C.: GPO, 1900.
"Untitled Editorial." *Denver Daily News*. August 12, 1890.
"Untitled Editorial." *New York Times*. July 12, 1888.
"Untitled Editorial." *New York Times*. December 27, 1889.
"Untitled Editorial." *New York Times*. December 24, 1891.
"Untitled Editorial." *New York Tribune*. July 25, 1890.
"Untitled Editorial." *Perth Amboy Republican*. October 18, 1889.
"Untitled Editorial." *Perth Amboy Republican*. March 28, 1890.

"Untitled Editorial." *Perth Amboy Republican*. September 12, 1890.
"Untitled Emancipation Day Article." *Herald* [Leavenworth, Kans.]. September 29, 1894.
"Untitled Pension Article." *Whig and Courier* [Bangor, Maine]. June 27, 1890.
"The Uprising for Pensions." *New York Times*. August 19, 1890.
"Verification of Pension Applications." *New York Tribune*. July 4, 1890.
The Veteran: Devoted to the Interests of the Grand Army of the Republic and Ex-Soldiers and Sailors. Columbus, Ohio: Gazette Printing House, 1881–82.
"Veterans in the Census: A Means to Help Grasping Pension Agents." *New York Times*. May 25, 1890.
"Veterans Unfit for War." *New York Times*. March 25, 1898.
"Volunteers and Regulars: Gossip of the National Encampment at Washington Which Has Just Closed." *Chicago Daily Inter-Ocean*. June 4, 1887.
Walker, C.I. (ed.). *Rolls and Historical Sketch of the Tenth Regiment, SO. CA. Volunteers in the Army of the Confederate States*. Charleston, S.C.: Walker, Evans, and Cogswell Printers, 1881.
"Wanting Pensions for All." *New York Times*. December 20, 1887.
"Washington Letter." *Perth Amboy Republican*. August 3, 1888.
"Washington Letter." *Perth Amboy Republican*. March 29, 1889.
"Washington Letter." *Perth Amboy Republican*. October 25, 1889.
Watkins, Samuel. *Company Aytch: A Sideshow of the Big Show*. New York: Plume Books, 1999.
"When the Boys in Blue Are Gone." Gardner, Mass.: George H. Ross, 1912.
Whitman, Walt. "The Real War Will Never Get in the Books." *Specimen Days*. Rpt. in *Leaves of Grass and Other Writings*. Ed. Michael Moon. New York: W. W. Norton, 2002.
"Why Colored Soldiers Are Not Subjects of Art." *Lowell Daily Citizen* [Lowell, Mass.]. May 2, 1879.
Wilkeson, Frank. *Recollections of a Private Soldier in the Army of the Potomac*. Freeport, N.Y.: Books for Libraries Press, 1972.
Willard, C. W. "The Business Era in Politics." *Rocky Mountain News* [Denver]. October 10, 1874.
Willett, Elbert Decatur (ed.). *History of Company B, 40th Alabama Regiment, Confederate States Army*. Anniston, Ala.: Norwood Printers, 1902.
Williams, George Washington. *A History of the Negro Troops in the War of the Rebellion, 1861–1865*. New York: Negro Universities Press, 1969.
Wilson, Joseph T. *The Black Phalanx*. New York: Arno Press and the New York Times, 1968.
Wilson, Keith (ed.). *Honor in Command: Lt. Freeman S. Bowley's Civil War Service in the 30th United States Colored Infantry*. Gainesville: U P of Florida, 2006.
Wing, Samuel. *The Soldier's Story: A Personal Narrative of the Life, Army Experiences and Marvelous Sufferings Since the War of Samuel Wing*. Philips, Maine: Phillips Phonograph Steam Book and Job Print, 1898.
Winn, Robert. *Winn-Cook Papers*. Filson Historical Society. Louisville, Ky.

Secondary Sources

Aaron, Daniel. *The Unwritten War: American Writers and the Civil War*. New York: Knopf, 1973.

Ackerman, Kenneth. *Dark Horse: The Surprise Election and Political Murder of President James A. Garfield*. New York: Carroll and Graf, 2003.

Adams, Larry. "Bakhtin and 'A Resumed Identity.'" *Ambrose Bierce Project Journal* 1.1 (2005). http://www.ambrosebierce.org/journal1adams.html.

Allred, Randall W. "'The Gilded Images of Memory': *The Red Badge of Courage* and 'The Veteran.'" *Stephen Crane in War and Peace: A Special Edition of War, Literature and the Arts* 18.1–2 (1999): 100–115.

Ampadu, Lena. "The Poetry of Paul Laurence Dunbar and the Influence of African Aesthetics." *We Wear the Mask: Paul Laurence Dunbar and the Politics of Representative Reality*. Ed Willie Harrell. Kent, Ohio: Kent State U P, 2010.

Andrew, Rod. "Soldiers, Christians, and Patriots: The Lost Cause and Southern Military Schools, 1865–1915." *Journal of Southern History* 64.4 (1998): 677–710.

Antoni, Robert. "Miss Ravenel's Conversion: A Neglected American Novel." *Southern Quarterly* 24.3 (1986): 58–63.

Balestrini, Nassim. "National Memory and the Arts in Paul Laurence Dunbar's War Poetry." *We Wear the Mask: Paul Laurence Dunbar and the Politics of Representative Reality*. Ed. Willie J. Harrell Jr. Kent, Ohio: Kent State U P, 2010.

Ball, Durwood. *Army Regulars on the Western Frontier, 1848–1861*. Norman: U of Oklahoma P, 2001.

Barton, Michael. "Did the Confederacy Change Southern Soldiers?" *The Old South in the Crucible of War*. Eds. Harry P. Owens and James J. Cooke. Jackson: U P of Mississippi, 2011.

Beaty, John O. *John Esten Cooke, Virginian*. Port Washington, N.Y.: Kennikat Press, 1965.

Becker, George. "Albion W. Tourgée: Pioneer in Social Criticism." *American Literature* 19.1 (1947): 59–72.

Bederman, Gail. *Manliness and Civilization: A Cultural History of Gender and Race in the United States, 1880–1917*. Chicago: U of Chicago P, 1995.

Bell, Jack. *Civil War Heavy Explosive Ordinance: A Guide to Large Artillery Projectiles, Torpedoes, and Mines*. Denton: U of North Texas P, 2003.

Belz, Herman. *Emancipation and Equal Rights: Politics and Constitutionalism in the Civil War Era*. New York: W. W. Norton, 1978.

Benfey, Christopher. *The Double Life of Stephen Crane*. New York: Knopf, 1992.

Benton, Josiah Henry. *Voting in the Field: A Forgotten Chapter of the Civil War*. Norwood, Mass.: Plimpton Press, 1915.

Bercovitch, Sacvan. *The American Jeremiad*. Madison: U of Wisconsin P, 1978.

Berdal, Mats. *Disarmament and Demobilisation After Civil Wars*. The International Institute for Strategic Studies: Adelphi Paper 303. New York: Oxford U P, 1996.

Berkove, Lawrence I. *A Prescription for Adversity: The Moral Art of Ambrose Bierce*. Columbus: Ohio State U P, 2002.

Berry, Mary. *Military Necessity and Civil Rights Policy: Black Citizenship and the Constitution, 1861–1868*. Port Washington, N.Y.: Kennikat Press, 1977.

Blair, William. *Cities of the Dead: Contesting Memory of the Civil War in the South, 1865–1914*. Chapel Hill: U of North Carolina P, 2004.

Blight, David. *Beyond the Battlefield: Race, Memory, and the American Civil War*. Amherst: U of Massachusetts P, 2002.

———. *Frederick Douglass's Civil War: Keeping Faith in Jubilee*. Baton Rouge: Louisiana State U P, 1989.

———. *Race and Reunion: The Civil War in American Memory*. Cambridge, Mass.: Harvard U P, 2001.

Bloom, Harold (ed.). *Stephen Crane's Red Badge of Courage: Modern Critical Interpretations*. Philadelphia: Chelsea House, 2004.

Bolton, Matthew. "*The Red Badge of Courage* in the Context of the 1890s." *The Red Badge of Courage*. Ed. Eric Carl Link. Pasadena, Calif.: Salem Press, 2010.

Bonekemper, Edward H., III. *Ulysses S. Grant: A Victor, Not a Butcher*. Washington, D.C.: Regnery, 2010.

Booraem, Hendrik. *The Road to Respectability: James A. Garfield and His World, 1844–1852*. Lewisburg, Pa.: Bucknell U P, 1988.

Borgstrom, Michael. "Face Value: Ambivalent Citizenship in *Iola Leroy*." *African American Review* 40.4 (2006): 779–93.

Bower, Stephen E. "The Theology of the Battlefield: William Tecumseh Sherman and the U.S. Civil War." *Journal of Military History* 64.4 (2000): 1005–34.

Boyd, Melba Joyce. *Discarded Legacy: Politics and Poetics in the Life of Frances E. W. Harper, 1825–1911*. Detroit: Wayne State U P, 1994.

Bradburn, Douglas. *The Citizenship Revolution: Politics and the Creation of the American Union, 1774–1804*. Charlottesville: U of Virginia P, 2009.

Bratton, Mary Jo. "John Esten Cooke and His 'Confederate Lies.'" *Southern Literary Journal* 13.2 (1981): 72–91.

Broomall, James. "Personal Confederacies: War and Peace in the American South, 1840–1890." Ph.D. diss. University of Florida. 2011.

Brown, Bill. *The Material Unconscious: American Amusement, Stephen Crane, and the Economics of Play*. Cambridge, Mass.: Harvard U P, 1996.

Bruce, Dickson. *Black American Writing from the Nadir: The Evolution of a Literary Tradition, 1877–1915*. Baton Rouge: Louisiana State U P, 1989.

Bruce, Robert V. *Lincoln and the Tools of War*. Fwd. by Benjamin P. Thomas. Urbana: U of Illinois P, 1989.

Brumm, Ursula. "Definitions of Southern Identity in the Civil War Novels of John Esten Cooke." *Rewriting the South: History and Fiction*. Eds. Lothar Honninghausen and Valeria Lerda. Tübingen: Francke, 1993.

Brundage, W. Fitzhugh. "Race, Memory, and Masculinity: Black Veterans Recall the Civil War." *The War Was You and Me: Civilians in the American Civil War*. Ed. Joan E. Cashin. Princeton, N.J.: Princeton U P, 2002.

Buck, Paul H. *The Road to Reunion: 1865–1900*. Boston: Little, Brown, 1937.

Buinicki, Martin. "John W. De Forest's *Miss Ravenel's Conversion* and the Limits of Sentimental Citizenship." *American Literary Realism* 39.1 (2006): 48–63.
Burbick, Joan. *Healing the Republic: The Language of Health and the Culture of Nationalism in Nineteenth-Century America*. New York: Cambridge U P, 1994.
Busey, John W., and David G. Martin (eds.). *Regimental Strengths and Losses at Gettysburg*. 4th ed. East Windsor, N.J.: Longstreet House, 2005.
Caccavari, Peter. "Reconstructing Reconstruction: Region and Nation in the Work of Albion Tourgée." *Regionalism Reconsidered: New Approaches to the Field*. Ed. David Jordan. New York: Garland, 1994.
Calhoun, Charles W. (ed.). *The Gilded Age: Perspectives on the Origins of Modern America*. 2nd ed. New York: Rowman and Littlefield, 2007.
Campbell, Christopher D. "Conversation Across a Century: The War Stories of Ambrose Bierce and Tim O'Brien." *War, Literature, and the Arts* 10.2 (1998): 267–88.
Campbell, Jacqueline Glass. *When Sherman Marched North from the Sea: Resistance on the Confederate Home Front*. Chapel Hill: U of North Carolina P, 2003.
Carnes, Mark C. "Middle-Class Men and the Solace of Fraternal Ritual." *Meanings for Manhood: Constructions of Masculinity in Victorian America*. Eds. Mark C. Carnes and Clyde Griffen. Chicago: U of Chicago P, 1990.
Caron, Timothy P. "'How Changeable Are the Events of War': National Reconciliation in the *Century Magazine*'s 'Battles and Leaders of the Civil War.'" *American Periodicals* 16.2 (2006): 151–71.
Carruthers, Sharon. "'Old Soldiers Never Die': A Note on Col. John L. Burleigh." *Studies in the Novel* 10.1 (1978): 158–60.
Caruth, Cathy (ed.). *Trauma: Explorations in Memory*. Baltimore: Johns Hopkins U P, 1995.
———. *Unclaimed Experience: Trauma, Narrative, and History*. Baltimore: Johns Hopkins U P, 1996.
Casper, Scott E. *Constructing American Lives: Biography and Culture in Nineteenth-Century America*. Chapel Hill: U of North Carolina P, 1999.
Cassandra, Jackson. "'I Will Gladly Share with Them My Richer Heritage': Schoolteachers in Frances E. W. Harper's *Iola Leroy* and Charles Chesnutt's *Mandy Oxendine*." *African American Review* 37.4 (2003): 553–68.
Caudill, Edward, and Paul Ashdown. *Sherman's March in Myth and Memory*. New York: Rowman and Littlefield, 2008.
Cecelski, David S., and Timothy B. Tyson (eds.). *Democracy Betrayed: The Wilmington Race Riot of 1898 and Its Legacy*. Chapel Hill: U of North Carolina P, 1998.
Cetina, Judith. "A History of Veterans' Homes in the United States, 1811–1930." Ph.D. diss. Case Western Reserve University. 1977.
Cimbala, Paul, and Randall Miller. *Union Soldiers and the Northern Home Front: Wartime Experiences, Postwar Adjustments*. New York: Fordham U P, 2002.
Clarke, Frances. "'Let All the Nations See': Civil War Nationalism and the Memorialization of Wartime Volunteerism." *Civil War History* 52.1 (2006): 66–93.
Clark, James. *The Murder of James A. Garfield: The President's Last Days and the Trial and Execution of His Assassin*. New York: McFarland and Co., 1994.

Clendenning, John. "Visions of War and Versions of Manhood." *Stephen Crane in War and Peace: A Special Edition of War, Literature and the Arts* 18.1–2 (1999): 23–34.
Coffman, Edward M. *The Old Army: A Portrait of the American Army in Peacetime, 1784–1898.* New York: Oxford U P, 1986.
Cohen, Nancy. *The Reconstruction of American Liberalism, 1865–1914.* Chapel Hill: U of North Carolina P, 2002.
Cooper, Jerry. *The Rise of the National Guard: The Evolution of the American Militia, 1865–1920.* Lincoln: U of Nebraska P, 1997.
Cornish, Dudley Taylor. *The Sable Arm: Negro Troops in the Union Army, 1861–1865.* New York: W.W. Norton, 1966.
Couser, G. Thomas. "Writing the Civil War: Ambrose Bierce's 'Jupiter-Doke, Brigadier-General.'" *Studies in American Fiction* 18.1 (1990): 87–98.
Cox, Caroline. *A Proper Sense of Honor: Service and Sacrifice in George Washington's Army.* Chapel Hill: U of North Carolina P, 2004.
Cox, James. "*The Red Badge of Courage*: The Purity of War." *Southern Humanities Review* 25.4 (1991): 305–20.
Crackel, Theodore J. *Mr. Jefferson's Army: Political and Social Reform of the Military Establishment, 1801–1809.* New York: New York U P, 1987.
Crane, Gregg D. *Race, Citizenship, and Law in American Literature.* New York: Cambridge U P, 2002.
Cunliffe, Marcus. *Soldiers and Civilians: The Martial Spirit in America, 1775–1865.* Boston: Little, Brown, 1968.
Davidson, Cathy N. (ed.). *Critical Essays on Ambrose Bierce.* Boston: G. K. Hall and Co., 1982.
———. *The Experimental Fictions of Ambrose Bierce: Structuring the Ineffable.* Omaha: U of Nebraska P, 1984.
Davidson, Cathy N., and Jessamyn Hatcher (eds.). *No More Separate Spheres! A Next Wave American Studies Reader.* Duke U P, 2002.
Davis, Linda. *Badge of Courage: The Life of Stephen Crane.* New York: Houghton Mifflin, 1998.
Davis, Stephen. "'A Matter of Sensational Interest': The *Century* 'Battles and Leaders Series.'" *Civil War History* 27.4 (1981): 338–49.
Dawes, James. *The Language of War: Literature and Culture in the U.S. from the Civil War Through World War II.* Cambridge: Harvard U P, 2002.
Dean, Eric T. *Shook over Hell: Post-traumatic Stress, Vietnam, and the Civil War.* Cambridge: Harvard U P, 1997.
Dearing, Mary R. *Veterans in Politics: The Story of the GAR.* Baton Rouge: Louisiana State U P, 1952.
Denholm, Anthony. *France in Revolution: 1848.* New York: John Wiley and Sons, 1972.
DePastino, Todd. *Citizen Hobo: How a Century of Homelessness Shaped America.* Chicago: U of Chicago P, 2003.
Dicken-Garcia, Hazel. *Journalistic Standards in Nineteenth-Century America.* Madison: U of Wisconsin P, 1989.

Diffley, Kathleen. *Where My Heart Is Turning Ever: Civil War Stories and Constitutional Reform*. Athens: U of Georgia P, 1992.

Dingledine, Don. "'The Whole Drama of the War': The African American Soldier in Civil War Literature." *PMLA* 115.5 (2000): 1113–17.

Duveau, Georges. *1848: The Making of a Revolution*. New York: Random House, 1967.

Elliott, Mark. *Color-Blind Justice: Albion Tourgée and the Quest for Racial Equality from the Civil War to Plessy vs. Ferguson*. New York: Oxford U P, 2006.

Emanuel, James. "Racial Fire in the Poetry of Paul Laurence Dunbar." *A Singer in the Dawn: Reinterpretations of Paul Laurence Dunbar*. Ed. Jay Martin. New York: Dodd, Mead, and Co., 1975.

Emberton, Carole. "'Only Murder Makes Men': Reconsidering the Black Military Experience." *Journal of the Civil War Era* 2.3 (2012): 369–93.

Emmert, Scott. "Reversals in the Fortunes of War: Ambrose Bierce, Literary Naturalism, and 'One of the Missing.'" *Ambrose Bierce Project Journal* 1.1 (2005). http://www.ambrosebierce.org/journal1emmert.html.

Ernest, John. "From Mysteries to Histories: Cultural Pedagogy in Frances E. W. Harper's *Iola Leroy*." *American Literature* 64.3 (1992): 497–518.

Escott, Paul D. *Military Necessity: Civil–Military Relations in the Confederacy*. Westport, Conn.: Praeger Security International, 2006.

Fabian, Ann. *The Unvarnished Truth: Personal Narratives in Nineteenth-Century America*. Berkeley: U of California P, 2000.

Fahs, Alice. *The Imagined Civil War: Popular Literature of the North and South, 1861–1865*. Chapel Hill: U of North Carolina P, 2001.

———. "The Market Value of Memory: Popular War Histories and the Northern Literary Marketplace, 1861–1868." *Book History* 1.1 (1998): 107–39.

Faust, Drew Gilpin. *This Republic of Suffering*. New York: Knopf, 2008.

Fehrenbacher, Don. *The Dred Scott Case: Its Significance in American Law and Politics*. New York: Oxford U P, 1978.

Fellman, Michael. *Citizen Sherman: A Life of William Tecumseh Sherman*. New York: Random House, 1995.

Fick, Thomas H. "Genre Wars and the Rhetoric of Manhood in Miss *Ravenel's Conversion from Secession to Loyalty*." *Nineteenth Century Literature* 46.4 (1992): 473–94.

Fleche, Andre. "'Shoulder to Shoulder as Comrades Tried': Black and White Union Veterans and Civil War Memory." *Civil War History* 51.2 (2005): 175–201.

Foos, Paul. *A Short, Offhand, Killing Affair: Soldiers and Social Conflict During the Mexican-American War*. Chapel Hill: U of North Carolina P, 2002.

Foner, Eric. *Free Soil, Free Labor, Free Men: The Ideology of the Republican Party Before the Civil War*. New York: Oxford U P, 1995.

———. *Reconstruction: America's Unfinished Revolution, 1863–1877*. New York: Harper and Row, 1988.

Foner, Philip. *The Great Labor Uprising of 1877*. New York: Monad Press, 1977.

Foreman, P. Gabrielle. "'Reading Aright': White Slavery, Black Referents, and the Strategy of Histotextuality in *Iola Leroy*." *Yale Journal of Criticism* 10.2 (1997): 327–54.

Förster, Stig, and Jörg Nagler (eds.). *On the Road to Total War: The American Civil War and the German Wars of Unification, 1861–1871*. New York: Cambridge U P, 1997.

Foster, Gaines. "Coming to Terms with Defeat: Post-Vietnam America and the Post–Civil War South." *Virginia Quarterly Review* 66.1 (1990): n.p.

———. *Ghosts of the Confederacy: Defeat, the Lost Cause, and the Emergence of the New South, 1865 to 1913*. New York: Oxford U P, 1987.

Fredrickson, George. *The Inner Civil War: Northern Intellectuals and the Crisis of the Union*. New York: Harper and Row, 1965.

Freud, Sigmund. "Psychoanalysis and the War Neuroses." *The Standard Edition of the Complete Psychological Works of Sigmund Freud*. Vol. 17. Ed. James Strachey. London: Hogarth Press, 1955.

Furgurson, Ernest B. *Not War But Murder: Cold Harbor, 1864*. New York: Alfred A. Knopf, 2000.

Gallagher, Gary W. *The Confederate War: How Popular Will, Nationalism, and Military Strategy Could Not Stave Off Defeat*. Cambridge, Mass.: Harvard U P, 1997.

———. *The Union War*. Cambridge, Mass.: Harvard U P, 2011.

Gannon, Barbara. *The Won Cause: Black and White Comradeship in the Grand Army of the Republic*. Chapel Hill: U of North Carolina P, 2011.

Gaston, Paul M. *The New South Creed: A Study in Southern Myth-Making*. New York: Knopf, 1970.

Gatewood, Willard. *Aristocrats of Color: The Black Elite, 1880–1920*. Fayetteville: U of Arkansas P, 2000.

Gayle, Addison. "Literature as Catharsis: The Novels of Paul Laurence Dunbar." *A Singer in the Dawn: Reinterpretations of Paul Laurence Dunbar*. Ed. Jay Martin. New York: Dodd, Mead, and Co., 1975.

Geary, James. *We Need Men: The Union Draft in the Civil War*. DeKalb: Northern Illinois U P, 1991.

Gibson, Donald. *The Red Badge of Courage: Redefining the Hero*. Boston: Twayne, 1988.

Gilman, Sander L. *Disease and Representation: Images of Illness from Madness to AIDS*. Ithaca, N.Y.: Cornell U P, 1988.

Glasner, David. "Crisis of 1873." *Business Cycles and Depressions: An Encyclopedia*. Ed. David Glasner. New York: Garland, 1997.

Glatthaar, Joseph T. *Forged in Battle: The Civil War Alliance of Black Soldiers and White Officers*. New York: Free Press, 1990.

Glickstein, Jonathan. *Concepts of Free Labor in Antebellum America*. New Haven, Conn.: Yale U P, 1991.

Goler, Robert. "Loss and the Persistence of Memory." *Literature and Medicine* 23.1 (2004): 160–83.

Gosling, F. G. *Before Freud: Neurasthenia and the American Medical Community, 1870–1910*. Urbana: U of Illinois P, 1987.

Grant, Susan-Mary. "The Lost Boys: Citizen-Soldiers, Disabled Veterans, and Confederate Nationalism in the Age of People's War." *Journal of the Civil War Era* 2.2 (2012): 233–59.

Grattan, C. Hartly. *Bitter Bierce: A Mystery of American Letters*. New York: Doubleday, 1929.
Grenander, Mary. *Ambrose Bierce*. New York: Twayne, 1971.
Griffin, Martin. *Ashes of the Mind: War and Memory in Northern Literature, 1865–1900*. Amherst: U of Massachusetts P, 2009.
Grimsley, Mark. *And Keep Moving On: The Virginia Campaign, May–June 1864*. Lincoln: U of Nebraska P, 2002.
———. *The Hard Hand of War: Union Military Policy Toward Southern Civilians, 1861–1865*. New York: Cambridge U P, 1995.
Gross, Theodore L. "The Fool's Errand of Albion W. Tourgée." *Phylon* 24.3 (1963): 240–54.
Grossman, Lt. Col. Dave. *On Killing: The Psychological Cost of Learning to Kill in War and Society*. New York: Little, Brown, 1996.
Guemple, Michael. "A Case for the Appleton *Red Badge of Courage*." *Resources for American Literary Study* 21.1 (1995): 43–57.
Haack, Kathleen, Ekkehardt Kumbier, and Sabine C. Herpertz. "Illnesses of the Will in 'Pre-psychiatric' Times." *History of Psychiatry* 21.3 (2010): 261–77.
Habegger, Alfred. "Fighting Words: The Talk of Men at War in *The Red Badge of Courage*." *Fictions of Masculinity: Crossing Cultures, Crossing Sexualities*. Ed. Peter Murphy. New York: NYU Press, 1994.
Hagerman, Edward. *The American Civil War and the Origins of Modern Warfare: Ideas, Organization, and Field Command*. Bloomington: Indiana U P, 1988.
———. "Union Generalship, Political Leadership, and Total War Strategy." *On the Road to Total War: The American Civil War and the German Wars of Unification, 1861–1871*. Eds. Stig Förster and Jörg Nagler. New York: Cambridge U P, 1997.
Hahn, Steven. *A Nation Under Our Feet: Black Political Struggles in the Rural South from Slavery to the Great Migration*. Cambridge, Mass.: Belknap Press of Harvard U P, 2003.
Halbwachs, Maurice. *On Collective Memory*. Chicago: U of Chicago P, 1992.
Hallwas, John. "Civil War Accounts as Literature: Illinois Letters, Diaries, and Personal Narratives." *Western Illinois Regional Studies* 13.1 (1990): 46–60.
Harrari, Yuval Noah. "Military Memoirs: A Historical Overview of the Genre from the Middle Ages to the Late Modern Era." *War in History* 14.3 (2007): 289–309.
———. *The Ultimate Experience: Battlefield Revelations and the Making of Modern War Culture, 1450–2000*. New York: Palgrave Macmillan, 2008.
Harrell, Willie. "'Nemmine. You Got to Git Somebody Else to Ring Yo' Ol' Bell Now': Nigger Ed and the Rhetoric of Local Color Realism and Racial Protest in Dunbar's *The Fanatics*." *We Wear the Mask: Paul Laurence Dunbar and the Politics of Representative Reality*. Ed. Willie J. Harrell Jr. Kent, Ohio: Kent State U P, 2010.
Harris, M. Keith. *Across the Bloody Chasm: The Culture of Commemoration Among Civil War Veterans*. Baton Rouge: Louisiana State U P, 2014.
Harwell, Richard Barksdale. "John Esten Cooke, Civil War Correspondent." *Journal of Southern History* 19.4 (1953): 501–16.

Henken, Elissa R. "Taming the Enemy: Georgian Narratives About the Civil War." *Journal of Folklore Research* 40.3 (2003): 289–307.
Hess, Earl J. *The Rifle Musket in Civil War Combat: Reality and Myth*. Lawrence: U P of Kansas, 2008.
———. "Tactics, Trenches, and Men in the Civil War." *On the Road to Total War: The American Civil War and the German Wars of Unification, 1861–1871*. Eds. Stig Förster and Jörg Nagler. New York: Cambridge U P, 1997.
———. *Trench Warfare Under Grant and Lee: Field Fortifications in the Overland Campaign*. Chapel Hill: U of North Carolina P, 2013.
———. *The Union Soldier in Battle: Enduring the Ordeal of Combat*. Lawrence: U P of Kansas, 1997.
Higgins, Andrew. "Reconstructing Rebellion: The Politics of Narrative in the Confederate Memoir." *Mississippi Quarterly* 58.1–2 (2004–5): 119–39.
Hijiya, James. *J. W. De Forest and the Rise of American Gentility*. Hannover, N.H.: U P of New England. 1988.
Hilkey, Judy. *Character Is Capital: Success Manuals and Manhood in Gilded Age America*. Chapel Hill: U of North Carolina P, 1997.
Hirshson, Stanley P. *The White Tecumseh: A Biography of General William T. Sherman*. New York: John Wiley and Sons, 1997.
Hoffman, Daniel. "Crane's Decoration Day Article and *The Red Badge of Courage*." *Nineteenth Century Fiction* 14.1 (1959): 78–80.
Hoganson, Kristen. *Fighting for American Manhood: How Gender Politics Provoked the Spanish-American and Philippine-American Wars*. New Haven, Conn.: Yale U P, 1998.
Holberton, William. *Homeward Bound: The Demobilization of the Union and Confederate Armies, 1865–1866*. Mechanicsville, Pa.: Stackpole Books, 2001.
Hollandsworth, James. *The Louisiana Native Guards: The Black Military Experience During the Civil War*. Baton Rouge: Louisiana State U P, 1995.
Hounshell, David. *From the American System to Mass Production: The Development of Manufacturing in the United States, 1800–1932*. Baltimore: Johns Hopkins U P, 1984.
Hughes, Jennifer. "The Politics of Incongruity in Paul Laurence Dunbar's *The Fanatics*." *African American Review* 41.2 (2007): 295–301.
Hunter, Adrian. "Obscured Hurts: The Civil War Writing of Henry James and Ambrose Bierce." *War, Literature, and the Arts* 14.1–2 (2002): 280–92.
Hunter, Devin. "Illinois Civil War Volunteer Regiment Histories and Cultural Memory, 1875–1890." Conference Paper. The Conference on Illinois History. Springfield, Ill. October 13, 2006.
Huntington, Samuel P. *The Soldier and the State: The Theory and Politics of Civil–Military Relations*. Cambridge, Mass.: Harvard U P, 1957.
Hunt, Nigel. *Memory, War, and Trauma*. New York: Cambridge U P, 2010.
Hunt, Robert. *The Good Men Who Won the War: Army of the Cumberland Veterans and Emancipation Memory*. Tuscaloosa: U of Alabama P, 2010.
Huston, James. *Securing the Fruits of Labor: The American Concept of Wealth Distribution, 1765–1900*. Baton Rouge: Louisiana State U P, 1998.

Inge, M. Thomas. "Sam Watkins and the Fictionality of Fact." *Rewriting the South: History and Fiction*. Eds. Lothar Honninghausen and Valeria Lerda. Tübingen: Francke, 1993.
Jackson, Blyden. *A History of Afro-American Literature: Volume I, the Long Beginning, 1746–1895*. Baton Rouge: Louisiana State U P, 1989.
Jackson, Gregory. "'A Dowry of Suffering': Consent, Contract, and Political Coverture in John W. De Forest's Reconstruction Romance." *American Literary History* 15.2 (2003): 276–310.
Jackson, Stanley W. *Melancholia and Depression: From Hippocratic Times to Modern Times*. New Haven, Conn.: Yale U P, 1990.
James, Jennifer. *A Freedom Bought with Blood: African American War Literature from the Civil War to World War II*. Chapel Hill: U of North Carolina P, 2007.
Janney, Caroline E. *Remembering the Civil War: Reunion and the Limits of Reconciliation*. Chapel Hill: U of North Carolina P, 2013.
Janoff-Bulman, Ronnie. *Shattered Assumptions: Towards a New Psychology of Trauma*. New York: Free Press, 1992.
Jarrett, Gene Andrew. *Deans and Truants: Race and Realism in African American Literature*. Philadelphia: U of Pennsylvania P, 2007.
Johanningsmeier, Charles. "The 1894 Syndicated Newspaper Appearances of *The Red Badge of Courage*." *American Literary Realism* 40.3 (2008): 226–47.
———. *Fiction and the American Literary Marketplace: The Role of the Newspaper Syndicates, 1860–1900*. New York: Cambridge U P, 1997.
Johannsen, Robert W. *To the Halls of the Montezumas: The Mexican War in the American Imagination*. New York: Oxford U P, 1985.
John, Arthur. *The Best Years of the Century: Richard Watson Gilder, Scribner's Monthly, and Century Magazine, 1870–1909*. Urbana: U of Illinois P, 1981.
Johnson, Steven K. "Uncanny Burials: Post–Civil War Memories in Chopin and Bierce." *Ambrose Bierce Journal* 2.1 (2006). http://www.ambrosebierce.org/journal2johnson.html.
Jones, P. M. (ed.). *Forgotten Soldiers: Murphysboro's African-American Civil War Veterans*. Murphysboro, Ill.: n.p., 1994.
Jordan, Brian Matthew. "'Living Monuments': Union Veteran Amputees and the Embodied Memory of the Civil War." *Civil War History* 57.2 (2011): 121–52.
Joshi, S. T., and David Schultz (eds.). *Ambrose Bierce: An Annotated Bibliography of Primary Sources*. Westport, Conn.: Greenwood, 1999.
Juhasz, Paul. "'No Matter What the Actual Hour May Be': Time Manipulation in the Works of Ambrose Bierce." *Ambrose Bierce Project Journal* 4.1 (2008). http://www.ambrosebierce.org/journal4juhasz1.html.
Kaplan, Amy. "Romancing the Empire: The Embodiment of American Masculinity in the Popular Historical Novel of the 1890s." *American Literary History* 2.4 (1990): 659–90.
Kaser, David. *Books and Libraries in Camp and Battle: The Civil War Experience*. Westport, Conn.: Greenwood Press, 1984.
Kawash, Samira. *Dislocating the Color Line: Identity, Hybridity, and Singularity in African-American Literature*. Stanford, Calif.: Stanford U P, 1997.

Keely, Karen. "Marriage Plots and National Reunion: The Trope of Romantic Reconciliation in Postbellum Literature." *Mississippi Quarterly* 51.4 (1998): 621-48.
Kelly, Patrick J. *Creating a National Home: Building the Veterans' Welfare State, 1860-1900*. Cambridge, Mass.: Harvard U P, 1997.
———. "The Election of 1896 and the Restructuring of Civil War Memory." *Civil War History* 49.3 (2003): 254-80.
Kemble, C. Robert. *The Image of the Army Officer in America: Background for Current Views*. Westport, Conn.: Greenwood Press, 1973.
Kern, Stephen. *The Culture of Time and Space, 1880-1918*. Cambridge, Mass.: Harvard U P, 2003.
Kettner, James. *The Development of American Citizenship, 1608-1870*. Chapel Hill: U of North Carolina P, 1978.
Kimball, William J. "Realism in Sidney Lanier's *Tiger-Lilies*." *South Atlantic Bulletin* 36.2 (1971): 17-20.
Kimmel, Michael. *Manhood in America: A Cultural History*. 2nd ed. New York: Oxford U P, 2006.
Klement, Frank. *The Limits of Dissent: Clement L. Vallandigham and the Civil War*. Lexington: U P of Kentucky, 1970.
Knouff, Gregory T. *The Soldiers' Revolution: Pennsylvanians in Arms and the Forging of Early American Identity*. University Park: Pennsylvania State U P, 2004.
Langston, Thomas S. *Uneasy Balance: Civil-Military Relations in Peacetime America Since 1783*. Baltimore: Johns Hopkins U P, 2003.
Lanier, Leonard. "Appealing to Different Virginias: Readjusters, Redeemers, and Richmond Civil War Veterans." Conference Paper. Virginia Forum. Lexington, Va. March 26, 2011.
Laurie, Bruce. *From Artisans to Workers: Labor in Nineteenth-Century America*. New York: Hill and Wang, 1989.
Lee, A. Robert. "The Fiction of Paul Laurence Dunbar." *Negro American Literature Forum* 8.1 (1974): 166-75.
Lentz, Perry. *Private Fleming at Chancellorsville*. Columbia: U of Missouri P, 2006.
Leys, Ruth. *Trauma: A Genealogy*. Chicago: U of Chicago P, 2000.
Light, James F. *John William De Forest*. New York: Twayne, 1965.
Limon, John. *Writing After War: American War Fiction from Realism to Postmodernism*. New York: Oxford U P, 1994.
Linares, Claudia. *The Civil War Pension Law*. Center for Population Economics Working Paper Series. November 2001.
Linderman, Gerald F. *Embattled Courage: The Experience of Combat in the American Civil War*. New York: Free Press, 1987.
Logue, Larry. *To Appomattox and Beyond: The Civil War Soldier in War and Peace*. Chicago: Ivan R. Dee, 1996.
Logue, Larry, and Michael Barton. *The Civil War Veteran: A Historical Reader*. New York: New York U P, 2007.
Logue, Larry, and Peter Blanck. *Race, Ethnicity, and Disability: Veterans and Benefits in Post-Civil War America*. New York: Cambridge U P, 2010.

Long, David. *The Jewel of Liberty: Abraham Lincoln's Re-election and the End of Slavery.* Mechanicsville, Pa.: Stackpole Books, 1994.

Long, Lisa A. *Rehabilitating Bodies: Health, History, and the American Civil War.* Philadelphia: U of Pennsylvania P, 2004.

Lubetkin, M. John. *Jay Cooke's Gamble: The Northern Pacific Railroad, the Sioux, and the Panic of 1873.* Norman: U of Oklahoma P, 2006.

Mahon, John K. *History of the Militia and the National Guard.* New York: Macmillan, 1983.

Manning, Chandra. "Working for Citizenship in Civil War Contraband Camps." *Journal of the Civil War Era* 4.2 (2014): 172–204.

Mariani, Giorgio. "Ambrose Bierce's Civil War Stories and the Critique of the Martial Spirit." *Studies in American Fiction* 19.2 (1991): 221–28.

Marshall, Nicholas. "The Great Exaggeration: Death and the Civil War." *Journal of the Civil War Era* 4.1 (2014): 3–27.

Marszalek, John F. *Sherman: A Soldier's Passion for Order.* Carbondale: Southern Illinois U P, 1993.

Marten, James. "Exempt from the Ordinary Rules of Life." *Civil War History* 47.1 (2001): 57–70.

———. *Sing Not War: The Lives of Union and Confederate Veterans in Gilded Age America.* Chapel Hill: U of North Carolina P, 2011.

Mattingly, Cheryl. *Healing Dramas and Clinical Plots: The Narrative Structure of Experience.* New York: Cambridge U P, 1998.

McClintock, Megan J. "Civil War Pensions and the Reconstruction of Union Families." *Journal of American History* 83.2 (1996): 456–80.

McClurken, Jeffrey W. *Take Care of the Living: Reconstructing Confederate Veteran Families in Virginia.* Charlottesville: U of Virginia P, 2009.

McConnell, Stuart. *Glorious Contentment: The Grand Army of the Republic, 1865–1900.* Chapel Hill: U of North Carolina P, 1992.

McPherson, James. *Battle Cry of Freedom.* New York: Ballantine Books, 1988.

———. *For Cause and Comrades: Why Men Fought in the Civil War.* New York: Oxford U P, 1998.

———. "From Limited War to Total War in America." *On the Road to Total War: The American Civil War and the German Wars of Unification, 1861–1871.* Eds. Stig Förster and Jörg Nagler. New York: Cambridge U P, 1997.

———. *The Negro's Civil War: How American Negroes Felt and Acted During the War for the Union.* Urbana: U of Illinois P, 1982.

McWilliams, Dean. *Charles W. Chesnutt and the Fictions of Race.* Athens: U of Georgia P, 2002.

Miller, Edward A., Jr. (ed.). *The Black Civil War Soldiers of Illinois: The Story of the Twenty-Ninth U.S. Colored Infantry.* Columbia: U of South Carolina P, 1998.

Miller, Jeffrey. "Redemption Through Violence: White Mobs and Black Citizenship in Albion Tourgée's *A Fool's Errand*." *Southern Literary Journal* 35.1 (2002): 14–27.

Mims, Edwin. *Sidney Lanier.* Boston: Gordon, 1905.

Mitchell, Lee Clark. *New Essays on the Red Badge of Courage*. New York: Cambridge U P, 1986.

Mitchell, Reid. *Civil War Soldiers*. New York: Viking Press, 1988.

———. *The Vacant Chair: The Northern Soldier Leaves Home*. New York: Oxford U P, 1993.

Mixon, Wayne. *Southern Writers and the New South Movement, 1865–1913*. Chapel Hill: U of North Carolina P, 1980.

Moody, Wesley. *Demon of the Lost Cause: Sherman and Civil War History*. Columbia: U of Missouri P, 2011.

Morris, Roy, Jr. *Ambrose Bierce: Alone in Bad Company*. New York: Crown, 1995.

———. "On Whose Responsibility? The Historical and Literary Underpinnings of *The Red Badge of Courage*." *Memory and Myth: The Civil War in Fiction and Film from Uncle Tom's Cabin to Cold Mountain*. Eds. David B. Sachsman, S. Kittrell Rushing, and Roy Morris Jr. Lafayette, Ind.: Purdue U P, 2007.

———. "'So Many Needless Dead': The Civil War Witness of Ambrose Bierce." *Memory and Myth: The Civil War in Fiction and Film from Uncle Tom's Cabin to Cold Mountain*. Eds. David B. Sachsman, S. Kittrell Rushing, and Roy Morris Jr. Lafayette, Ind.: Purdue U P, 2007.

Mulderink, Earl F., III. "A Different Civil War: African American Veterans in New Bedford, Massachusetts." *Union Soldiers and the Northern Home Front: Wartime Experiences, Postwar Adjustments*. Eds. Paul A. Cimbala and Randall M. Miller. New York: Fordham U P, 2002.

Murdock, Eugene. *One Million Men: The Civil War Draft in the North*. Westport, Conn.: Greenwood Press, 1980.

Neely, Mark E., Jr. *The Civil War and the Limits of Destruction*. Cambridge: Harvard U P, 2007.

———. *Fate of Liberty: Abraham Lincoln and Civil Liberties*. New York: Oxford U P, 1992.

———. "Was the Civil War a Total War?" *Civil War History* 50.4 (2004): 434–58.

Nelson, Dana. "Sympathy as Strategy in Hope Leslie." *The Culture of Sentiment: Race, Gender, and Sentimentality in 19th-Century America*. Ed. Shirley Samuels. New York: Oxford U P, 1992.

Nelson, Larry E. *Bullets, Ballot, and Rhetoric: Confederate Policy for the United States Presidential Contest of 1864*. University: U of Alabama P, 1980.

Nelson, Megan Kate. *Ruin Nation: Destruction and the American Civil War*. Athens: U of Georgia P, 2012.

Newell, Clayton R., and Charles R. Shrader. "The U.S. Army's Transition to Peace, 1865–66." *Journal of Military History* 77.3 (2013): 867–94.

Newhouse, Wade. "Reporting Triumph, Saving a Nation: 'Interesting Juxtapositions' in John W. De Forest's Civil War." *Studies in American Fiction* 32.2 (2004): 165–83.

Nora, Pierre. "Between Memory and History: Les Lieux de Memoire." *Representations* 26 (1989): 7–24.

Oberly, James W. *Sixty Million Acres: American Veterans and the Public Lands Before the Civil War*. Kent, Ohio: Kent State U P, 1990.

O'Brien, Tim. "How to Tell a True War Story." *The Things They Carried*. New York: Broadway Books, 1990.
Olson, Otto. *Carpetbagger's Crusade: The Life of Albion Winegar Tourgée*. Baltimore: Johns Hopkins U P, 1965.
Orr, Timothy. "A Viler Enemy in Our Rear: Pennsylvania Soldiers Confront the North's Antiwar Movement." *The View from the Ground: Experiences of Civil War Soldiers*. Ed. Aaron Sheehan-Dean. Lexington: U P of Kentucky, 2007.
Orvell, Miles. *The Real Thing: Imitation and Authenticity in American Culture, 1880–1940*. Chapel Hill: U of North Carolina P, 1989.
Owens, David M. *The Devil's Topographer: Ambrose Bierce and the American War Story*. Knoxville: U of Tennessee P, 2006.
Painter, Nell Irvin. *Exodusters: Black Migration to Kansas After Reconstruction*. New York: W. W. Norton, 1979.
Pennebaker, James W., and Janel D. Seagal. "Forming a Story: The Health Benefits of Narrative." *Journal of Clinical Psychology* 55.10 (1999): 1243–54.
Persons, Stow. *The Decline of American Gentility*. New York: Columbia U P, 1973.
Pesking, Allan. *Garfield: A Biography*. Kent, Ohio: Kent State U P, 1978.
Pittman, Coretta. "Rhetorical Accountability: Paul Laurence Dunbar's Search for 'Representative' Men." *We Wear the Mask: Paul Laurence Dunbar and the Politics of Representative Reality*. Ed. Willie J. Harrell Jr. Kent, Ohio: Kent State U P, 2010.
Pizarro, Judith, Roxane Cohen, Silver, and JoAnn Prause. "Physical and Mental Health Costs of Traumatic War Experiences Among Civil War Veterans." *Archives of General Psychiatry* 63 (2006): 193–200.
Pizer, Donald. "Henry Behind the Lines and the Concept of Manhood in *The Red Badge of Courage*." *Stephen Crane Studies* 10.1 (2001): 2–7.
Prucha, Francis Paul. *Broadax and Bayonet: The Role of the United States Army in the Development of the Northwest, 1815–1860*. Lincoln: U of Nebraska P, 1967.
Purcell, Sarah J. *Sealed with Blood: War, Sacrifice, and Memory in Revolutionary America*. Philadelphia: U of Pennsylvania P, 2002.
Pursell, Carroll. *The Machine in America: A Social History of Technology*. Baltimore: Johns Hopkins U P, 1995.
Putney, Martha. *Black Sailors: Afro-American Merchant Seamen and Whalemen Prior to the Civil War*. New York: Greenwood Press, 1987.
Ramold, Steven. *Slaves, Sailors, Citizens: African Americans in the Union Navy*. DeKalb: Northern Illinois U P, 2002.
Raynor, Sharon. "'Sing A Song Heroic': Paul Laurence Dunbar's Mythic and Poetic Tribute to Black Soldiers." *We Wear the Mask: Paul Laurence Dunbar and the Politics of Representative Reality*. Ed. Willie J. Harrell Jr. Kent, Ohio: Kent State U P, 2010.
Reardon, Carol. *With a Sword in One Hand and Jomini in Another: The Problem of Military Thought in the Civil War North*. Chapel Hill: U of North Carolina P, 2012.
Regosin, Elizabeth. *Freedom's Promise: Ex-slave Families and Citizenship in the Age of Emancipation*. Charlottesville: U P of Virginia, 2002.
Reid, Richard M. *Freedom for Themselves: North Carolina's Black Soldiers in the Civil War Era*. Chapel Hill: U of North Carolina P, 2008.

———. "USCT Veterans in Post–Civil War North Carolina." *Black Soldiers in Blue: African American Troops in the Civil War Era.* Ed. John David Smith. Chapel Hill: U of North Carolina P, 2002.

Resch, John. *Suffering Soldiers: Revolutionary War Veterans, Moral Sentiment, and Political Culture in the Early Republic.* Amherst: U of Massachusetts P, 1999.

Revell, Peter. *Paul Laurence Dunbar.* Boston: Twayne, 1979.

Reynolds, Larry. *European Revolutions and the American Literary Renaissance.* New Haven: Yale U P, 1988.

Richardson, Heather Cox. *The Death of Reconstruction: Race, Labor, and Politics in the Post–Civil War North, 1865–1901.* Cambridge, Mass.: Harvard U P, 2001.

Robertson, Michael. *Stephen Crane, Journalism, and the Making of Modern American Literature.* New York: Columbia U P, 1997.

Roberts, Timothy. *Distant Revolutions: 1848 and the Challenge to American Exceptionalism.* Charlottesville: U of Virginia P, 2009.

Robinett, Jane. "The Narrative Shape of Traumatic Experience." *Literature and Medicine* 26.2 (2007): 290–311.

Robinson, Armistead L. "Not North of Dixie's Line: The Social Limitations and Political Implications of the Wartime Emancipation Process." *Soldiers and Civilians: The U.S. Army and the American People.* Eds. Garry D. Ryan and Timothy K. Nenninger. Washington, D.C.: National Archives and Records Administration, 1987.

Robinson, Lillian. "Paul Laurence Dunbar: A Credit to His Race?" *African American Review* 41.2 (2007): 215–25.

Robison, Lori. "An 'Imperceptible Infusion' of Blood: Iola Leroy, Racial Identity, and Sentimental Discourse." *Genre* 37.3–4 (2004): 433–60.

Roggenkamp, Karen. *Narrating the News: New Journalism and Literary Genre in Late-Nineteenth-Century American Newspapers and Fiction.* Kent, Ohio: Kent State U P, 2005.

Rosenburg, R. B. *Living Monuments: Confederate Soldiers' Homes in the New South.* Chapel Hill: U of North Carolina P, 1993.

Rosen, George. "Nostalgia: A 'Forgotten' Psychological Disorder." *Psychological Medicine* 5.4 (1975): 340–54.

Rotundo, Anthony. *American Manhood: Transformations in Masculinity from the Revolution to the Modern Era.* New York: Basic Books, 1993.

Royster, Charles. *A Revolutionary People at War: The Continental Army and American Character, 1775–1783.* Chapel Hill: U of North Carolina P, 1986.

Samito, Christian. *Becoming American Under Fire: Irish Americans, African Americans, and the Politics of Citizenship During the Civil War Era.* Ithaca, N.Y.: Cornell U P, 2009.

Samuels, Shirley (ed.). *The Culture of Sentiment: Race, Gender, and Sentimentality in 19th-Century America.* New York: Oxford U P, 1992.

Sandage, Scott A. *Born Losers: A History of Failure in America.* Cambridge, Mass.: Harvard U P, 2005.

Savage, Kirk. *Standing Soldiers, Kneeling Slaves.* Princeton, N.J.: Princeton U P, 1997.

Scary, Elaine. *The Body in Pain: The Making and Unmaking of the World*. New York: Oxford U P, 1985.

Schaefer, Michael. "'Heroes Had No Shame in Their Lives': Manhood, Heroics, and Compassion in *The Red Badge of Courage* and 'A Mystery of Heroism.'" *War, Literature, and the Arts* 18.1–2 (2006): 104–13.

———. *Just What War Is: The Civil War Writings of De Forest and Bierce*. Knoxville: U of Tennessee P, 1997.

Schivelbusch, Wolfgang. *The Culture of Defeat: On National Trauma, Mourning, and Recovery*. New York: Picador, 2003.

Schmidt, Peter. *Sitting in Darkness: New South Fiction, Education, and the Rise of Jim Crow Colonialism, 1865–1920*. Oxford: U P of Mississippi, 2008.

Shaffer, Donald R. *After the Glory: The Struggles of Black Civil War Veterans*. Lawrence: U of Kansas P, 2004.

Shay, Jonathan. *Achilles in Vietnam: Combat Trauma and the Undoing of Character*. New York: Scribner, 1995.

Short, Joanna. "Confederate Veteran Pensions, Occupation, and Men's Retirement in the New South." *Social Science History* 30.1 (2006): 75–101.

Silber, Nina. *The Romance of Reunion: Northerners and the South, 1865–1900*. Chapel Hill: U of North Carolina P, 1993.

Skelton, William B. *An American Profession of Arms: The Army Officer Corps, 1784–1861*. Lawrence: U P of Kansas, 1992.

Skocpol, Theda. *Protecting Soldiers and Mothers: The Political Origins of Social Policy in the United States*. Cambridge, Mass.: Harvard U P, 1992.

Skocpol, Theda, and Jennifer Lynn Oser. "Organization Despite Adversity: The Origins and Development of African American Fraternal Associations." *Social Science History* 28.3 (2004): 367–437.

Slap, Andrew. *The Doom of Reconstruction: The Liberal Republicans in the Civil War Era*. New York: Fordham U P, 2010.

Smith, John David (ed.). *Black Soldiers in Blue: African American Troops in the Civil War Era*. Chapel Hill: U of North Carolina P, 2004.

Smith, Ronald. *Sports and Freedom: The Rise of Big-Time College Athletics*. New York: Oxford U P, 1988.

Smyth, Joshua, Nicole True, and Joy Souto (eds.). "Effects of Writing About Traumatic Experiences: The Necessity for Narrative Structuring." *Journal of Social and Clinical Psychology* 20.2 (2001): 161–72.

Smythe, Ted Curtis. *The Gilded Age Press, 1865–1900*. Westport, Conn.: Praeger Press, 2003.

Snyder, R. Claire. *Citizen-Soldiers and Manly Warriors: Military Service and Gender in the Civic Republican Tradition*. New York: Rowman and Littlefield, 1999.

Sobel, Robert. *Panic on Wall Street: A Classic History of America's Financial Disasters—with a New Exploration of the Crash of 1987*. New York: Truman Talley Books/E. P. Dutton, 1988.

Solomon, Eric. "A Gloss on *The Red Badge of Courage*." *Modern Language Notes* 75.2 (1960): 111–13.

———. "The Novelist as Soldier: Cooke and De Forest." *American Literary Realism* 19.3 (1987): 80–88.
Sperber, Jonathan. *The European Revolutions, 1848–1851*. New York: Cambridge U P, 1994.
Stanley, Amy Dru. *From Bondage to Contract: Wage Labor, Marriage, and the Market in the Age of Slave Emancipation*. New York: Cambridge U P, 1998.
Starke, Aubrey H. *Sidney Lanier: A Biographical and Critical Study*. Chapel Hill: U of North Carolina P, 1933.
Stowell, David (ed.). *The Great Strikes of 1877*. Urbana: U of Illinois P, 2008.
Summers, Mark Wahlgren. *The Era of Good Stealings*. New York: Oxford U P, 1993.
———. *Railroads, Reconstruction, and the Gospel of Prosperity: Aid Under the Radical Republicans, 1865–1877*. Princeton: Princeton U P, 1984.
Strauss, Tracy L. "Trauma's Dialectic in Civil War Literature and Film." *War Literature and the Arts* 20.1–2 (2008): 206–24.
Tal, Kalí. *Worlds of Hurt: Reading the Literatures of Trauma*. New York: Cambridge U P, 1996.
Tang, Edward. "Writing the American Revolution: War Veterans in the Nineteenth-Century Cultural Memory." *Journal of American Studies* 32.1 (1998): 63–80.
Taylor, Eric. "Confederates Against Confederates: William Mahone, the Lost Cause, and Political Insurgency in Virginia, 1876–77." Conference Paper. Virginia Forum. Newport News, Va. April 17, 2010.
Terry, Jennifer. "When Dey 'Listed Colored Soldiers': Paul Laurence Dunbar's Poetic Engagement with the Civil War, Masculinity, and Violence." *African American Review* 41.2 (2007): 269–75.
Thomas, Emory M. *The Confederacy as a Revolutionary Experience*. Columbia: U of South Carolina P, 1992.
Thompson, Todd. "Reconstructive Realism: Satire in *Miss Ravenel's Conversion from Secession to Loyalty*." *Journal of American Culture* 29.4 (2006): 425–36.
Thomson, Rosemarie Garland. *Extraordinary Bodies: Figuring Physical Disability in American Culture and Literature*. New York: Columbia U P, 1997.
Tolnay, Stewart, and E. M. Beck. *A Festival of Violence: An Analysis of Southern Lynchings, 1882–1930*. Urbana: U of Illinois P, 1995.
Tomblin, Barbara. *Bluejackets and Contrabands: African Americans and the Union Navy*. Lexington: U P of Kentucky, 2009.
Townsend, Kim. *Manhood at Harvard: William James and Others*. New York: W.W. Norton, 1996.
Trachtenberg, Alan. *The Incorporation of America: Culture and Society in the Gilded Age*. New York: Hill and Wang, 1982.
Trent, Logan Douglas. *The Credit Mobilier*. New York: Arno Press, 1981.
Trudeau, Noah Andre. *Like Men of War: Black Troops in the Civil War, 1861–1865*. Boston: Little, Brown, 1998.
Utley, Robert. *Frontier Regulars: The United States Army and the Indian, 1866–1891*. New York: MacMillan Publishing Co., 1973.
———. *Frontiersmen in Blue: The United States Army and the Indian, 1848–1865*. Lincoln: U of Nebraska P, 1981.

Van der Kolk, Bessel A. "The Body Keeps the Score: Approaches to the Psychobiology of Posttraumatic Stress Disorder." *Traumatic Stress: The Effects of Overwhelming Experience on Mind, Body, and Society*. Eds. Bessel van der Kolk, Alexander McFarlane, and Lars Weisaeth. New York: Guilford Press, 1996.

———. "Trauma and Memory." *Traumatic Stress: The Effects of Overwhelming Experience on Mind, Body, and Society*. Eds. Bessel van der Kolk, Alexander McFarlane, and Lars Weisaeth. New York: Guilford Press, 1996.

Van der Kolk, Bessel, Alexander McFarlane, and Lars Weisaeth (eds.). *Traumatic Stress: The Effects of Overwhelming Experience on Mind, Body, and Society*. New York: Guilford Press, 1996.

Van Wagenen, Michael Scott. *Remembering the Forgotten War: The Enduring Legacies of the U.S.-Mexican War*. Amherst: U of Massachusetts P, 2012.

Vetter, Charles Edmund. *Sherman: Merchant of Terror, Advocate of Peace*. Gretna, La.: Pelican Publishing, 1992.

Wachtell, Cynthia. *War No More: The Antiwar Impulse in American Literature, 1861–1914*. Baton Rouge: Louisiana State U P, 2010.

Wang, Xi. *The Trial of Democracy: Black Suffrage and Northern Republicans, 1860–1910*. Athens: U of Georgia P, 1997.

Warren, Craig. *Scars to Prove It: The Civil War Soldier and American Fiction*. Kent, Ohio: Kent State U P, 2009.

Washington, Versalle F. *Eagles on Their Buttons: A Black Infantry Regiment in the Civil War*. Columbia: U of Missouri P, 1999.

Wecter, Dixon. *When Johnny Comes Marching Home*. Boston: Houghton Mifflin, 1944.

Weigley, Russell F. "The American Civil–Military Cultural Gap: A Historical Perspective, Colonial Times to the Present." *Soldiers and Civilians: The Civil–Military Gap and American National Security*. Eds. Peter D. Feaver and Richard H. Kohn. Triangle Institute for Security Studies. Cambridge, Mass.: MIT Press, 2001.

Weihong, Julia Zhu. "The Absurdity of Henry's Courage." *Stephen Crane Studies* 10.2 (2001): 2–11.

Welke, Barbara. *Law and the Borders of Belonging in the Long Nineteenth-Century United States*. New York: Cambridge U P, 2010.

Wertheim, Stanley. *A Stephen Crane Encyclopedia*. Westport, Conn.: Greenwood Press, 1997.

Westwood, Howard. *Black Troops, White Commanders, and Freedmen During the Civil War*. Carbondale: Southern Illinois U P, 1992.

White, Jonathan W. "Canvassing the Troops: The Federal Government and the Soldier's Right to Vote." *Civil War History* 50.3 (2004): 291–317.

Whites, Lee Ann. *The Civil War as a Crisis in Gender: Augusta, Georgia, 1860–1890*. Athens: U of Georgia P, 1995.

Wicker, Elmus. *Banking Panics of the Gilded Age*. New York: Cambridge U P, 2000.

Wiebe, Robert. *The Search for Order, 1877–1920*. New York: Hill and Wang, 1967.

Williams, Andreá. *Dividing Lines: Class Anxiety and Postbellum Black Fiction*. Ann Arbor: U of Michigan P, 2013.

Williams, Heather Andrea. "'Commenced to Think Like a Man': Literacy and Manhood in African American Civil War Regiments." *Southern Manhood: Perspectives on Masculinity in the Old South*. Eds. Craig Thompson Friend and Lorri Glover. Athens: U of Georgia P, 2004.

Williams, Kenny J. "The Masking of the Novelist." *A Singer in the Dawn: Reinterpretations of Paul Laurence Dunbar*. Ed. Jay Martin. New York: Dodd, Mead, and Co., 1975.

Williams, Rusty. *My Old Confederate Home: A Respectable Place for Civil War Veterans*. Lexington: U P of Kentucky, 2010.

Wills, Jack. "John Esten Cooke." *Dictionary of Literary Biography*, Volume 248: *Antebellum Writers in the South, Second Series*. Ed. Kent Ljungquist. Detroit: Gale Group, 2001.

Wilson, Christopher Kent. "Winslow Homer's *The Veteran in a New Field*: A Study of the Harvest Metaphor and Popular Culture." *American Art Journal* 17.4 (1985): 2–27.

Wilson, Edmund. *Patriotic Gore: Studies in the Literature of the American Civil War*. New York: Oxford U P, 1962.

Windars, Richard Bruce. *Mr. Polk's Army: The American Military Experience in the Mexican War*. College Station: Texas A&M U P, 1997.

Wolford, Chester L. *The Anger of Stephen Crane*. Lincoln: U of Nebraska P, 1983.

Wright, Nathalia. "The East Tennessee Background of Sidney Lanier's *Tiger-Lilies*." *American Literature* 19.2 (1947): 127–38.

Wyllie, Irvin. *The Self-Made Man in America: The Myth of Rags to Riches*. New York: Free Press, 1954.

Yarborough, Richard. "Race, Violence, and Manhood: The Masculine Ideal in Frederick Douglass's 'The Heroic Slave.'" *Frederick Douglass: New Literary and Historical Essays*. Ed. Eric Sundquist. New York: Cambridge U P, 1990.

Young, Elizabeth. *Disarming the Nation: Women's Writing and the American Civil War*. Chicago: U of Chicago P, 1999.

———. "Warring Fictions: *Iola Leroy* and the Color of Gender." *American Literature* 64.2 (1992): 273–97.

Zornow, William Frank. *Lincoln and the Party Divided*. Norman: U of Oklahoma P, 1954.

Index

107th United States Colored Troops, 61
141st Illinois Regiment, 59

Acres of Diamonds (Conwell), 62
Across the Bloody Chasm (Harris), 167n6
"The Affair at Coulter's Notch" (Bierce), 99
African American community: ambivalence toward the perceived value of military service, 16, 131, 132, 146–59, 162; Emancipation Day celebrations, 146, 191n43; racial uplift and the search for new role models in the Jim Crow era, 145–47
African American military service: black community ambivalence toward the perceived value of, 16, 131, 132, 146–59, 162; differences between the experiences of black and white troops, 135, 161; histories of, 131–32, 160–61; the quest for citizenship rights and, 130, 132–39, 161; racial discrimination experienced during the Civil War, 130–31, 161; response of black veterans to the decline in the perceived value of, 131–32, 159–62; in the U.S. Navy, 187n4, 188–89n17
African American soldiers: combat and, 136–38; denial of the right to serve as officers, 142, 190n32; enlistment in the Union army, 188n11; military service and a change in identity, 130; military service and the quest for citizenship rights, 130, 132–39, 161; pay inequalities, 138–39. *See also* United States Colored Troops
African American veterans: assaults on in the 1880s and 1890s, 159–60; banding together of, 141; declining stature of in the post-Reconstruction era, 131, 142, 144–45, 162; demobilization, 140–41; histories of black military service, 131–32, 160–61; interracial veterans' groups, 160; military service and a change in identity, 130; military service and the quest for citizenship rights, 130, 132–39, 161; positive impact of during Reconstruction, 131, 141–42, 162; racial discrimination experienced during military service,

130–31, 161, 188–89n17; racial uplift and the search for new role models in the Jim Crow era, 145–47; rearguard defense of martial manhood, 159–62; reintegration experience, 10, 15–16; response to the decline in the perceived value of military service by the black community, 131–32, 159–62; of the Revolutionary War, 140; as targets of racial violence, 161; voting rights and, 139–40
Alger, Russell, 182–83n5
"An American Goddess Between Veterans of Two Wars," 127, *128*
army camps: black troops and, 135
Arp, Bill, 181n47
artisanal manhood: Civil War veterans and the struggle for, 48–49, 54–63; *Figs and Thistles* as a corporate jeremiad, 67–73; Homer's *The Veteran in a New Field* and, 51–54; ideal of, 49–54; the revival of the natural gentleman in *The Heir of Gaymount*, 63–67
autobiographical sketches: of Ambrose Bierce, 79, 96–98

Bacheller, Irving, 122
Ball, Durwood, 37
Barber, William Harrison, 24–25
Bates, Henry, 144
Beaty, John, 65
Belo, A. H., 110
Bierce, Ambrose: effect of combat trauma on, 79, 181n55; importance of stories and sketches as a narrative of Civil War experience, 13–14, 75; witness to the "authentic" horror of war in the writings of, 79–80, 82, 83, 95–103
Bigelow, Kathryn, 166
Binder, Henry, 118, 185–86n34
The Black Phalanx (Wilson), 16, 160
Blair, Montgomery, 28
Blakeslee, B. F., 21
Blight, David, 80, 178n4
Blue-Gray reunions, 3
Bond, Daniel, 8

Bostick, Dudley and Stephen, 144–45
Boynton, H. V., 84–85
Bricks Without Straw (Tourgée), 68
Brown, Bill, 126
Bryant, A. R., 139

Caruth, Cathy, 78
Century, 81
Chesnutt, Andrew Jackson, 142
Chesnutt, Charles, 142, 147, 155
Chicago Daily Inter-Ocean, 72, 146
Chicago Record, 147
Chicago Tribune, 133
Christian Recorder, 133, 139, 158
Churchill, Amos, 59
Cincinnati Gazette, 84
Cincinnatus, 51
citizenship: black military service and the quest for citizenship rights, 130, 132–39, 161; legal confusion around, 133, 135; linked to manhood and military service, 111
citizen-soldier concept: in *Miss Ravenel's Conversion*, 18, 34, 35–39, 46
civilian anxieties: about soldiers returning home, 10–12, 17, 27–30; wounded warrior imagery and the dispelling of, 17–18, 30–34
Civil War: black military service and the quest for citizenship rights, 130, 132–39, 161; Confederate strategy in, 6–7; demobilization experiences in the Union and Confederate armies, 19–24; government expenditures on veteran pensions, 183n8 (*see also* veteran pensions); Grant's strategies and tactics, 6, 7–8, 169n19; impact on fiction, 5; "modernity" or "totality" of, 5–8, 164; racial discrimination experienced by black troops during, 130–31, 161; Sherman's "march to the sea," 5, 87–89; as a transformative experience altering veteran self-identity, 163–66
Civil War memoirs: analysis of veteran reintegration and, 8–9; *Company Aytch*, 13, 14, 74–75, 80, 82–83, 90–95; important works, 74–75; narrative expectations of the civilian audience and, 81; period of greatest publication, 74; relationship between trauma and narrative, 78–83; Sherman's *Memoirs*, 13, 14, 80, 81–82, 83–90; shortage of black veteran narratives, 15–16; sources of inner turmoil in, 81–83; trauma and the veteran, 75–78; troubled nature of, 13–14; veteran self-identity and, 75, 80–81; the writings of Ambrose Bierce, 13–14, 75, 79–80, 82, 83, 95–101
Civil War monuments, 109
Civil War veterans: active management of Civil War remembrance, 111–13; aging veterans and the intergenerational struggle with the younger male generation, 14–15, 104–5, 113–29; artisanal manhood and the quest for postwar employment, 48–49; claims to representational authority of "their war," 2; cultural burden of, 110–13; Decoration Day parades and the distinction between living memory and history, 109–10; demobilization (*see* demobilization); impact of the war on, 8; interracial veterans' groups, 160; links between manhood, citizenship, and service, 111; mortality in the 1890s, 110; pensions, 106–10, 183n8; the postwar "road to reunion" and, 3, 167n6; reactions to wounded warrior imagery, 18–19; reintegration (*see* veteran reintegration); self-identity (*see* veteran self-identity); Spanish-American War and, 126–29; struggle for artisanal manhood and, 48–49, 54–63 (*see also* artisanal manhood); trauma and, 75–78, 178n4; as U.S. presidents, 105; view of war service as "experience," 9
Claverack College, 114
Cleveland, Grover, 105
Cold Harbor, Battle of, 8
college sports, 115, 184–85n23
The Colored Patriots of the American Revolution (Nell), 140
"The Colored Soldiers" (Dunbar), 146, 148–49
Columbia Herald, 91
combat trauma: Civil War veterans and, 75–78, 178n4; commanding officers and, 83; relationship to narrative, 78–83. *See also* trauma
commanding officers: combat trauma and, 83; war memoirs and, 90–95. *See also* Grant, Ulysses S.; Sherman, William Tecumseh
Company Aytch (Watkins): ambivalence of psychic closure in, 80; importance as a personal narrative of Civil War experience, 74–75; influence of regimental histories and tall tales on, 91–92; limitations of personal narratives and, 91; publication of, 91; sources of inner turmoil and the struggle with traumatic memory, 13, 82–83; types of sketches in and the challenge to communal ties, 92–95; veteran self-identity and, 14

Index

Confederate army: experiences of demobilization, 19–20; strategy in the war, 6–7
Confederate Veteran, 77, 113
Confederate veterans: John Cooke and the return of the natural gentleman in *The Heir of Gaymount*, 63–67 (see also *The Heir of Gaymount*); ineligibility for federal pensions, 106; meaning of reunions, 3; struggle for artisanal manhood and, 58–59; veteran self-identity and the management of Civil War remembrance, 113; wounded warrior imagery and the search for empathy in *Tiger-Lilies*, 18–19, 34, 39–47. *See also* Civil War veterans
Confiscation Acts, 187n1, 188n11
Conwell, Russell, 62
Cooke, John Esten: belief in the efficacy of good character, 62; natural gentleman concept and, 176n43; on realist fiction, 67. *See also The Heir of Gaymount*
Cooper, James Fenimore, 176n40
corporate capitalism: Albion Tourgée's critiques of, 12–13, 67–73, 177n48; veterans' rejection of, 50
corporate jeremiad, 12–13, 67–73
Crane, Stephen: college athletics and, 115, 184–85n23; intergenerational struggle with aging veterans and, 14–15, 104–5, 113–29; newspaper writings of, 115–18; origins of *The Red Badge of Courage*, 114–18; "realistic" account of war and, 5; transcendent experience of war, 126; "The Veteran," 14–15, 123–25; as a war correspondent, 15, 125–26. *See also The Red Badge of Courage*
Crédit Mobilier scandal, 177n53
Cummings, Charles L., 54–58, 175n17
Curry, Jonas, 20

Da Costa, J. M., 76–77
Daily Gazette (Emporia, Kansas), 146
Dean, Eric, 75–76, 77
Decoration Day: newspaper articles and *The Red Badge of Courage*, 116–18; parades, 109–10, 126
De Forest, John William: war experience of, 34. *See also Miss Ravenel's Conversion from Secession to Loyalty*
demobilization: civilian anxieties about veterans returning home, 10–12, 17, 27–30; conflicting emotions of veterans, 24–27; experiences in the Union and Confederate armies, 19–24; experiences of black soldiers, 140–41; veterans' anxieties about social status, 26–27; wounded warrior imagery, 17–18
Denver Daily News, 108
DePastino, Todd, 61
Dependent Pension Act, 106–7
"The Devil's Dictionary" (Bierce), 98
The Dial, 121
disabled veterans: struggle for artisanal manhood and, 54–59
double-consciousness, 147
Douglass, Frederick, 132–33
Downs, Levy, 61
Dred Scott decision, 132
Dunbar, Joshua, 148
Dunbar, Paul Laurence: ambivalence toward the significance of black military service in the works of, 16, 131, 146, 147–55, 162; family history, 148; influence of the generation gap on the attitudes of, 155; mask metaphor and, 147

economic panics, 48–49
Emancipation Day, 146, 191n43
Emancipation Proclamation, 133
empathy: the search for in *Tiger-Lilies*, 18–19, 34, 39–47
"The Empty Sleeve at Newport," 30, 32–34
Exodusters, 145

Fairfax, Alfred, 145
The Fanatics (Dunbar), 16, 146, 150–55
Faust, Drew Gilpin, 178n4
Fellman, Michael, 85
Fick, Thomas, 36
fiction: analysis of veteran reintegration through, 8–9; concern with finding the "real" war, 5; depiction of civilian anxieties about soldiers returning home, 10–12; depiction of demobilization, 22–23; depiction of the societal consequences of the veterans' exclusive sense of self, 14–15; depiction of the troubled nature of veterans' memories, 13–14; depiction of veterans' reentry into society, 12–13; impact of the Civil War on, 5; reactions to civilian anxieties and wounded warrior imagery by veteran authors, 18–19, 34–47; shift in the conception of veterans, 5. *See also individual works*
Field, Joseph, 21–22

Fifteenth Amendment, 142
Fifth Connecticut Regiment, 21
Fifth Regiment, U.S. Colored Troops, 141
Fifty-Fifth Illinois Regiment, 24
Fifty-Fifth Massachusetts Regiment, 139, 148
Fifty-Fourth Massachusetts Regiment, 133, 138–39
Fifty-Second Virginia Regiment, 58
Figs and Thistles (Tourgée): artisanal manhood and, 48; on civilian employment and the reentry of veterans into society, 12–13; constancy of good character in, 62–63; James Garfield and, 72
Finch, Edwin, 26
First Confiscation Act, 188n11
First Louisiana Native Guards, 138
flashbacks, 100
Foner, Eric, 142
A Fool's Errand (Tourgée), 68
Fortieth Alabama Regiment, 20
Forty-Ninth Ohio Regiment, 21
Forty-Ninth Pennsylvania Regiment, 24–25
Fourteenth Amendment, 133, 142
Fourth U.S. Colored Heavy Artillery, 144
Frank Leslie's Illustrated Newspaper, 51, 53, 54
Freedom's Lawmakers (Foner), 142

Galveston News, 109–10, 111–13
Gannon, Barbara, 15
Garfield, James, 72
gender relations: separate spheres concept, 172n37; wounded warrior imagery and, 30–34
German prose romance, 40
Gettysburg, Battle of, 8
Gilded Age: economic panics and strikes, 48–49; ideal of artisanal manhood, 49–54
Goodman, Duke, 113
Grand Army Journal, 59
Grant, Ulysses S.: burlesqued in "Jupiter Doke, Brigadier-General," 181n60; government corruption under the presidency of, 49, 177n53; narrative of the Battle of Shiloh, 81; perspective on his own participation in the war, 89; strategies and tactics as general of the army, 6, 7–8, 169n19
"The Gratitude of a Nation" (Crane), 116, 117–18
The Great War Relic, 54–58
Gullason, Thomas, 116

Hall, James Henry, 133
Halleck, Henry, 86–87, 89

Hampton, Wade, 89
Harari, Yuval Noah, 164
Harper, Frances Ellen Watkins: ambivalence toward the significance of black military service in the works of, 16, 146–47, 156–59, 162; desire for a moral equivalent of war, 158; *Minnie's Sacrifice*, 158, 193n71
Harper's Weekly, 10, 30, 136, 137
Harris, Keith, 167n6
"Have We Come to Caesarism?", 28–29
Hayes, Rutherford B., 49
The Heir of Gaymount (Cooke): belief in the efficacy of good character in, 62; return of the natural gentleman in, 63–67; return of veterans to civilian employment in, 12, 13, 48
heroic odes, 149
Hilkey, Judy, 62
history: living memory and, 109. *See also* military histories
Hitchcock, Ripley, 122, 123, 186n34
Hoffman, Daniel, 116
Hoganson, Kristin, 104–5
Holmes, Oliver Wendell, 80–81, 165
Homer, Winslow, 10, 30–32, 51–54
Homestead Acts, 175n29
homesteading, 60
Hood, John Bell, 86
Howells, William Dean, 148
"How to Tell a True War Story" (O'Brien), 166
The Hurt Locker (film), 166, 194n6

indirect narration: in public criticism of veteran pensions, 107–9
Iola Leroy (Harper), 16, 146, 156–59
irritable heart, 76–77

James, William, 115, 158
Janet, Pierre, 77, 179n9
Janney, Caroline, 167n6
Janoff-Bulman, Ronnie, 89, 94–95
jeremiad: concept of, 69, 177n49; Albion Tourgée's corporate jeremiad, 12–13, 67–73
Jim Crow era: black ambivalence toward the perceived value of military service, 16, 131, 132, 146–59, 162; declining stature of black veterans and, 131, 142, 144–45, 162; racial uplift and the search for new black role models, 145–47
Johnson, Robert, 81
Jomini, Antoine-Henri, 6

Index

Jones, William, 59
"Jupiter Doke, Brigadier-General" (Bierce), 98–99, 181n60

Kay, T. F. M., 145
Kemble, C. Robert, 37

labor: Civil War veterans and the struggle for artisanal manhood, 48–49, 54–63; strikes, 49
Lanier, Sidney: war experience of, 34. *See also* Tiger-Lilies
Lentz, Perry, 184n18
Leys, Ruth, 78–79
Linderman, Gerald, 81, 193–94n3
The Little Regiment (Crane), 123
living memory: history and, 109
"Lost Generation" writers, 9, 165
Louisiana Native Guard, 138, 190n32
Lowrey, Gad, 60
Lyrics of Love and Laughter (Dunbar), 150
Lyrics of Lowly Life (Dunbar), 148

Mabin, James H., 144
Majors and Minors (Dunbar), 148
manhood and masculine identity: black veterans and a rearguard defense of martial manhood, 159–62; citizen-solider concept in *Miss Ravenel's Conversion* and, 35–39; cultural burden of Civil War veterans and, 119–13. *See also* artisanal manhood
"march to the sea," 5, 87–89
"Marines Signaling Under Fire" (Crane), 125–26
The Marrow of Tradition (Chesnutt), 155
Marrs, Elijah, 133, 135, 136, 138
Marshall, Henry Grimes, 24
Marszalek, John, 87–88
Marten, James, 167n6
martial manhood: black veterans and a rearguard defense of, 159–62
Marvin, Edwin, 21
McClellan, George, 28–29
McClure's magazine, 123
McClurg, Alexander C., 121
McIntyre, James, 161
melancholy, 77–78, 179n8
memoirs. *See* Civil War memoirs
Memoirs (Sherman): ambivalence of psychic closure in, 80; contemporary reactions to, 84–85; importance as a narrative of traumatic experience, 74–75; inner turmoil and the struggle with traumatic memory, 13, 81–82; reasons for the writing and publishing of, 83–84, 85; reflections on the wartime death of friends, 89–90; Sherman's defense of his wartime actions, 85–89; veteran self-identity and, 14
memory: distinction between living memory and history, 109; obsessive memory as the cause of melancholy or nostalgia, 77–78; veterans and the active management of Civil War remembrance, 111–13. *See also* traumatic memory
Merrill, George, 113
Mexican War veterans, 4
military histories: of African American service, 131–32, 160–61; influence of regimental histories on *Company Aytch*, 91–92
Militia Act of 1862, 138, 188n11
Mills, George Henry, 19
Minnie's Sacrifice (Harper), 158, 193n71
Miss Ravenel's Conversion from Secession to Loyalty (De Forest): biographical details in, 34; defense of the citizen-soldier concept in, 18, 34, 35–39, 46; depiction of demobilization and the conflicting emotions of veterans, 22–23, 25–26; divisions between regulars and volunteers in, 168n8; reaction to civilian anxieties about returning veterans, 10, 11, as a reconciliation romance, 35
Mitchell, Reid, 26
"modern" war: the Civil War and, 5–8, 164; impact on soldiers, 8
moral equivalent of war, 115, 158
"More Than Half Are Dead" (poem), 109–10
Mynheer Dutchman, 92

narrative indirection: in public criticism of veteran pensions, 107–9
narratives: characteristics of personal narratives, 91; *Company Aytch*, 13, 14, 74–75, 80, 82–83, 90–95; relationship to trauma, 78–83. *See also* Civil War memoirs
Nash, Charles, 144
The Nation, 17, 27–29, 52–53
natural gentleman: John Cooke and, 176n43; gentry and, 176n40; the return of in *The Heir of Gaymount*, 62, 63–67
Nell, William Cooper, 140
New Orleans Daily Picayune, 126–27
New York Herald, 17
New York Press, 116
New York Times, 107–8, 127–29, 161

INDEX

New York Tribune, 116
"New York Veterans Ready" (Shaw), 127–28
Ninety-Fifth Illinois Regiment, 26–27
Ninety-Fourth Ohio Regiment, 23–24
Ninety-Third Illinois Regiment, 60
nonfiction: analysis of veteran reintegration through, 8–9. *See also* Civil War memoirs; military histories; narratives
Nora, Pierre, 109
nostalgia, 77–78, 179n8

O'Brien, Tim, 166
obsessive memories, 77–78
"One of the Missing" (Bierce), 99
"Ought Soldiers to Vote?" (newspaper editorial), 29
"Our Watering Places—The Empty Sleeve at Newport" (Homer), 10, 30–32
Overland Campaign, 7

Palmer, John, 111
Payne, John H. B., 139
Pennebaker, James W., 79
pension agents, 107
pensions. *See* veteran pensions
Personal Memoirs (Grant), 89
personal narratives: characteristics of, 91; *Company Aytch*, 13, 14, 74–75, 80, 82–83, 90–95
Petersburg siege, 7, 8
Philadelphia Times, 107
Pinchback, P. B. S., 142–43
posttraumatic stress disorder (PTSD), 75–76, 178–79n5
Private Fleming at Chancellorsville (Lentz), 184n18
Progress of a Race, 159
"Protecting a Colored Veteran" (newspaper article), 161

Race and Reunion (Blight), 178n4
race riots, 155
racial discrimination: experienced by black troops during the Civil War, 130–31, 161; impact on black veterans, 16; in the U.S. Navy, 188–89n17
racial uplift: the ambivalent legacy of the U.S. Colored Troops, 139–45; black ambivalence toward the perceived value of military service and, 131, 132, 146–59, 162; black veterans and a rearguard defense of martial manhood, 159–62; military service and a change in identity, 130; military service and the quest for citizenship rights, 130, 132–39, 161; the search for new role models in the Jim Crow era, 145–47
racial violence, 156, 161, 193n72
railroad strikes, 49
Ramsey, Alex, 84–85
realist fiction, 67
"Recession Never" (Dunbar), 147–48
reconciliation romances, 35
Reconstruction: positive impact of black veterans during, 131, 141–42, 162; Albion Tourgée on the failure of in *Figs and Thistles*, 67–73
The Red Badge of Courage (Crane): contemporary responses to, 121; Crane's newspaper writings and, 115–18; Crane's "The Veteran" and, 123–25; foreshadowing in, 120; and the intergenerational struggle between aging veterans and younger males, 14–15, 104, 105, 113–23; manuscript version, 118, 185–86n34; origins of, 114–18; publication history, 121–23; syndicated and book versions, 122–23; traditional views of, 113–14
Reed, George, 55
regimental histories, 91–92
Regular Army: citizen-soldier concept in *Miss Ravenel's Conversion* and, 18, 34, 35–39, 46; divisions between regulars and volunteers, 168nn8–9
Reid, Richard, 141
Reid, Whitelaw, 107–8
Remembering the Civil War (Janney), 167n6
Resch, John, 18
"A Resumed Identity" (Bierce), 100–3
reunions, 3
Revolutionary War era: black veterans, 140; views of a standing army in, 171n27; views of veterans in, 4
"road to reunion" theme/narrative, 3, 167n6
"Robert Gould Shaw" (Dunbar), 146, 148, 150
Robson, John, 58–59
Royster, Charles, 171n27

San Francisco Daily Evening Bulletin, 84
Savage, Kirk, 109
Second Confiscation Act, 187n1
Second Iraq War, 166
Second Massachusetts Heavy Artillery, 21–22
service pension plan, 106

INDEX 233

Seventy-Fourth Regiment, U.S. Colored Troops, 142
Shattered Assumptions (Janoff-Bulman), 94–95
Shaw, Albert D., 127–28
Sherman, William Tecumseh: defense of his wartime actions, 85–89; effect of combat trauma on, 79; feud with H. V. Boynton, 84–85; importance of the *Memoirs* as a narrative of traumatic experience, 74–75; inner turmoil and the struggle with traumatic memory, 13, 81–82; "march to the sea," 5, 87–89; reasons for writing and publishing *Memoirs*, 83–84, 85; reflections on the wartime death of friends, 89–90; trauma narrative and psychic closure, 80; veteran self-identity and, 14
Sherman's Historical Raid (Boynton), 84
Shook over Hell (Dean), 75–76
short stories: of Ambrose Bierce, 95–96, 98–103
Sickles, Daniel, 124–25, 186n49
Simpson, Mark, 53
Sing Not War (Marten), 167n6
Sixteenth Connecticut Regiment, 21
Sixteenth North Carolina Regiment, 19
Sixtieth Regiment, U.S. Colored Infantry, 144
Sixty-Second Regiment, U.S. Colored Troops, 140
Smith, Charles Henry, 181n47
soldiers' homes, 77, 106, 179n10
soldier vote, 28–29
southern gentleman: reinvention of in *The Heir of Gaymount*, 63–67
Southwestern Christian Advocate, 146
Spanish–American War, 15, 126–29
St. Louis Globe-Democrat, 84
state asylums, 77
Stephens, George E., 138–39
strikes, 49
suffering soldier image, 18, 46
Suffering Soldiers (Resch), 18
Surry of Eagle's Nest (Cooke), 63

Tal, Kalí, 80
Tales of Soldiers and Civilians (Bierce), 79–80
tall tales, 92
"Teaching the Negro Recruits the Use of the Minie Rifle" (engraving), 136, *137*
Tenth South Carolina Regiment, 20
Third Louisiana Native Guards, 138
Thirty-Fifth Regiment, U.S. Colored Troops, 141
Thirty-Fourth Illinois Regiment, 60
This Republic of Suffering (Faust), 178n4
Thomas, George Henry, 84
Tiger-Lilies (Lanier): on the brutalization process in war, 41–43; exploration of the survival instinct in, 43–44; German prose romance and, 40; reaction to civilian anxieties about returning veterans, 10, 11–12; "war flower" metaphor, 41, 173n60; wounded warrior imagery and the search for empathy in, 18–19, 34, 39–47
Tourgée, Albion Winegar: artisanal manhood and, 48; combat experiences of, 177n50; corporate jeremiad and critiques of corporate capitalism, 12–13, 67–73, 177n48; disillusionment of, 165. See also *Figs and Thistles*
Trachtenberg, Alan, 50
tragic mulatta tales, 156
tramps, 61
trauma: Civil War veterans and, 75–78, 178n4; definitions of, 94–95; posttraumatic stress disorder, 75–76, 178–79n5; relationship to narrative, 78–83
traumatic memory: contradictory nature of, 80; emergence of veteran self-identity and, 80–81, 103; Pierre Janet's concept of, 179n9
Trumbull, Lyman, 142
Turner, Aaron S., 23–24
Turner, Henry M., 145
Twelfth United States Heavy Artillery, Colored, 138
Twenty-Eighth Michigan Regiment, 54
Twenty-Fifth Corps, U.S. Colored Troops, 189n28
Twenty-Fourth Regiment, U.S. Colored Troops, 133
Twenty-Ninth U.S. Colored Infantry, 145

Union army: black military service and the quest for citizenship rights, 130, 132–39, 161; enlistment of black soldiers, 188n11; experiences of demobilization, 20–24; Grant's strategies and tactics, 6, 7–8, 169n19; racial discrimination experienced by black troops in, 130–31, 161; Sherman's "march to the sea," 5, 87–89; veteran pensions, 106–10, 183n8
Union Pacific Railroad, 177n53
Union veterans: interracial veterans' groups, 160; meaning of reunions, 3. See also Civil War veterans

United States Colored Troops (USCT): declining stature of veterans in the post-Reconstruction era, 142, 144–45; demobilization, 140–41; denial of the right for black soldiers to serve as commissioned officers, 142, 190n32; differences between the experiences of black and white troops, 135; formation of, 135; pay inequalities and, 138–39; positive impact of veterans during Reconstruction, 141–42
"unwritten war" theme/narrative, 2
U.S. Navy, 187n4, 188–89n17
U.S. presidents, 105

Vallandigham, Clement, 152, 192n59
van der Kolk, 78
"The Veteran" (Crane), 14–15, 123–25
The Veteran in a New Field (Homer), 51–54
veteran pensions: government expenditures on, 183n8; perceived as a burden to the country, 106–10
veteran reintegration: analysis through works of fiction and nonfiction, 8–9; civilian anxieties about soldiers returning home, 10–12, 17, 27–30; civilian employment and reentry into society, 12–13; discourse and distance between veterans and civilians, 19; experience of black veterans, 10, 15–16; societal consequences of the veterans' exclusive sense of self, 14–15; stages of, 9–10; turn to memory, 13–14; wounded warrior imagery, 17–19
veterans: problem of how to address, 1–2; shifting conceptions of, 2, 4–5. *See also* Civil War veterans
veteran self-identity: active management of Civil War remembrance and, 113; Civil War memoirs and, 80–81; exclusive nature of, 14, 75; societal consequences of, 14–15, 103; traumatic memory and the emergence of, 80–81, 103; war as a transformative experience and, 163–66

"The Veteran's Memories" (etching), 111–13, 117
"Veterans' Ranks Thinner by a Year" (Decoration Day article), 116–17
Vietnam veterans, 75–76
volunteers: citizen-soldier concept in *Miss Ravenel's Conversion*, 18, 34, 35–39, 46; divisions between regulars and volunteers, 168nn8–9; length of service and reenlistment, 192n58
voting rights: black veterans and, 139–40

Walker, C. I., 20
Wallace, Lew, 114–15
Walls, Josiah T., 144
war correspondents, 15, 125–26
war literature: origin in America, 9
War of 1812 veterans, 4
Washington Daily Intelligencer, 17
Watkins, Francis Ellen, 131
Watkins, Sam: effect of combat trauma on, 79; inner turmoil and the struggle with traumatic memory, 13, 82–83; publication of *Company Aytch*, 91; trauma narrative and psychic closure, 80; veteran self-identity and, 14. *See also Company Aytch*
Weekly Anglo-African, 138
"We Wear the Mask" (Dunbar), 147
"What I Saw of Shiloh" (Bierce), 79, 96–98
Williams, George Washington, 131–32, 145, 146
Wilson, Christopher Kent, 51–52
Wilson, Edmund, 173n61, 176n39
Wilson, Joseph, 16, 131–32, 146, 160, 162
"wily slave" archetype, 156
Windars, Richard Bruce, 168n9
Winters, Elhanon, 60
wounded warrior imagery: and the dispelling of civilian anxieties about veterans, 17–18, 30–34; figure of the suffering soldier and, 18, 46; reactions to in fiction by veteran authors, 18–19, 34–47; roots of, 27–30

RECONSTRUCTING AMERICA
Andrew L. Slap, series editor

Hans L. Trefousse, *Impeachment of a President: Andrew Johnson, the Blacks, and Reconstruction.*

Richard Paul Fuke, *Imperfect Equality: African Americans and the Confines of White Ideology in Post-Emancipation Maryland.*

Ruth Currie-McDaniel, *Carpetbagger of Conscience: A Biography of John Emory Bryant.*

Paul A. Cimbala and Randall M. Miller, eds., *The Freedmen's Bureau and Reconstruction: Reconsiderations.*

Herman Belz, *A New Birth of Freedom: The Republican Party and Freedmen's Rights, 1861 to 1866.*

Robert Michael Goldman, *"A Free Ballot and a Fair Count": The Department of Justice and the Enforcement of Voting Rights in the South, 1877–1893.*

Ruth Douglas Currie, ed., *Emma Spaulding Bryant: Civil War Bride, Carpetbagger's Wife, Ardent Feminist—Letters, 1860–1900.*

Robert Francis Engs, *Freedom's First Generation: Black Hampton, Virginia, 1861–1890.*

Robert F. Kaczorowski, *The Politics of Judicial Interpretation: The Federal Courts, Department of Justice, and Civil Rights, 1866–1876.*

John Syrett, *The Civil War Confiscation Acts: Failing to Reconstruct the South.*

Michael Les Benedict, *Preserving the Constitution: Essays on Politics and the Constitution in the Reconstruction Era.*

Andrew L. Slap, *The Doom of Reconstruction: The Liberal Republicans in the Civil War Era.*

Edmund L. Drago, *Confederate Phoenix: Rebel Children and Their Families in South Carolina*.

Mary Farmer-Kaiser, *Freedwomen and the Freedmen's Bureau: Race, Gender, and Public Policy in the Age of Emancipation*.

Paul A. Cimbala and Randall Miller, eds., *The Great Task Remaining Before Us: Reconstruction as America's Continuing Civil War*.

John A. Casey Jr., *New Men: Reconstructing the Image of the Veteran in Late-Nineteenth-Century American Literature and Culture*.